THE
FUSE
BOX

THE
FUSE
BOX

Essays on writing
from Victoria University's
International Institute of Modern Letters

Edited by Emily Perkins and Chris Price

Victoria University Press

TE WHARE WĀNANGA O TE ŪPOKO O TE IKA A MĀUI

VICTORIA
UNIVERSITY OF WELLINGTON

VICTORIA UNIVERSITY PRESS
Victoria University of Wellington
PO Box 600 Wellington
vup.victoria.ac.nz

A catalogue record for this book is available from the
National Library of New Zealand.

Printed by Printlink

Contents

Contributors

Pip Adam's short-story collection *Everything We Hoped For* and novels *I'm Working on a Building* and *The New Animals* are published by Victoria University Press. Her work has also appeared in *Sport*, *Glottis*, *Turbine*, *Hue & Cry* and *Landfall*. She teaches short fiction at the IIML and is a member of Write Where You Are, a charity which teaches creative writing in prisons. Pip also makes 'Better Off Read', a podcast about reading and writing.

Tusiata Avia has travelled the world performing her one-woman poetry show, based on her 2004 collection *Wild Dogs Under My Skirt*. Residencies she has held include the Fulbright Pacific Writer's Fellowship at University of Hawai'i and the Ursula Bethell Writer in Residence at University of Canterbury. She was the 2013 recipient of the Janet Frame Literary Trust Award. Until recently Avia taught creative writing and performing arts at the Manukau Institute of Technology. Her other poetry collections are *Bloodclot* (2009) and *Fale Aitu | Spirit House* (2016), shortlisted for the 2017 Ockham NZ Book Awards. She is published by Victoria University Press.

Hera Lindsay Bird was born in 1987 in Thames, New Zealand. Her debut collection of poetry *Hera Lindsay Bird* was published in 2016 with Victoria University Press and won both the Jessie Mackay Best First Book of Poetry for 2017 and the Sarah Broom Poetry Prize for 2017. She has an MA in poetry from the IIML, where she was awarded the 2011 Adam Prize. Her work has been featured in *Vice*, *i-D* magazine and the *Guardian*.

William Brandt has an MA in creative writing from the IIML at Victoria University. His short fiction collection *Alpha Male* won the Montana Award for Best First Book. His novel *The Book of the Film of the Story of My Life* has been published in New Zealand, the United Kingdom and the United States. He teaches short fiction at the IIML and is a member of Write Where You Are, a charity which teaches creative writing in prisons.

James Brown's poetry books are *Go Round Power Please* (winner of the Jessie Mackay Best First Book of Poetry Award), *Lemon*, *Favourite Monsters*, *The Year of the Bicycle* and *Warm Auditorium*. He is the author behind the useful non-fiction chapbook *Instructions for Poetry Readings*, and in 2005 edited *The Nature of Things: Poems from the New Zealand Landscape*. He has been a finalist in the Montana New Zealand Book Awards three times. James convenes the poetry workshop at the IIML. His new collection *Floods Another Chamber* is due for publication by Victoria University Press in 2017.

Stephen (also Steph or Stephanie) Burt is Professor of English at Harvard and the author of several books of poetry and literary criticism, most recently *The Poem Is You: 60 Contemporary American Poems and How to Read Them* (Harvard University Press, 2016). A new book of Steph's own poems, *Advice from the Lights*, will be published by Graywolf Press in late 2017.

Rajorshi Chakraborti was born in Calcutta, India. He is the author of four novels and a collection of short fiction. Two of his books have been shortlisted for the Crossword Book

Award in India. He also teaches creative writing at Rimutaka Prison as part of the Write Where You Are collective. Rajorshi's new novel, *The Man Who Would Not See*, is due out for release in New Zealand next year.

Stella Duffy is an award-winning writer with over sixty short stories, fourteen written and devised plays and fifteen novels published in fifteen languages. The network HBO has optioned her *Theodora* novels for television. She has twice won the CWA Short Story Dagger and twice won Stonewall Writer of the Year. Her latest novel, *The Hidden Room*, was published by Virago in May 2017. Stella has also worked in theatre for over thirty-five years as an actor, director, playwright and facilitator. She is the founder and co-director of the Fun Palaces campaign for cultural democracy. In 2016 there were over 292 Fun Palaces across the world, in the United Kingdom, Ireland, Norway, France, Australia and New Zealand, and 124,000 people took part. In the Queen's Birthday Honours 2016 she was awarded the OBE for Services to the Arts. She grew up in Tokoroa and lives in London.

Ken Duncum lives in Wellington where he is director of the MA scriptwriting programme at the IIML. He is an award-winning writer for theatre, television and radio, and has spent a year in Menton, France, as the 2010 New Zealand Post Mansfield Prize winner. Publications include two volumes of collected plays (*Plays 1: Small Towns and Sea*, and *Plays 2: London Calling*), his play *Cherish*, and a volume of early plays co-written with Rebecca Rodden (*BATS Plays*). He is currently working on *The Nightdress*, a musical based on a famous Victorian murder case.

Gigi Fenster has a PhD from the IIML at Victoria University. She has been published in various literary journals, and her novel *The Intentions Book* was a finalist in the New Zealand Post Book Awards for 2013. She teaches at Rimutaka Men's Prison.

Patricia Grace is the author of seven novels, five short-story collections and several children's books. Awards for her work include the Deutz Medal for Fiction for the novel *Tu* and the New Zealand Fiction Award for *Potiki*. She was also awarded the Literaturpreis from Frankfurt for *Potiki*. *Dogside Story* was longlisted for the Booker Prize and winner of the Kiriyama Pacific Rim Fiction Prize. Her latest novel, *Chappy*, was a finalist in the Ockham New Zealand Awards for fiction and winner of Ngā Kupu Ora Award 2016. Patricia has received the Prime Minister's Award for Literary Achievement and the Neustadt International Prize for Literature sponsored by the University of Oklahoma. She was a recipient of the Distinguished Companion of the New Zealand Order of Merit (DCNZM) in 2007 and has received honorary doctorates for literature from Victoria University of Wellington in 1989, and the World Indigenous Nations University in 2016.

Briar Grace-Smith is of Ngā Puhi descent and is a writer of plays, short fiction and screenplays. She was an inaugural recipient of the Arts Foundation Laureate award (2000), the Creative New Zealand writer in residence at Victoria University (2003) and recipient of Te Pou Marohi Ngā Aho Whakaari Award (2016). Her plays include *Ngā Pou Wāhine*, *When Sun and Moon Collide*, *Purapurawhetū* and *Paniora!* Her television work includes *Fishskin Suit, Kaitangata Twitch, Being Eve* and *Billy*. Her feature film *The Strength of Water* premiered at the Rotterdam and Berlin Film Festivals, receiving the New Zealand Writers Guild award for best script (2010). The comedy horror *Fresh Meat* played at various festivals including the Tribeca Film Festival (2013). Briar has worked as a Development Executive for the New Zealand Film Commission and has directed two short films, *Nine of Hearts* and *Charm*, part of *Waru* – eight films by Māori women – to premiere in 2017.

Gary Henderson is a New Zealand playwright, director and teacher whose work is produced locally and internationally. His scripts have been published by Playmarket in New Zealand and by Bloomsbury Methuen Drama in London. His most well travelled play is *Skin Tight,* written in 1994. In 2016 a French translation by Xavier Mailleux – *Te tenir contre moi* – was produced by Théâtre L'Instant in Montréal. Other work includes *Mo & Jess Kill Susie*, *An Unseasonable Fall of Snow, Home Land* and *Peninsula*, and the radio plays *The Moehau* and *News Bomb.* Henderson's most recent work was *Shepherd*, which he directed at the Court Theatre in Christchurch in 2015. His current projects are the libretto for a new opera co-commissioned by New Zealand Opera, Victorian Opera and West Australian Opera, and a new play for the Court. He also teaches a workshop on writing for theatre at the IIML. In November 2013 Henderson received the Playmarket Award acknowledging his significant artistic contribution to New Zealand theatre.

Lloyd Jones's books include *The Book of Fame*, *Biografi*, *Mister Pip*, *Hand Me Down World*, and most recently a memoir, *A History of Silence*. His new novel will be published in early 2018.

Elizabeth Knox is the author of twelve novels and three novellas. *The Vintner's Luck* won the Deutz Medal for Fiction in the 1999 Montana New Zealand Book Awards, and the Tasmania Pacific Region Prize, and is published in ten languages. *Dreamhunter* won the 2006 Esther Glen Medal. *Dreamhunter*'s sequel *Dreamquake*, 2007, was a Michael L Printz Honor book for 2008 and, in the same year, was named an ALA, a CCBC, Booklist, and New York Library best book. A collection of essays, *The Love School*, won the biography and memoir section of the New Zealand Post Book Awards in 2009. *Mortal Fire* won a New Zealand Post Children's Book Award and was a finalist in the LA Times Book Awards.

Elizabeth's latest book is the horror/science fiction novel, *Wake*. Elizabeth is an Arts Foundation Laureate and was made ONZM in 2002. In 2017 she taught the first world-building workshop at the IIML. She lives in Wellington with her husband, Fergus Barrowman, and her son, Jack.

Tina Makereti writes novels, essays and short fiction. In 2016 she won the Pacific Regional Commonwealth Short Story Prize with her story 'Black Milk'. Tina teaches creative writing at Massey University, and established the Māori & Pasifika Creative Writing Workshop at the IIML in 2014. Her novel *Where the Rēkohu Bone Sings* (2014) was longlisted for the Dublin Literary Award and won the Ngā Kupu Ora Aotearoa Māori Book Award for Fiction, also won by her short story collection, *Once Upon a Time in Aotearoa* (2010). She has had residencies in Frankfurt and the Randell Cottage, Wellington, and is recipient of numerous awards including the Beatson Fellowship. With Witi Ihimaera, she is the editor of a new anthology of Māori and Pasifika fiction, *Black Marks on the White Page* (2017). She is of Ngāti Tūwharetoa, Te Ati Awa, Ngāti Rangatahi Pākehā and, according to family stories, Moriori descent.

Bill Manhire started teaching creative writing at Victoria University in the mid-1970s, and retired as director of the IIML in 2013. His books include a collected stories, *The Stories of Bill Manhire*, and a *Selected Poems*. There is also a volume of critical essays, *Doubtful Sounds*. His most recent publications are a book of poems, *Some Things to Place in a Coffin*, and a collection of riddles *Tell My My Name*, set to music by Norman Meehan and voiced by Hannah Griffin. He lives in Wellington.

Tom McCrory is the writer of many plays including *French Kiss* (Independent Top 10, Edinburgh Festival), *Life on Mars*, which premiered at the Riverside Studios, London, *Faith* (Adam Play Reading Award Winner), *The Last 27 Days of Childhood* and *Significance*, highly commended at the 2015

Playmarket Adam Play Awards. With Nina Nawalowalo he is co-founder of internationally acclaimed Pacific visual theatre company The Conch. Their work has toured nationally and internationally and had seasons at the Sydney Opera House and London's Barbican Centre. Tom has worked extensively as a movement teacher including at the Young Vic London, Bristol Old Vic, Rose Bruford Drama School, California State University Fullerton, East 15 Acting School and the Shanghai Theatre Academy, and was a senior movement teacher at Mountview Drama School, London. For fifteen years he worked as head of the Movement Programme at Toi Whakaari: New Zealand Drama School.

Nina Nawalowalo is artistic director of The Conch. Her work has been presented at over forty festivals including the London International Mime Festival, British Festival of Visual Theatre, Ulster Comedy Festival, Moscow Arts Festival, the Magic Castle (Los Angeles) and the London International Workshop Festival. Her awards include the International Brotherhood of Magicians Comedy Award, the Creative New Zealand Pacific Innovation and Excellence Award and the Outstanding Theatre Award in Edinburgh 2014. Her internationally acclaimed work with The Conch has included *Vula*, which enjoyed a three-week season at the Sydney Opera House, a six-city tour of Holland and a ten-night sold-out season at the London Barbican Theatre. It was commissioned by the New Zealand International Festival, which toured it to Fiji and Sydney. In 2016 Nina had two of her works programmed into the Auckland Arts Festival and concluded an eight-city sold-out tour of *The White Guitar*, which won an Excellence Award at the Auckland theatre awards.

Emily Perkins is the author of short stories and novels including the books *Not Her Real Name*, *Novel About My Wife* and *The Forrests*. She is the co-writer of the feature film *The Rehearsal*, adapted from the Eleanor Catton novel.

Her reworking of Ibsen's *A Doll's House*, commissioned by Auckland Theatre Company, has been produced in Auckland and Wellington. Awards for Emily's books include the Montana New Zealand Book Award, the Geoffrey Faber Award (UK), and the Believer Book of the Year (US). She has held the Buddle Findlay Sargeson Residency and in 2011 was named an Arts Foundation Laureate. In 2017 she was awarded MNZM in the Queen's Birthday Honours. Emily is a senior lecturer at the IIML, where she convenes the MA workshop in fiction.

Chris Price is a past editor of *Landfall*, has worked in publishing, and was for many years coordinator of the New Zealand Festival's Writers and Readers Week. She is the author of three poetry collections and the genre-hopping *Brief Lives*, which takes its impetus from a sixteenth-century biographical dictionary. In 2002 *Husk* won the Best First Book of Poetry award, and Chris was awarded the Katherine Mansfield Fellowship in 2011. Her interest in science has seen her contribute to the physics-literature collaboration *Are Angels OK?* and the German-New Zealand Transit of Venus Poetry Exchange. She convenes the poetry and creative non-fiction MA workshop at the IIML, where she is also series editor of *Best New Zealand Poems*.

Victor Rodger is an award-winning playwright of Samoan and Scottish descent whose work deals with race and sexuality. His plays include *Black Faggot*, *My Name Is Gary Cooper* and *Sons*. He is currently the writer in residence at Victoria University of Wellington.

Mary Ruefle's many poetry collections include a *Selected Poems*, *Trances of the Blast* and the erasure book *A Little White Shadow*. Her essays are collected in *Madness, Rack, and Honey*, and she has also written two books of short prose pieces, *The Most of It* and *My Private Property*. Ruefle is the recipient of numerous honours, including a Guggenheim Fellowship. She gave a masterclass at the IIML in 2013.

Damien Wilkins is the author of nine novels, two short-story collections and a book of poems. He has won the New Zealand Book Award for Fiction and a Whiting Award from the Whiting Foundation, New York. He has also written for the stage and for television. He is a founding editor of the literary magazine *Sport*. In 2008 Damien was awarded the Katherine Mansfield Fellowship and he received an Arts Foundation Laureate Award in 2013. As a musician and songwriter, he records under the name The Close Readers and has released three albums. He is the director of the IIML at Victoria University of Wellington. His most recent novel is *Lifting*.

Charlotte Wood is the author of five novels and two books of non-fiction. Her novel *The Natural Way of Things* won the 2016 Stella Prize, the Indie Book of the Year and Australia's Prime Minister's Literary Award for Fiction, and has been published throughout Europe, Britain and North America. Her latest book is *The Writer's Room*, a collection of interviews with authors about the writing process.

Ashleigh Young works as an editor at Victoria University Press in Wellington. Her poetry and essays have been widely published in print and online journals, including *Tell You What: Great New Zealand Non-fiction*, *Five Dials* (UK) and *The Griffith Review* (Australia). She gained an MA in Creative Writing from the IIML in 2009, winning the Adam Prize. Her first book was the poetry collection *Magnificent Moon* (Victoria University Press, 2012), followed by the essay collection *Can You Tolerate This?* (Victoria University Press, 2016), for which she won the 2017 Windham-Campbell Literature Prize for non-fiction and the and the 2017 Royal Society Te Apārangi Award for General Non-Fiction.

Acknowledgements

We would like to thank Holly Hunter and Fergus Barrowman of Victoria University Press and our colleagues at the International Institute of Modern Letters. We are grateful to the following authors, publishers and institutions for permission to adapt and reproduce some of the material in this book:

Thanks to Darren Glass for the cover image, from 'Cosmo Flying Disc 2000'.

Mary Ruefle (inside front cover), from *The Mansion*, p. 53 (Seattle: Wave Books, n.d.). *The Mansion* appears online in its entirety at maryruefle.com.

James Brown, 'The Day I Stopped Writing Poetry', *Favourite Monsters* (Wellington: Victoria University Press, 2002).

John Dennison, 'Errata' (plus Eileen Duggan errata slip), *Otherwise* (Auckland: Auckland University Press, 2015).

A version of Tusiata Avia's essay was first delivered as one of the Conchus Conversations by Pasifika women artists at the Conchus Summit, held at Circa Theatre, Wellington, in February 2017.

An earlier version of Stephen Burt's 'Controlled Experiments (in Poetry)' was delivered as a talk at Rutgers University in 2014; the author is grateful to Rebecca Porte and Rachel Feder for the invitation, and to the Department of English there.

Gary Henderson's essay is adapted from an address delivered at the Feast of New Theatre forum held in Christchurch in 2007.

Elizabeth Knox's essay is partly adapted from her Frank

Sargeson Memorial Lecture delivered at the University of Waikato in 2016.

Damien Wilkins's essay is the slightly amended text of his Inaugural Professorial Lecture given at Victoria University of Wellington in 2014, and was first published in *Sport 43*, edited by Fergus Barrowman with Kirsten McDougall and Ashleigh Young.

The photograph on p. 106 is from Dennis McEldowney. (1957). *The World Regained*, 2nd ed., 2001. Auckland: Auckland University Press.

Charlotte Wood's interview with Lloyd Jones was first published in *The Writer's Room: Conversations about Writing*, Charlotte Wood (Sydney: Allen & Unwin, 2016), reproduced with permission of Allen & Unwin Pty Ltd.

Briar Grace-Smith's interview with Patricia Grace is transcribed from an event presented on 18 July 2016 as part the Writers on Mondays series (produced by the International Institute of Modern Letters) at Te Papa Tongarewa, Wellington.

Emily Perkins's essay is adapted from a keynote address given to the Australasian Association of Writing Programs conference at Massey University in 2014. The theme for the conference was 'Minding the Gap'.

Hera Lindsay Bird's poem 'Untitled 404' was first published in a limited edition by City Gallery Wellington and Victoria University Press, January 2017, in conjunction with the exhibition *Cindy Sherman*. Thanks are also due to Tracey Monastra (City Gallery Wellington) for her assistance with this inclusion.

Cindy Sherman, *Untitled #404*, 2000 (inside back cover) is reproduced courtesy of the artist and Metro Pictures, New York.

Introduction

Emily Perkins and Chris Price

'A story brings with it a world,' write Nina Nawalowalo and Tom McCrory. 'If we listen, it tells us how it wants to be told.' 'Get on with it,' says Stella Duffy. Bill Manhire quotes Louis Pasteur, 'chance favours only the prepared mind', but also Lawrence Raab: 'Beginning poets need to learn how to be stupid.' What do you choose to write? Why? And how do you go about it? When we first conceived of this book, these were our questions – as much as we know there are no definitive answers to *how* and *what* and *why*, there is only a wavering beam of light floating about in the dark, hoping to land on something we can walk towards.

Here you will find writers coming at writing from without – what they find in the world – and within – how that world makes them feel, think and create. These essays and interviews tell of the joy of writing and its urgency, and look at how the act itself works on the writer and on its audience – not that it always needs a wide audience, as is shown by the Write Where You Are Collective, whose work teaching writing in prisons upends some received ideas about what writing is for. These pieces, we hope, show that ways into creativity are everywhere, even when there are obstacles in our heads, in our lives and in culture itself. The contributors to this book are some of Aotearoa's most defining writers and some of the new guard: they've both been fresh arrivals to literature and learned what it takes to keep on going; they bring many different experiences, questions and offerings with them.

This book, then, is for anyone with that persistent buzzing urge to write who doesn't know where to begin; it's for a curious reader; and it is for established writers who themselves wonder about the spark: where the impulses and the ideas come from. It's also about the current – what to do with those ideas, and how to maintain energy and discipline through a long project or a writing life. It's about finding the flow. How to know what's vital, and how to get close to the heat without being burned. It's full of connected and sometimes opposing elements: planning and accidents; total permission and moral responsibility; music and silence; faith and doubt; vision and revision; tradition and the brand new voice. It's also full of encouraging overlaps, where one essayist, writing alone on a theme of their own choosing, expresses common ground or shares a metaphor with another ostensibly solo artist: we are not really alone in the dark. In gathering these pieces together we hope readers will be able to make their own connections and will come away feeling charged and inspired, ready to write.

What does it mean to write about writing? How can one murky process be illuminated using only the same tools for that process we have in the first place? The uncertainty inherent in exploring the territory is often expressed in the anti-maxim 'There are no rules'. It comes from, perhaps, that sense of the approximate – the gap that a writer must try to close between what *is* and what we are able to describe; what is not, and what we are able to imagine. It comes also from a sense of the vastness, variety and inbuilt contradictions of the terrain: one morning it is true that planning is a waste of time; the next morning (or the next poem, next novel), it is not. But despite the unease, putting it into words is the only way we can communicate what we do. Discounting MRI scans, no one can see the landscape inside a writer's mind, so it's the happy task of these essays to illuminate what's in there, just as it's the task of fiction, drama and poetry to show us around inside those unseen parts of inner life. These ventures into clarity about the writing process might double back or end in the woods or lead to sudden clifftops, but there's always another path, a fresh view from the top of a tree, another ridge above the one you're on. The all-important mystery is never completely solved. The more we know, the more there is to know. The more we understand, the broader our horizons.

The pieces in this book cover poetry, drama, fiction and creative non-fiction. It's our hope that poets will find as much in the essays by fiction writers or dramatists as the other way around. When it comes to creative practice, and to finding the conditions to maintain it, we have more in common than formal demarcations would suggest. We hope that art-makers from other media, or practitioners of other forms, will find something here too, just as we can take the guidelines for yoga and rugby and needlework and apply them to writing. (Touch. Pause. Engage.) We hope that whatever stage you are at in the writing life, there will be writers here who speak to you.

Our day jobs are as teachers of creative writing at Victoria University's International Institute of Modern Letters, which in 2011 drew on its community to compile *The Exercise Book*, a collection of writing prompts and constraints to stimulate ideas. You might think of *The Fuse Box* as something of a companion volume, digging deeper into process, motivation and inspiration to enlarge on those hands-on exercises. Once again, it's through the IIML that we've been fortunate to come into contact with the contributors to this book. Some of these writers teach alongside us; some have been international visitors; others have spoken at our reading series Writers on Mondays, or been connected through the many live wires that make up the Aotearoa New Zealand literary grid. This community is ever expanding, and we've only been able to capture some of its many lights here; there are many other Fuse Boxes to be made – the imagination is a renewable resource. For now, we hope the guidance and honesty of these writers delivers a welcome jolt or a warm buzz. Enlightenment. A connection.

THE FUSE BOX

The Day I Stopped Writing Poetry

James Brown

The day I stopped writing poetry
I felt strangely serene.
Back when I first started, I had no idea
what I was trying to do: get something out, perhaps,
and I suppose 'art' had something
to do with it. There's a tempting simplicity
about poetry; you don't necessarily need
the room, the desk, the glowing typewriter
– a scrap of paper and a pencil will suffice.
Some of my tidier lines often came to me
on the bus or while I was just lumping along;
they'd be dancing or singing away in my head
while I grinned helplessly at the passing world
until I could arrange to meet them somewhere.
But of course the passing world passes by,
and poetry isn't prose, or Java, and in the end
the time/money equations just don't add up.
Poetry's biggest strength is also its biggest weakness.
Remember I said how poetry doesn't need
the desk, the 2000-words-before-breakfast, etc?
Well, I lied (something else poetry's good at).
More often than not it does, and you find yourself locked
in the doll's house of your skull for days, months, years eve

trying to find a way out.
Sometimes you do, sometimes you don't – that's by the by –
the point is you haven't finished a novel
or a short story, or got anywhere near Java,
and there are bills to pay, children to feed, etc.
So the day I stopped writing poetry
I felt strangely serene.
3.44 am, Wednesday, November the 3rd, 1999.
That was it – finished.

Continuing

Elizabeth Knox

At some point in every writer's life they'll find themselves facing the question, 'Why write?' Because it can be a lonely slog, and you have to like it. Because it's always been difficult to make any money, and it's even more difficult now.

Young writers, those with fire in their bellies, never think, 'Why write?' What they think, and should, is, 'Why not?' I used to think, 'Why not?' Mostly in response to the surprisingly many people confidently prepared to ask, 'Who are *you* to think you can do this?' I got into the healthy, bloody-minded habit of asking, 'Why not me?' And the thing is, that however difficult the lonely slog, it becomes normal. I'm aware that mine isn't a life a lot of writers have. Lots of them have jobs teaching writing. Or have jobs in order to supplement their writing. I've been lucky. Also I've been sequestered. And that has been for the most part wonderful. But it isn't easy, and eventually that defiant but joyful, 'Why not?' turns into, 'Why? Why write?'

When I was younger I used to write things down in my journal as if doing so would make some difference. I had an idea of myself as a witness, and that there was something intrinsically useful in my going about the world noticing things. Processing them, and making a record.

When I first read *King Lear* in the seventh form, I was struck by Lear's proposal to Cordelia that they be like God's spies. He is so happy to have found the daughter who loves him, so happy to be with her that the prospect of being tossed in a jail cell with her only means *with her*. Sharing the same air with Cordelia is now more precious to Lear than his kingdom, than being a king and having the gift of the kingship, of power; those things he had and failed to use wisely. But this moment in the play is not just a straightforward portrait of a man reunited with his daughter, two people for whom the society of each other is sufficient. It is also that, somehow, they've been elevated to a position where they belong more to God. If they can't judge like God judges, they can at least witness like God. Like God and *for* God. At least until 'He who parts us shall bring a brand from heaven / And fire us hence like foxes.'

So, about writing I always thought, 'At least there's this being one of God's spies.' But when you put pen to paper, even in a journal, you have to imagine that someone might read what you're writing. You don't have to imagine they'll be interested; it's just being heard, whispering into the box of a book, closing the lid, and leaving it lying around for a very long time in the hope that someone will pick it up, open it, and hear you confiding.

I had the idea that the private act of seeing things and thinking about them was somehow useful to the good order of the universe, and that maybe my small understandings might help facilitate the tendency to things being understood. As if to be unheard, and not to have faith that you can be heard, is entropy. I believed, for a start, in writing *my* story, or the way I saw things, and then just stories, whatever was in my gift – which is to say, in my power to give.

But time goes on, and things happen that are ordinary, because they happen to pretty much fifty-one per cent of the population. You become invisible. The first several times that you order a cup of coffee in a cafe and the waitstaff forget your order it's a great surprise. And then it happens again, and again. And you think, 'Ah well, I've become invisible.' Now, invisibility has an upside as well as a downside, but that's a whole other story. But if that commonplace occurrence coincides with an ever-shrinking pool of readers, not just for you, but for everybody; with reading being, every year, less a natural activity; then things feel a bit more acute.

I wasn't a reader until I was eight. My older sister told me stories and we played games – often lying in bed in the dark – so, games made solely of words. Later I was a keen but slow reader who couldn't write. I kept playing imaginary games, ferociously and voraciously, and holding everything in my head. Persuading people with my voice, and being persuaded by their voices.

My first relationship with story was as spoken narrative, and *then* as written. I fell from speaking into books. Later, with almost everyone else, I fell out of books into movies and television. And, like many others, I lost some faith in the *necessary* supremacy of that old wonderful thing of looking at a page, and interpreting the black marks on the white, and creating in my head the world that the words convey. But throughout my fall I retained my faith that reading books, particularly fiction, is better for us. The way a novel makes space inside us because the words have to be turned into a garden, a haunted house, a street, a wasteland; into people, and animals wild and domestic; into weather. The words only do some of the work of making the world. It's a collaboration: the reader makes the world out of what the words have summoned in them, and that world makes room for itself inside the reader. The reader's interior grows. And that is good for us. It doesn't just feel good because it's pleasurable, it also feels good because it's exercise at the cellular level. And we do know now that there is such a thing as exercise at the cellular level. Reading fiction is health-giving; it makes you calm and orderly, and a person with fluent feelings. So, I believe in books and reading. But because I'm a pessimist I don't believe that enough other people do, or can be made to.

My imagination and my faith can't keep on fighting the good fight. What good is it for me to write books? Well, as my father used to say, 'Art is inner order.' And I think that every time I get myself into a state of grace where I stop being a believer who has faith in writing and start being a mystic who has communion with it, then delightful things are possible.

For the past eight or so years I've had a fascination with my own ready-to-hand stories whose basic world-building, or problematic premises, are derived from episodes of my imaginary game, the game I share with my younger sister, Sara, and for many years shared with a friend. That double ownership is significant. My two most recently published novels, *Mortal Fire* and *Wake*, have plots derived from episodes of the game, two each, played with my friend and with my sister. It worked like this: Sara and I were stuck for an idea we could agree on, and I reached for a plot that was tried-and-true because I'd already played it with my friend. I reused the setup. The thing about the games that became *Mortal Fire* and *Wake* was that, because I did them twice, I was able to see with greater clarity what possibilities might be produced by the same setup.

The story that became *Mortal Fire*, in its first iteration, was entirely peopled by adult characters. It was set in an isolated snowbound place. There was a house like the Beast's castle, without invisible servants, but where the house cleaned and maintained itself and its chattels by mending everything at midnight, and where time, folding back on itself this way, had slowed to a crawl. All the Beast's castle stuff ended up in the book. There was a magician deemed too powerful to be permitted freedom, who was trapped by a spell that governed both him and the house. Much of that ended up in the book. In its second iteration – the one played with Sara – the story centred much more around a juvenile magic user who, as it turned out, was the only person who could release the magician from the house. The house was situated in an isolated valley, a pastoral paradise. The magician's jailers were his cousins, now much older than him, and they were keeping him prisoner not just because they were afraid of him, but to punish him for something that happened in a local coal mining disaster decades before. The second story is much closer to the plot of *Mortal Fire*. However, the novitiate was male, not female, and not a Pacific Islander, and the setting wasn't my invented South Pacific island continent, Southland, and it wasn't 1959.

I have no record of either of these games. Even the second one with Sara was before we began recording ourselves; before 2004, when we discovered Skype. Sara has been living in Australia since 1992, so we must have been playing while she was on holiday with me, Fergus and Jack in Golden Bay.

My experiences with *Wake* and *Mortal Fire* encouraged me to think that the stories that had excited me, when I first collaboratively made them, might be used like nets to catch the bait running in the river, tasty sustaining ideas I wanted to chew on. Though the stories are collaborative, Sara and I share them out; we get to call dibs on what we think we might use in our writing. Sara currently has a novel with an agent in the States, a fantasy with Mafiosi using demons as muscle. *Very Minor Demons* is substantially based on an episode of our game. I have a nearly finished young adult book called *Kings of this World*, a school story and speculative fiction set in Southland. It's also based on a game, but is much further from its source. With these setups Sara and I have a record of how the whole thing played out, our voices on Skype, making up the stories together.

The trick of making use of these My Food Bag narratives is to recognise what will work in a novel as opposed to an imaginary game. Imaginary games have heat and immediacy, their worlds have to be solid enough for their characters to inhabit them, and their plots can't have gaping holes. Their plots evolve, and don't tend to tidy themselves as they go. We're very good at remembering who knows what, but can be a little extravagant with psychology if it's more productive of drama. What we can pull off in the heat of a played moment won't necessarily work in a novel. So using a game as the basis for a novel means you have to have the judgement to go 'this' but not 'that'.

Writing *Kings of this World*, I was very grateful for the play of ideas in the original game. Ideas were articulated in conversations between the characters, which were naturally spirited because Sara and I were also arguing things out – principally whether or not people are inherently good. But the plot was a dog's breakfast, so I had to start again from the ground up. I had to ask myself, 'What are these kids doing when they're getting to know each other? Having Jane Austen's *Emma*-like assumptions about what's going on around them, and nurturing each other's willingness to interfere in people's lives?' I had all that, so was it possible to germinate a plot out of misunderstandings, accidents and mischances? But if I did that I'd be writing a comedy, and it wasn't enough for me to be writing a comedy when I wanted to write a thriller. A thriller with a speculative fiction plot that was also a Southland book. I had to come up with a thriller plot that wouldn't just accommodate the comedy, but somehow rise out of it, out of gossip and conniving, and youthful high spirits. I was doing pretty well, but then I made an injurious decision that *Kings* needed to be a short book, and the first of two, so that I could get a sale quickly and help pay for the new garage and terrace and deck we were building.

Then, as soon as I'd declared that the book was part one of two, I realised that the material I had for a second book wasn't going to shape itself into a novel-like entity. Shortly I'll take *Kings* apart, put it back together again and finish it, as book one of one.

Anyway, I can't help but think that apart from mistakes fostered by pressing financial concerns most of my difficulties were produced by my being like a frugal home handyman who tells himself that, since he got the demolition windows for next to nothing, the kitchen he's trying to build must shape itself around them. And then, once his extension is well underway, the home handyman finds he has insoluble difficulties with his indoor–outdoor flow.

What happened to me is what happens to the person who starts with a given, and then has to shape the whole thing, and its needs, around something they already have. My method might have worked with *Wake* and *Mortal Fire*, but with those novels I didn't have enchanting pre-existing voices whispering their jokes and arguments in my ear.

So – with the demolition windows problem, the having-a-record problem, it is still possible to figure out what bits of lively business you can use, and what to reject. But that's far less of a challenge than establishing the integrity of the whole picture. Your characters may be delightfully alive, but characters appear in what happens, and if you change what you must of what happens, you are inevitably going to alter the way in which those characters reveal themselves.

I have a lot of sympathy for the scriptwriters of rebooted franchises, and admiration for those who do it well. Take Marvel's *Luke Cage* on Netflix. How do you make sense of the manly man in Harlem in the twenty-first century, whose standard curse is 'Sweet Christmas!'? Well – you have him trained mercilessly by his friend the barber's adherence to a swear jar in an effort to keep the language of the street out of his establishment. It's fascinating to witness the ingenuity of writers coping with their own famous franchise's demolition windows.

In the end I think the major problem I had in using a given, even one with verve, and sturdy story legs, is that doing so didn't leave any room for other things that would have turned up if I wasn't so wrapped up in the problem of having the whole room look right with the house.

Fortunately for the plus column of the 'Why write?' ledger I'm having a very different experience with the adult novel I'm now near to finishing.

The Absolute Book turned up, like *Dreamhunter* and *The Vintner's Luck*, out of the ether, and is using me to get itself written.

In his 1993 *Listener* review of my second novel *Treasure* Brian Boyd says: 'Knox seems a realist by nature but a metaphysician by inclination, a magpie who can swoop on glittering detail but would prefer to be a Phoenix.' Later he kindly and privately qualified his remark: 'The magpie and Phoenix was an image with a semi-private echo of Isaiah Berlin on the hedgehog (who knows one big thing), and the fox (who knows many little things): Berlin compared Tolstoy to a brilliant fox who thought it was more important to be a hedgehog. Not bad company for you.'

Perhaps what I know as a writer – after many novels – is that the one big thing can only appear as a dark place in the sky, discernible because of the otherwise – the myriad visible stars.

Besides, it seems to me that in order to write many novels it might be useful to be a bird of the Corvidae family – that is, a magpie, a crow, a jay, a rook, a jackdaw. Or a raven. Each novel has a different thing it wants, and needs to do. It's a centrifuge that mixes. It's a centrifuge that separates. It's a spinning body creating its own gravity.

There's a lot of talk about 'finding your own fictional voice', because so many of our ideas about writing fiction are shaped by the kindly pedagogical concerns of creative writing classes. But you don't find *your* voice, you find the voice of that particular book, of a first book, a second book, a fourth, a tenth and a thirteenth. Each has its own tone it wants to take. And if I was trying to be helpful I could talk about tone. But beyond tone and voice there's a quality that feels more telling to me when I'm trying to define the virtues of books that I'm really excited by, or when I recognise in my own work a necessity to the creation that isn't coming out of my interest in the characters, or the plot, or the kind of language I'm using, but is more simply a property of the book's vibe of being alive.

By that I mean not just how Elizabeth Knox the writer feels about human existence, but how the untethered, reactive, feeling entity, who is making it all up, feels at that particular moment, the moment of beginning the book, the moments of continuing the book. The book that is not a calibration of existence, but one day with a certain kind of weather, a memorable whole, like the interval between waking up and going to sleep. What I think I find in the novels I'm most excited by, and what I'm after in my own work, is a vibe of being alive that belongs generally to – well – I want to say each writer, but of course not all writers have one. Perhaps each considerable writer has one. And by considerable I don't mean literary, I mean a writer whose vitality has been transmitted to their work. I can make compelling arguments for the vibe of life of Lee Child, or Georgette Heyer, just as I can for Hilary Mantel, Elizabeth Gaskell or Margaret Mahy. This vibe of life is one of the reasons we choose to be constant readers of certain writers. We like what they do, but we also like the way they make us see the world, or feel about it. We like how they make us feel when we are in their world, and therefore how we feel once we've finished the book, and are returned to our everyday with something about our sensibilities, our thought processes, our grit and appetite, altered. That's my explanation of why we love and cleave to particular authors: their vibe of life. But it isn't a satisfactory explanation of what, if you're a novelist, you're looking for in each of your own books as it yields its purpose to you. I think of that thing as the book's *aura*: borrowing from the New Age. A glow coming off the created thing, which belongs to its life and its character, and tells us something about where it's been, even if *it's never been anywhere*. A book begins, and it hasn't been anywhere. Sometimes a book begins whose degree of never having been anywhere before its appearance feels as if it's in the territory of Annunciation and Nativity.

I am reminded of the afternoon when our son Jack finally appeared in my hospital room at Wellington Women's. He'd been in neonatal for two days, and because of blood loss and my healing caesarean incision, I'd only visited him to breastfeed. He turned up very suddenly, at dinner-time, because, while eating her dinner, his mother had begun sobbing that she wanted her baby. And then his father started crying too. I figure we must have been overheard. Jack appeared twenty minutes later, in his plastic cradle. They put him between my bed and Fergus's chair, and we proceeded to get cricks in our necks just staring at him. One thing we couldn't take our eyes off was his quizzical and daunting single eyebrow lift. His left eyebrow would go up as if he couldn't quite believe what he was being presented with. And Fergus remarked that he thought he had cultivated that expression himself over many years. But Jack was born with it. And perhaps Fergus had been too, and might that not mean that his character was shaped by his facial expression rather than the other way around?

There is the idea that a soul comes into the world with the body, that the soul is unstained, but somehow perfectly formed, although the child still has to grow as a person in the world. That idea may be a bit of Western dualism, but at least to some extent it rises out of observation: the marvel of being surprised by a grandparent's expression on a toddler's face. Not just the shadow of an expression, but a thing so powerfully reminiscent that it is as if the expression has arrived containing the whole texture of the grandparent's life and experience.

There are books that, when you're their author, seem to appear in the same way, stainless and finished, rather than formed in the forge of writing, as if you, the writer, hadn't sat there with all the hard labour and hard thinking of making the book's body. No – the book arrives trailing clouds of glory as if pencil on paper has summoned hitherto invisible realities that want to organise themselves out of nothing, using a writer's own character and experience.

From very early in my life I had a delight in how things

were connected. Connected in the world by use and influence, and how I was able to connect them myself in my head. I think my delight had something to do with my puzzlement at my stupidity when it came to writing – that is, writing as opposed to reading. I'm certain now that I had dysgraphia of the dyslexic type. I could read, and comprehend what I'd read, and verbally answer questions about what I'd read, and I could read out loud, but I could scarcely write. It was natural for all my too many primary schools to assume that, since I could read, my writing could only be laboured and abysmal because I was lazy, stubborn and uncooperative. It was the 1960s, and I was a girl, so pains were never taken. For example, when in standard two I was asked to produce two pages on the life cycle of a butterfly, I produced two pages of two words per line, in columns down the left and right hand side of the page, the teacher decided I was being either insolent or indolent. But it was like this: whenever I had a pen in my hand, I also had a great glass wall in front of me. I was all in and no out, so, although I was reading and thinking and making connections, whatever I learned I had to hold in my head, like water in cupped hands, waiting on the cup, the bucket, the lakebed.

My mind now pretty much works like everyone else's, but is shaped by this early intense practice of recognising how information connected up so that it might support itself instead of requiring me to support it by recording all its facets as they revolved in empty space. My mind has a very strong habit of seeing patterns, because a pattern is easier to hold in your head than its pieces.

Stories have legacies in our limbic systems. Something that is there for any storyteller to use. The audience doesn't need to know about earlier appearances and interpretations of a particular story – of an invisible monster, a human-shaped monster, a charming human-shaped heart-usurping monster, a monster made by an ambitious scientist, a monstrous God who never answers prayers, or the animal who talks and still curls up beside you like an ordinary cat, but who isn't there the moment it's most wanted. Of course it's nice for the audience to know – to have the deep, nuanced, textured experience of the story because of all the connections it makes. Constant readers, or watchers, people with a degree of appetite and experience and a good memory, *get* stuff when you give it to them. Those people know that they haven't learned most of what they know in order of its appearance in the world. They understand they might have met the monster in a joke, before meeting it in its myth.

The great and ancient beast we encounter in a television programme might owe much to H P Lovecraft's Cthulhu, but the energy of that creature is also the inheritance of all people in a house or a landscape with older occupants. It's our sense of how recently we've been the pinnacle predator, and how tenuously we are a pinnacle predator whenever we're by ourselves. It's our short period of remove from the time when we had no news of what was on the other side of the river, or why the mountain in whose shadow we lived would sometimes growl and glow. We may have left much of that behind us – or at least know what's choking us when the wall of ash washes over us. Yet as surely as being in fear and uncertainty can leave its mark on a developing child's DNA so that child's *children* will inherit a poorly extinguished anxiety, then our stories, and our response to them, have been shaped by all those years of not knowing what it was we could hear at night, behind the wind.

I first met one of my favourite monsters in a joke. At Christmas when I was nine someone gave my mother a card with the three wise men on it, two of them pink with anger and embarrassment, saying to the third, who was holding one end of a rope: 'We said *frankincense* . . .' Then, when the card opened, there on the end of the rope was a louring, greenish monster with bolts in his neck.

I didn't get the joke. But I knew it was a joke, and a story. Seeing my intrigue Mum explained Frankenstein's monster.

And, since she liked her facts straight, and was the kind of mother who took pains to make sure they were, she also explained how Frankenstein was the man who made the monster, not the monster, who had no name, and how lots of people got that wrong. I'd already realised there was some connection between the monster and the Gruesome Twosome of the Hanna-Barbera *Wacky Races*, a cartoon about a cross-country race, where the Gruesome Twosome drove a car that looked like a haunted house. One of the Twosome was a massive, monster-like individual with a bowl haircut and a turtleneck sweater – a kind of 60s hipster Frankenstein's monster. I made that connection. I began to build up a concordance of the story. A concordance which in time assembled itself in order of provenance – in this case Mary Shelley's book, a product of a ghost story challenge at the Villa Diodati with Shelley and Claire Clairmont, Lord Byron and Dr Polidori. First there was the book, and then later appearances, canon and otherwise, and, as with all my concordances, the information was also in order of what mattered most to me. I did that throughout my childhood and teens, and retained my habit of accepting the premises of an invention, or at least waiting to see how things might fit together. It was clear to me that there were no lame ideas. If an idea was limping its shoes might arrive at any moment. Its shoes, its horse and carriage, its rocket ship, its wings. Which isn't to say that the adult me hasn't thrown up her hands in disgust when faced with a story that is half-baked or inconsistent or derivative – derivative rather than open to influence – or, worst of all, a story that stacks its dice.

An acceptance of premises is the absolutely necessary prerequisite of the willing suspension of disbelief, that which lets us enjoy stories and not be those people who like to say, with an uneasy superiority, that they only read non-fiction. Because they 'want to learn something'.

It's the existence of all my concordances that have determined my mode of operation as a writer, how I like to

take a thing, or more often several things, with the charge
of a mythical legacy, and use them to my own purposes.
Because they are attractive to me and I want to pick them
up and handle them. Because they are meaningful to me and
I want to get into conversation with them. Because they are
comforting to me and I want to slip them under my pillow
when I sleep.

So. Why write? When it's often very difficult? Because if
you're lucky, and you keep at it long enough, and honestly,
if you stay by the sundial, and don't chase any of the things
beckoning you from the ends of the avenues – like your own
insufficient idea of fame; or money; or the approval of your
family and admiration of your friends; or the admiration
of your community, or arts funding bodies, or the public,
whoever they are – if you stay by the sundial, the sun will
come, will show you your shadow, and give you the time.
Then, if you're very lucky, it might give you your Absolute
Book.

Turnips

James Brown

Alphabet forms provide a frame – the illusion of order. I always think about form and how it might aid or reflect a poem's content in some way. But sometimes, such as here, a form is merely something to hang the words on, the alphabet as repository and index. Forms also counter free verse's tyranny of choice by imposing imaginative challenges: what in the weird world am I going to put for K, for example?

Books. How can you write if you don't like reading? But it's more than that. At some point, I discovered reading could make me laugh and cry. 'Singing in her song she died, / The Lady of Shalott.' I don't think written words work that way for everyone. In my mind there's a quote that goes something like, 'Reading is useful because it allows us to do nothing while believing a whole lot of stuff is getting done.' I thought it was from a Dean Young poem, but I can't find it. Now I'm hoping it's actually me!

Clichés. The germs in good writing, or so we're told. Yet our daily language is largely composed of clichés, and overwritten poetry is often the result of people straining to write in fresh and original ways because poetry is supposed to be above daily language. Yawn. Clichés exist in all levels of language. To deny them is to invent a new language, one that only you understand and that will inevitably also recycle its imagery. Communication is about recycling. Maybe the issue is more about how and where you use clichés. I used to think ending a poem on a cliché was a complete no-no until I read the concluding line of 'The Hand' by Mary Ruefle.

> The teacher repeats the question.
> Outside the window, on an overhanging branch,
> a robin is ruffling its feathers
> and spring is in the air.

Coherence. Contradictions. One does not necessarily preclude the other. Expansive poet Walt Whitman's famous lines from 'Song of Myself' explain how points in different directions can cheerfully coexist:

> Do I contradict myself?
> Very well then I contradict myself,
> (I am large, I contain multitudes.)

An old epic poem celebrating US plurality is probably the wrong place to mention compression. Or the right place.

Creating something is cathartic. 'Action causes more trouble than thought,' wrote Jenny Holzer, and while words might provoke action they're not actions themselves. Writing about digging a hole is not the same as digging a hole. Writing is momentous and empty. Readers cause all the trouble.

Discovery. Fiction writer Donald Barthelme wrote an excellent essay called 'Not-Knowing', in which he argues not only for not knowing where you're heading but also not knowing where you've got to. Poetry loves ambiguity, multiplicity, possibility. Who knows where this will end up.

Experimentation. Note to self: do more of this. Word processor Kenneth Goldsmith has grumbled that poetry still has a marginalised avant-garde distinct from mainstream poetry, whereas in the visual arts what was once considered avant-garde is now mainstream. But isn't the avant-garde and experimental meant to be outside the mainstream? And mainstream poetry has moved from where it was when avant-garde art first began baffling audiences (most obviously, free verse has long since superseded regular metres and rhyme schemes). That said, personal poems (see Personal poetry), give or take a few formal fluctuations, have been poetry's dominant mode for a long time now. It's too easy to default to writing lyrical first-person poems because we've come to think of poetry as the go-to form for expressing personal emotion. And subject verb object is how we're taught to communicate. Dog bites man. Man bites dog. If we stray too far outside that, we risk losing our audience. And yet it's good to push language about a bit, isn't it? Man bites dog dog man bites. Woof. Oof.

Found poetry. If, like me, you're not gifted and talented but reckon you can tell poetry from prose, then maybe you can assemble a poem using found phrases and sentences. There aren't hard and fast rules for this, except to say that lifting individual words from a text and piecing them together in the manner of fridge magnet poetry is asserting too much creative control. And finding a beautiful piece of prose and introducing line breaks and re-presenting it as a beautiful poem doesn't count either. You're supposed to transform the material into something new. Erase stuff, reorder, and maybe introduce line breaks and stanzas. The grey area is joining different phrases. You could, for example, find this in the above:

> If, like me, you're gifted and talented
> you can tell hard rules from
> fridge magnet poetry.
> A beautiful poem doesn't count.
> Erase, for example, the above.

Flarf poetry is like found poetry in that it involves collage, but it lifts material from all over the place and is relaxed about adapting it. Flarf started as a joke. Around the early 2000s, a group of US poets were trying to write bad poetry – poetry that was clunky, incoherent, tuneless, banal, oafish – whatever poetry isn't meant to be. Hmmm, and where might you find a ready source of such language? Yep, pretty soon the Flarfers were using internet searches to generate material. While some lines are hilarious, the trouble with a lot of Flarf poems is they go on too long and often still sound too like their tedious internet sources. The 'movement' probably peaked around 2010. Fun thought: was Ern Malley actually the first Flarf poet?

Freedom. Writing poetry is the one area of my life where I make all the rules. And if I don't like them, I change them. And if I don't like the results, I don't show anyone. That's the difference between writing and publishing: writing permits failure. Write to please yourself first and foremost.

God. God is proof of our need and ability to imagine a being mightier than ourselves and our boss at work. This god recognises our hard, unacknowledged toil and suffering, and delivers justice. God is the power of our imagination and the power of our imagination is god.

Grand themes. Let them go. No subject is too trivial. The grand also exists in the seemingly unimportant. A moment in 'The Hand' by Mary Ruefle:

You don't raise your hand and there is
some essential beauty in your fingers,
which aren't even drumming, but lie
flat and peaceful.

Heat. Humiliation. Humbleness. Hard work. Sometimes a poem lands on your plate fully formed, sometimes you hack away at it for years before going back to what you had in the first place, which still isn't quite right.

Humour. Poetry is frequently too earnest (see Grand themes).

O no. Then list with tearful eye,
Whilst I his fate do tell.
His soul did from this cold world fly,
By falling down a well.

Emmeline Grangerford 'could rattle off poetry like nothing . . . just so it was sadful', says an impressed Huck Finn. 'Poor Emmeline made poetry about all the dead people when she was alive, and it didn't seem right that there warn't nobody to make some about her, now she was gone; so I tried to sweat out a verse or two myself, but I couldn't seem to make it go, somehow.' Gosh, could it be possible to be funny and serious at the same time? Who'd have thought? Mark Twain doesn't show us any of Huck's verse, but I suspect it would have been better than Emmeline's.

Ideas. Words are ideas. Read the amazing essay 'Variations: A Return of Words' by poet Lyn Hejinian: 'Lucidities, or, lights (a starry angular). The staring bright varieties of word and idea . . . On the nectarine and the clarinet distinction casts a light, in its turn. One only has to look at a thing, and think a little.' You can find it on the internet.

Imagination. Hard to define, but you know when it isn't up to much. New clichés, the capacity to surprise, true wit . . . the more you read the more you realise how rarely writers get struck by lightning. That's because the sacrifices required – time on golf courses in thunderstorms while waving nine irons at god – can be too great.

Imitation. If imitation is the sincerest form of flattery, then plagiarism is the sincerest form of imitation. Discuss. Actually, it's quite hard to mimic your favourite writers because you are you and they are they. Try writing your version of a favourite poem. Imitate what it makes you think or feel, but transplant it into your own world. Steal its essence, not its bricks and mortar, and no one will know. Steal its bricks and mortar, and everyone will recognise a pale, wonky copy.

Imperfection. Some poems are perfectly cut diamonds, and it's hard when writing not to have perfection as your unattainable goal. But sometimes flaws are more interesting because of their capacity to surprise. I'm not arguing for howlingly bad lines (or am I?), but for sighs, hiccups, stutters, snorts, etc. – the little awkwardnesses that make writing human.

Irony. Somewhat maligned after postmodernism all but exhausted the knowing wink, I still think there's a place for saying the opposite of what you mean. Perhaps it's to do with degree. No such thing as too much sarcasm. Yeah, right.

James. It's hard to escape yourself, but poetry gives you the chance to imagine what it might be like to be somebody else . . . somebody bright, sensitive, gorgeous, witty, funny, insightful, spiritual, arty, athletic, practical, respected, talented, modest and of course genuine.

Kaos versus order, though 'kaos' is definitely trying too hard to be clever (see Wit and Uncertainty). An essential truth about poems is they usually set up their rules of engagement in the first few lines. Crucial basics like tone, point of view, punctuation, form, layout – all the parts, props and players in the poem's film and soundtrack. You can break your own rules, but it's trickier to break a poem's, to step outside its defining parameters to where slithy toves might gyre and gimble in the wabe. If I'd a knowed what a trouble it was, I wouldn't a tackled it and ain't agoing to no more. Did you spot where 'The Jabberwocky' and Huck Finn weirdly entered the text and altered the tone? Yes ( ). No ( ). Would you like 'The Jabberwocky' or Huck Finn to appear again later? Yes ( ). No ( ).

'Longing, we say, because desire is full of endless distances.' ('Meditation at Lagunitas', Robert Hass.)

Music – as in the musicality of language and making things sound how you want them to sound. Music is great at communicating emotion, hence lyric poetry. But there are countless other possible soundscapes. The English language is actually full of rhymes, assonance, alliteration, etc. It's almost too easy to start singing when what you really need to do is listen.

Narrative desire. Readers want to know what happens next. Prose writers make full use of this desire, but it's often underutilised by poets. Many poems are simply descriptions of things or feelings. Colin McCahon was once challenged about whether painting would survive in a world of moving images. He said it would. Why? 'Because it *doesn't* move.' Good response. A poem can be a still life, but it can also be a movie. I used to write museum labels and what people wanted to read most were stories about the displayed objects rather than just descriptions of them.

Nearly nailed it. Ninety per cent there. Oh god, the unfinished poem. You scrawled something down, something overheard, half remembered, something from nowhere that popped into your head, and then you worked it up a bit later, but you were called away by friends, family, food, frolicking . . . and now you're trying to re-enter the poem. You call and call, but you can't hear it anywhere.

Not bad. The 'not bad' theory of poetry occurred to me as a teacher and reader of poetry. When I read poetry in literary magazines, I often find myself thinking, 'That one's not bad,' much more than, 'That one's good.' The prevailing 'not bad' level is maybe a result of creative writing courses like the one I convene because I can teach people how to avoid the common pitfalls of bad writing, but I'm not sure I can teach people to be good writers. That's something they have to work out for themselves. There's a yawning gulf between a poem that's not bad and one that's good, and crossing it is a major step, one all writers constantly struggle with. You need to find your own way.

Ordinariness. Our lives are, on the whole, not as exceptional as we'd like to think (see James). 'I've seen this happen in other people's lives and now it's happening in mine' (The Smiths). Writing gives you the chance to go beyond yourself, to experience, from the relative safety of your desk or laptop, an extraordinary air rushing through your wings (see Imagination).

Pay attention – that's what poets are always told. Pay attention to the world. Every little particular. For me, it's the opposite. I have to screen stuff out. The world is overwhelming. I feel as if I'm being assaulted by information. Not everything is significant. You don't need to hear every conversation, watch every unmissable mini-series, go to every exhibition. Life and poetry are the art of selection. 'One day you're in. And the next day, you're out.' (Heidi Klum, *Project Runway.*)

Performing your work is a necessary evil of poetry. Eventually, you will have to do it (see Shyness).

Personal poetry. 'Poor. Old. Tired. Horse.' ('Please', Robert Creeley.) Roger Horrocks wrote the following in *Landfall* 182 (June 1992):

> The narrow perspectives of the present are epitomised by the form that has dominated local poetry over the last decade – the 'personal poem,' short, anecdotal, usually in the first person, mostly prosaic in a free-verse way but climaxing in a little burst of lyricism. Such poetry invites the reader to share a humane space in which some likeable, liberal person (usually the poet) becomes a little more sensitive or learns some wry lesson about life. This genre has become a cliché . . . the ambitious sense of 'we' in *Landfall* in the 1940s has given way to a sprinkling of sensitive first persons.

That is not to say we should stop writing personal poems. Donald Barthelme explains why in his short story 'Rebecca':

> The story ends. It was written for several reasons. Nine of them are secrets. The tenth is that one should never cease considering human love. Which remains as grisly and golden as ever, no matter what is tattooed upon the warm tympanic page.

Even language poets and conceptual poets still pen the odd personal poem. It's not the personal poetry, it's *how* we're writing the personal poetry. Go directly to Experimentation. Do not pass Go. Do not collect $200.

Problems. 'The fatal problem with poetry: poems.' (Ben Lerner, *The Hatred of Poetry.*)

Questions, always questions.

Realism. For obvious reasons, realism is another easy default writing setting. Trying to think of non-realist genres, all I can come up with are science fiction, fantasy, surrealism, magic realism, postmodernism and fairy stories. Poetry often mitigates realism with plentiful imagery, but remains shackled to it nonetheless. Yet reality is simply that which you can be persuaded of. Here are the concluding lines to 'The Loser' by James Tate:

[. . .] Jenny walked into the kitchen and started
banging some pots and pans around. I shook my head and
  stood up.
Something was terribly wrong. An egg was hatching in
  my hand,
the egg of an otter. Otters don't lay eggs, but I was
  starving.

Reality? Not exactly. Truth? Feels spot on to me.

Shit detector (see Uncertainty). You need one, but you don't want it set too high or you'll abandon everything. Space and time are good for helping you assess and change things because your eye becomes more detached, until finally you can unscrew it and hold it at arm's length and gawp in amazement at the one-eyed fool who thought that zing-swing pun (see Wit) was so ace. If something still sounds good to you after a few weeks or months or years, that's a good sign.

Shyness. Writing gives me a way of interacting with people without having to chatter to them face-to-face in witty and charming ways. A radio show I once did provided the same sort of buffer. The small print in the writing contract is the live reading, which if you write poetry long enough you will eventually be called upon to give. Because I've been to readings where a poet's shyness has spoiled their poems (I've also seen plenty of poems ruined by poets a little too fond of the limelight), I've taught myself to at least deliver my poems as best I can. One saving grace is being able to read your poem on paper, rather than having to know your lines like an actor. Believe in your words, they are a safe house. Practise. When I read, I go into the words of the poem, which are the sound of the poem, which are the safe house of the poem. I'm still not much good at between-poem banter, but providing I can say a few things that the audience might need to know about the poem, I can lurch to the poem itself, the safe house of its sounds.

Silence.

So what? Remember Grand themes and how someone claiming to be me said no subject is too trivial? But skip to Pay attention ('Not everything is significant') and Ordinariness, where I brutally inform you that most lives are unexceptional and encourage you to look beyond yourself. Writing needs to see off the So what? response, which means *how* you write about something is more important than *what* you write about. Much more. Also, *why* write poetry? People often do things for money and recognition. Poetry brings little of either, so you need to write it for other reasons – the pleasure of creating something, catharsis, freedom . . . whatever pushes your pen. Only a small community are going to read what you write, and even fewer are going to say they like it. So what.

Stop making sense. Sound over sense. This is easier to say than do because making sense is how we're schooled in language. Yet there are many discourses that seem designed to obfuscate – legal, medical, theoretical, political, to name a few. And poetry is often exploring stuff that's hard to say, so it makes sense that often it might not. Readers differ over how obscure or obvious they like poems to be. As you become a better poetry reader, you become more comfortable with obscurity. That will stand you in good stead as a poet, too.

'The tip of the tongue.' I began to notice this phrase, or variations of it, cropping up in poems so often that at one time I started bookmarking them. It appears in poems by Andrew Johnston, Dorothy Porter (twice in one book), Craig Raine (twice in one book), Michael Harlow, Jennifer Kronovet, Carol Ann Duffy. Thinking about sound and sense, it's not hard to see why poets are attracted to it.

Turnips. 'They rode past a great many turnip fields / but as it was the wrong time of year, they didn't see any turnips.' (*The Epiplectic Bicycle*, Edward Gorey.) Keep writing and reading. Not all the time, necessarily. Try writing exercises. I've never managed to ring-fence writing times and have no doubt lost stuff because I've been unable to hold off the world. Sometimes you've got to give something up. If you can't, be secretive. Writing time attracts people. Stay up late, get up early. Tomorrow, a thin stem.

Uncertainty. I can't think of many areas of endeavour where uncertainty is so manifest. If you play sport, you know when you've played badly. If you listen to a singer, you know when they're out of tune. But deciding whether a line of poetry is or isn't working is much harder. Brian Turner said, 'If you are uneasy about some aspect of a poem – an image or a phrase – then usually you have cause to be.' In other words, go with your gut. It's good advice.

Urm, back to the singing metaphor. Singing in tune isn't essential when it comes to rock and roll. Attitude counts for a lot. Unless you're writing something akin to opera, it's the same with poetry. You don't need a great voice, in fact imperfections are fine because poetry has long since stage-dived off its pedestal. But you do need to be able to hear the poem's music or anti-music. Jumping styles mid-poem is possible, but tricky (see Kaos). I can't actually think of many poems with a lot of radical tonal shifts (some Flarf poems, perhaps). Mostly, you get varying moments of intensity, but the band at the end of the poem is still the one that began it.

V-sign. Peace, victory, up yours.

Wit (shafts of). Bill Manhire introduced me to the question 'Does this line seem a bit too pleased with itself?' Tread carefully around puns, double meanings, mellifluous lyricism. I was going to end this essay with 'It don't mean a thing, if it ain't got that zing', which now earns its place as an example of a line that's not nearly as witty as it wants to be.

Word-world equation. Surely most writers melt a few brain cells over how language represents the world, indeed *is* the world, at some point. 'I write / a world as good as its word' ('A Balanced Bait in Handy Pellet Form', Allen Curnow). I sometimes think of language as a building material and the poem as a 4D object, which is useful when trying to get your head round a poem's sound, shape, sense and context. But, a word of warning: poems that are too consciously about poetry are frequently boring.

Ex, as in former. Deep down, you know what you're prepared to part with and what you're not. The older you get, the older a poem gets, the easier it is to ditch lines.

You. I write mainly to please myself, but when it comes to publishing I am aware that there are readers making judgements. I don't want my poems to be too obvious or too obscure. I also don't want to seem excessively stupid, heartless, depraved, earnest, etc. Like most people, I want to be liked, but finally I'm more interested in being true to the poem than true to myself. Donald Barthelme, when asked about his audience, replied, 'I have a very clear idea of the people I'm writing for. They are extremely intelligent and they are also physically attractive.'

Zing. Zing is whatever you like. It's that special unfathomable something you get when you and language connect. You want it when you read, and you want it when you write. I must insist on zing.

Necessity Is the Mother of My Inventions

Nina Nawalowalo with Tom McCrory

Every day we are bombarded with stories. Gossip, conspiracy, news, fake news, facts and their alternatives fly at us from nowhere. Like any blitzkrieg, the purpose is to bring us to surrender. To experience powerlessness in the face of onslaught. Information has become an instrument of terror. The story has become severed from the teller and we are left seeking refuge, not knowing what to believe. Into the rubble steps a saviour who offers shelter, who tells us who to hate.

What can I do? As a storyteller I certainly don't want to add to the barrage. I don't want to stand in the midst of the noise shouting for your attention. And so, as a Pacific storyteller, I ask myself what is *needed*? Necessity is the mother of my invention.

The answer grows from my culture and my art form, theatre. Culture, because in the Pacific the essential story weaves me into the land, to an unbroken thread of people. Following back, I become trees and animals, forces of nature, gods and finally the first darkness itself. Theatre, because the story is never severed from the teller, who meets you face to face, on a real patch of ground, in real time, and has the courage to breathe the same air, to tell their truth.

I need theatre's silence and stillness and its listening . . .

Quietly I ask myself, as a Pacific theatre-maker and storyteller, 'What are the stories that need to be told?' The answer is: the stories that are *hidden*. I must unearth stories buried under the layers of others' narratives. I choose to serve the unheard. Whose story is told, and whose is hidden?

Whose story is valued? Whose worthless? Whose story polished with pride and put on the mantelpiece? And whose is shadowed in shame?

These are the questions that I, as a Pacific storyteller, must ask myself.

Whose story has become *history* itself? Whose version of the story underpins and controls the very social environment in which my own unfolds?

For me, the environment is not clouds, trees and water, but story. We hear daily of the destruction of the environment. But this destruction is itself driven by a story. Are these trees and water commodities? Resources, our ancestors, gods? Raw experience – or raw materials? How we describe the environment becomes how we relate to it. Nothing tells this story so clearly as what has been happening at Standing Rock, North Dakota, since 2016.

So I ask myself, what story do I need to share with you? I choose to take you into the story of the creation of *The White Guitar*.

The White Guitar follows the true story of the Luafutu family: patriarch John and sons Matthias and Malo (also known as platinum-selling hip hop artist Scribe). It takes us from a grandmother's dream of a better life in New Zealand, through the collision of that dream with the realities of hardship and loss in 1958 Ponsonby, to the Christchurch earthquake in 2011. It follows a man's journey from boyhood innocence into the heart of darkness – from being put in a boys' home for stealing a bicycle at age nine to becoming a state ward at twelve, experiencing violence, drug addiction, prison and gangs, to reveal the possibility of hope and overcoming of adversity through healing and inspiration.

The White Guitar is a redemption song dedicated to the uplifting power of culture, spirit and music – from the first songs of a grandmother, sung to her white guitar, to the power of rock and roll, from the beats of hip hop to the hymns of the church; music is the life-blood that pumps through the story's veins. It is uniquely told on stage by a father and his two sons against a backdrop of stunning audio-visual design, live music and illusion.

A work like *The White Guitar* is a rare experience in a career: where a play carries such significance for all concerned, where the creation process has a power to heal and change, and where raw performance power is amplified nightly by the audience, who resonate with the story but, moreover, are deeply affected by witnessing people telling the truth. The Luafutu family shows profound courage in doing this. As the father and his two sons say, 'The truth will set you free . . .'

On a tour of nine cities in New Zealand, with a standing ovation for every performance, *The White Guitar* has been historic and groundbreaking, a life-changing event for The Conch and New Zealand theatre. It has been a major achievement for Pacific theatre, and has laid to rest the falsehood that there is no audience for Pacific stories in the regions. Seeing an audience of 600 in the Napier Municipal Theatre, patched gang members alongside a Hawke's Bay Arts Festival crowd, leap to their feet in unison at curtain call, was an unforgettable experience.

We have subtly changed our environment. Or maybe we have deeply changed ourselves. By telling the truth of our story we stand taller, a little freer in our environment. Telling the story of *The White Guitar* requires courage . . . But *why*?

Because the truths it tells are hidden, buried by shaming, or suppressed because they reveal a society in denial of its own true story. Gangs, violence, drug addiction, imprisonment and abuse *are* hidden stories to those outside this reality. But so is the story of political resistance, uprising, creativity, music; the story of reclaiming identity; the transformation of the experience of racism into an identity not defined by another's standards. In a world where we are told we are beyond redemption, to be redeemed becomes a revolutionary act.

To tell the story of *The White Guitar*, or any Pacific story, requires us to create our own environment within this environment. A world within our world. It takes special conditions and relationships, a microclimate of trust in which the huge energy of supressed story can be released and fusions take place in the heat. New forms are created. It means holding the quality of listening so that the story can be told. We give each other the courage to reveal ourselves. This is the story of a process created in order to tell a story.

Matthias Luafutu came to Toi Whakaari: New Zealand Drama School when Conch co-founder Tom McCrory was head of movement. Matthias had been inspired to become an actor by Miranda Harcourt's performance of *Verbatim* while he was imprisoned. On his release he joined Jim Moriarty's theatre company Te Rākau and, encouraged by Jim's unstoppable enthusiasm, auditioned for Toi Whakaari and got in.

Tom was assigned as his personal tutor and they developed a close bond – mainly because Matthias tested every rule in the school and struggled in an environment at odds with his identity. After two years he left suddenly, leaving Tom a book, *A Boy Called Broke*, written by his father Fa'amoana in prison, to share the story of the environment he had grown up in and the reasons he had to leave Toi Whakaari. It was a story gifted to explain a story.

Now here's the thing: Matthias was one of the most talented

actors we had met, ever. He was a walking story that needed to be told. Ten years went by where our connection was held on to like a newspaper on a Wellington street. There was a sense of unfinished business.

In 2014, looking for the next Conch production, Tom turned back to *A Boy Called Broke*. Re-reading it, he noticed the subtitle: 'The story so far . . .' We realised that the story *since* then included Fa'amoana's two sons Matthias and Malo (Scribe). A journey from the environment of 1948 in Samoa to the present day . . . A father and his two sons on stage together . . . The idea created an explosion of excitement!

Creativity's first step is chemistry. We begin by placing together explosive elements. It is volatile, dangerous potentiality. Its second step is creating an environment in which the energy released by the chemical reaction is channelled *creatively*. Heat creates fluidity, and by skilfully working in the molten moment, new forms become possible.

So we made the call, and caught Matthias running in the rain down an Auckland street, hurrying to a twelve-hour shift at a glass factory. 'That would be amazing, Tom,' he said. 'I'd love to. But you've got to understand, I don't really talk to my old man.'

'Can I have his number?'

We cold-called Fa'amoana, and told him that his son was one of the most talented actors we'd ever met. That we loved him. That we'd read his book over and over again. That we believed the story needed to be told. Needless to say Fa'amona thought to himself, 'Who is this crazy palagi man who loves my son?' But he answered, 'If it's for my son, I'm in.' Of his brother, Scribe said the same.

And so a new story began. Weeks later we were having a meeting in Conch Records on Ponsonby Road, and Matthias was telling us stories. When he mentioned his grandmother used to have a white guitar, something clicked and I immediately knew this was the title. *The White Guitar*.

There is a profound relationship between our story and our social environment, the way the enviroment in which we live shapes our story, and how the story we tell ourselves daily shapes our future through actions and choices. Sometimes the stories we never tell anyone are those which shape our lives the most.

The question that presented itself to me was how to create the right working environment in which these men felt held, and to seek the doorway into this space. Though a safe room is important, it is the space between people, the relationships, that is the key to the work. The Conch is a family, and so a family met a family, and we built a trust from there.

I felt I needed a co-director with a deep understanding of script and a fearless ability to step into the fire with the men, and live. So I approached Jim Moriarty to hold the space with Tom and I.

The doorway for me is cultural: kaupapa Pasifika, vaka-Viti; the Fijian way. And so we began with sevu sevu, the kava ceremony. Only traditional culture creates an environment in which the full dimensions of a person can be acknowledged. For Fijians and Samoans alike, the kava ceremony is the chiefly way, the Vakaturaga. Through it I wanted to let the men know that I saw them for who they are: chiefs. That, however they may have been seen in the past, I honoured who they are as chiefs. Through them I acknowledged lines of people and the land; I acknowledged their mana. Mana is the beginning and the end for Pacific people, that from which we come and to which we return. Everything else is what happens in between. There exist environments that build our mana, and those that take it away.

The first day's work was a humbling journey, sitting in a small room, listening as the men told each other stories. Stories gave birth to other stories. The story of an arrest was told from the perspective of a father, then his son. The amazing thing was, this was happening for the first time. The father had never heard what it was like for his child to watch him be arrested by five policemen. Something extraordinary was happening. Because of the environment of listening, telling stories gave rise to realisations, realisations to understanding. Great lines sprang out and hooked ideas, inspired images.

An environment of creativity is woven from the threads of listening for the world that wants to emerge in the space between the creators. A story brings with it a world. If we listen, it tells us how it wants to be told.

Our next step was to move into the theatre. Held in the historic embrace of the Hannah Playhouse, Wellington, we gave ourselves five days to develop this work. And on the fifth day we invited an audience. We needed to know the shape of the story, so we created something of the beginning, middle and end, from which the story grew, encountered obstacles and returned to. Time is a great motivator! Limiting it focuses action, makes decisions necessary.

We are known for making visual theatre work. Key for me was to see how to create the picture, a stage image that expressed the layers of the story, its depth. I drew on the curve of the woven fale roof flickering with the light from a kerosene lamp; the curve of a bay in which a son fished with his father; the curve of the moon's edge; of the familiar hill; the seasons' cycles. The female form of a mother and her white guitar gave way to the hard edge of an electric light, to the straight lines of a Ponsonby street map, to the containment of a square room and, ultimately, a prison cell.

The environment of the present day co-exists with that of memory. We layered actions on stage with family photographs which, projected, took on the scale of their significance.

Most important of all to me was the presence of the female, literally, in the form of the grandmother, played by Tupe Lualua, whose white guitar became the symbol of creative resilience. The chief's daughter, the taupou, represents the sacred feminine, the highest values of traditional culture. The ancient covenant between male and female, which came to be replaced by the church and was broken. The mother is the superglue that binds a family together. The female has the power of forgiveness and redemption through unwavering love. The men's stories resonated in all these spaces like the strings of a guitar.

Of course the first audience completes the picture. They gave us the confidence to go on. And then Craig Cooper gave us a future by commissioning the work for the Christchurch Arts Festival 2015.

The next step was to write. The creative writing team, made up of Tom, Fa'amoana, Malo and Matthias, were joined by renowned writer Oscar Kightley, who gave his invaluable skill and perspective. The job was to map the narrative and find what was driving it. This was no mean feat. The story was epic, spanning sixty-three years, interweaving the lives of the three men.

Knowing what drives a story comes down to *why* it needs to be told. Knowing this helps you make decisions, tell the essential stories, find the essential truths. For us, this is a story about redemption, light that is found in the darkest hour.

Each man was given the stories he needed to write. The three returned to their different cities, Auckland, Christchurch and Wellington. Two months later, nine handwritten exercise books and a flurry of emails arrived at our house. Tom gave himself five days to read and edit these into the form of a script.

It was breathtaking that, though the men had written

separately, their stories *interwove*. Huge repeating cycles of experience rolled through generations. The words a father spoke to his son after beating him in a room in 1958 Ponsonby were repeated in a room in 1980s Christchurch: 'I only hit you because I love you.'

These stories became the text of a play. Imagery was written in. Embedded dialogue became characters to be played. Golden one-liners noted down in development were woven into speeches. Rap became the poetry of the prologue. The script was handed back to the men. It was a remarkable moment, as it contained stories they had never heard from each other, including their father's abuse in Kohitere boys' home. They saw their individual stories *as a whole*.

This point in the journey required deep courage again. The story needed to be told. But there was the personal question: why did the men need to tell it? What started as getting their son and brother's talent seen had become something much greater. They asked themselves why they would reveal all this so publicly.

Silent threats raise their heads in moments like this. People keep quiet for reasons. Society runs on terror. A bully only needs to hit you once: next time, just the thought of him is enough to make you beat yourself up. This is our environment, all the silent threats that cause us to not act. But as Martin Luther King said, 'Our lives begin to end the day we become silent about the things that matter.' This was a family committed to telling the truth. And so we pushed on.

We prepared meticulously: designed and built a set inspired by the legs of the kava bowl; created and refined all audio-visual material; created and rehearsed all illusions; refined and refined the script over many long nights at Jim Moriarty's kitchen table, powered by his rocket-fuel coffees.

I fuelled myself by watching the NWA video for 'Express

Yourself' on repeat, looking at the urban black males and their culture and setting, how they explore isolation, how the build-up of frustrations influences the imagery, rhythm and visual choreography.

When we stepped into three weeks' rehearsal, we were on top of our game. We were blessed to work in the Hannah Playhouse. For those three weeks it became our home. We worked in different spaces simultaneously. I would craft light and visual illusion on the stage, Jim would drill monologues and scenes in the green room, Tom and Fa'amoana would create the music in the bar area. We worked with what Jim would call *paepae*, three leaders picking upon the themes of each others' whaikōrero, knowing that the sum of the total meaning was greater than the individual's speech.

It was extremely hard at times. We hit walls where we needed to stop and sit, cry, smoke cigarettes, eat, talk or be silent. But there was a tremendous energy of love in the work. And in that environment great things become possible. Chris Winter brought the incredible cinematic dimension of a soundscape, Lisa Maule brought the brilliant environment of light, and I took a risk on a young Samoan design graduate, Owen McCarthy, to create an extraordinary realisation of the scripted audio-visuals. It paid off and he has not stopped working since. We were held by the technical wizardry of 'Magic' Mike Ainsworth and unseen performers Merlin Connell-Nawalowalo and Kasaya Manulevu.

Opening night came, and with it our first packed house and standing ovation, which was followed by fourteen more sold-out houses and standing ovations. In 2016 came another thirty, with eight thousand people seeing the work. This wave of acceptance washed away doubt and carried the men into a new understanding of the importance of their story. It enabled a greater objectivity over time, which helped us begin to craft the show as a work of art.

An audience is representative of a social environment. Theatre brings together a community to share an experience. This can create change.

The White Guitar is unique in my experience. In Christchurch it brought the Pacific community together with the traditional audience of the Court Theatre. It took an earthquake to unify them but when the lights came up, they leapt to their feet as one. In Auckland it brought together the Ponsonby community of 1968 with that of 2016. Two very different worlds coexisted for ninety minutes and laughed in very different places. Many for whom this was their first theatre performance sat with those for whom theatre is a regular Friday night. In Auckland the audience heard Albert Wendt stand and salute the Luafutu family alongside leaders of the Polynesian Panthers. Theatre has the power to change. *The White Guitar* could change the heart of someone who has only seen these stories in the media. It could change a fifteen-year-old schoolgirl who feels less alone because she is not the only one going through these things. This could change a woman who runs out into the street and calls her father for the first time in thirty years.

Theatre has a unique and powerful role to play in our environment. It takes courage to engage. With *The White Guitar* that courage began with the leadership of father Fa'amoana Luafutu, in his willingness to own his story. In doing so he opened the way for all – his sons, the creative team, the company and the audience. His actions powerfully demonstrate the way of the chief – an incredible fusion of boldness and humility. It has been impossible for us all to not be affected daily by this example. We all have our demons. We all have the potential for redemption.

One of our last performances was in the Pacific Unit of Spring Hill Corrections Facility. As I walked in through security I saw an environment made up almost entirely of Māori and Pacific men, inside a fence. The audience, made up of forty Pacific men, all serving long sentences, many for violence, met the performance of the Luafutu men, two of whom themselves have been in prison. I slowly watched the body language of the audience change as prison guards and prisoners alike were deeply moved by seeing their story told. There seemed only a millimetre of difference between the story of the Pacific prison guards and the inmates. The guards themselves stripped to the waist to siva alongside the inmates. At this moment all I saw was a room full of Pacific people.

Fa'amoana's words at the end of the performance will always stay with me: 'We spend our lives trying to be the hard man, forgetting that in the end we will have to face the hardest man of all, God.'

Just as we can create a unique environment in the rehearsal space, so we can in a theatre, one in which change becomes possible. People walk back into the night with a different story, a shifted perspective. And maybe, just maybe, this can change our environment.

I have at times, like all of us, felt overwhelmed by the barrage of noise and disembodied stories, by the dominance of the loudest voice. So when I ask what can I do for our world, my answer is: tell the truth as I see it. Create a quiet and stillness in which listening is possible, and share the stories that *need* to be told.

Lloyd Jones

An Interview with Charlotte Wood

'It would be difficult to think of another novelist quite as original or fearless as fifty-five-year-old New Zealand author Lloyd Jones,' wrote novelist Delia Falconer in *The Monthly* in 2010.

The author of fifteen books, including novels, short stories, fiction for children and a memoir, Jones came to international prominence in 2006 with *Mister Pip*, his extraordinary riff on Dickens's *Great Expectations* set in war-torn Bougainville, narrated by a fourteen-year-old girl. The novel won him many new admirers, as well as the Commonwealth Writers' Prize, and was shortlisted for the Booker. It was also made into a feature film starring Hugh Laurie in the title role.

Jones was born in Lower Hutt in the Wellington region of New Zealand in 1955. After attending Hutt Valley High School and Victoria University, he left his homeland and took off on a road trip across America, a journey that became a defining experience for him as a blossoming fiction writer.

He describes himself as a sports-mad kid until struck by meningitis at the age of nineteen – a temporary plunge into physical frailty that was a factor in turning his attention towards literature.

As well as the Commonwealth Writers' Prize, his work has garnered many other accolades, including the Tasmania Prize for Fiction, New Zealand's Deutz Medal for Fiction, the Kiriyama Prize, several Montana awards as well as many international shortlistings, including the Booker.

My first 'meeting' with Jones was not a meeting at all, but online, in a classroom. I took part in a webinar masterclass Jones gave about voice in fiction, held in Queensland and hosted by *Griffith Review* and its editor, Julianne Schultz. I found the way Jones spoke about fiction so fresh and exhilarating that as soon as the class finished I wrote asking for an interview.

Our conversation took place in Adelaide, at the townhouse Jones was renting while working at Adelaide University, where he had been invited as the first writer in residence for the university's J M Coetzee Centre for Creative Practice.

Jones describes himself as having a 'contrarian' nature, and certainly his fiction speaks of an impatience with rules and an urge to combat or challenge convention. The vastly different settings and material of his novels – his subject matter includes the civil war in Bougainville, painting, the birth of the All Blacks rugby team in 1905, the Argentinian tango in World War II New Zealand, African refugees in contemporary Germany, political intrigue in Albania – makes categorisation of his work impossible. He told me this striking change in each book's material is usually a reaction against the previous work, and he spoke often of the quest to discover 'a new way' of storytelling, or even of reading.

In conversation Jones is thoughtful and quiet, speaking of his own work with an unassuming thoroughness of self-examination. For a man of his achievements I also found him unusually modest.

While speaking carefully, he gives off an air of restless physical energy. When I arrived for the interview he shot out of the apartment to get a sandwich, then to unpeg some laundry, and then an unforeseen urgent request for a faxed document saw us break up the conversation with a brisk walk to the university, continuing to talk on the way. I was left with the sense of someone keen to keep moving – physically, intellectually and creatively – and it seems to me this restive, searching spirit may be the lifeblood of Jones's work.

CHARLOTTE WOOD:

You're in the middle of another book now, I understand; how far off do you think it is?

LLOYD JONES:

Oh God, that's a good question. I'm wrestling with two projects right now, but the one that's further down the track is problematic. Often my writing projects are. I mean, I call them 'writing projects'. I don't say 'I'm writing a novel', because it predetermines too much.

Often I get a bit caught up in trying to reject the conventions of narrative, which pushes me out into an area where it doesn't work, and then that kind of redirects me back to where I probably should have been all the way along. But temperamentally I'm not suited to doing this in a sensible way. [*laughs*]

I think too, with every project, that as much as you're trying to figure out how to write in a new way, you're also trying to show how something can be read in a new way. Inevitably for me it's always about finding the language; that's the key. The language will unlock everything. I'm not at all concerned about plot or anything like that. That will take care of itself if the language is there from the outset.

CHARLOTTE WOOD:

It's interesting you talk of going to a place that doesn't work and coming back. I've heard you speak about the centrepiece of *Mister Pip* as the 'fresco' of words and phrases written on a baby's bedroom walls – which has nothing to do with Bougainville or Dickens.

LLOYD JONES:

That's right.

CHARLOTTE WOOD:

Was that a starting point?

LLOYD JONES:

It was, and it's a very good example of what I'm talking about.
I had this notion that you could open a book up at random
and just dip into it and get something out of it, without the
usual sort of causality and narrative. But of course, it lacked
some kind of connective tissue. Why is this being written?
What's its reason to exist? If you can't answer that question,
something vital is missing – and it was. I mean, it was an
imaginative risk, but without the underpinning of some vital
need to be told. But that is a good illustration of how I was
sent back to a much more conventional mode of narrative –
not that it's all that conventional in the end, I don't think.
But I think it must be a personality trait, you know – I'm just
contrarian.

CHARLOTTE WOOD:

But it's brilliant, because it must push you somewhere very
original each time.

LLOYD JONES:

That's the hope. The hope is – and it's always a vain one, of
course – that you are going to uncover something new and
vital, and find a new way of telling. I think that's what it's
all about. I think every project really ought to begin with the
question: why am I writing what I'm writing?

CHARLOTTE WOOD:

But can you answer that question at the start?

LLOYD JONES:

Well, I sort of do . . . it may be a made-up proposition, and
it's just a starting point, that's all. But I'm writing to find out
the answer, to some extent. I'm writing to unlock something

I don't know exists. It's in me somewhere, and I'm in search of it. I'm trying to find this thing. It's exciting when you surprise yourself. Then you've tapped into something – if you are excited, then it will be exciting on the page.

CHARLOTTE WOOD:

And the energy comes from the discovery?

LLOYD JONES:

I think so. When you are on song you just find connection everywhere. The world just suddenly connects. And you can't believe nobody else has seen this, and you're a bit worried that somebody *might* have, because it's so obvious. That's when you're on song, when you have unlocked that thing. It's all there in the subconscious somewhere, waiting to be dragged up and connected and pieced together in an interesting way.

So I suppose the starting point is often artificial, and that's probably where dissatisfaction sits, and pushes you into a territory where you have to take more imaginative risks.

I'm really straining here to actually make sense of it, and in a way I don't want to because it's such a mysterious process, in every writing project. Like this thing I'm writing now; I mean, it's not working! Why isn't it working? You would think I would know by now, but I don't.

It's almost like every time I set out on a writing project I'm learning how to write all over again. But I've done it often enough now that I know the frustrations are all part of it.

CHARLOTTE WOOD:

Do you know at the start whether it's fiction or non-fiction, or is even that quite mysterious?

LLOYD JONES:

Well, if you want something new and surprising then I don't think you should acknowledge that, because it will just get steered into known territory. You'll feel like you are just pouring cement into a mould.

I often do, of course. Somebody will say, 'What are you working on?' and I'll say, 'I'm writing a novel.' But even when I say it I am inwardly wincing because . . . there are so many artificial demarcations around these categories, novels and so forth. I prefer just to think of it in terms of prose – and what happens, happens. Then at the end you look at it and say, 'Well, what's that?'

The only time I haven't really gone in for that, when I was aware that I was writing a particular genre, was the memoir, because I don't think you can fool around with the facts. I think you are rightly constrained by those. So I had no problems telling myself, 'I'm writing a memoir.'

As for the other stuff, I just suddenly feel encumbered somehow if I say, 'Yes, this is a novel.' Sure as hell it will look like a novel, it will obey the conventions of one, and so I will be walking in the hallways of tradition rather than the imagination.

CHARLOTTE WOOD:

What would happen if you did try and 'write a novel'? Does it just go dead for you?

LLOYD JONES:

Well, where it would go dead for me would be if I plotted something out. If I said, 'Right, this is going to be twenty-five chapters,' and I had notes for each chapter and all that sort of thing. I can't imagine why I would write that thing; it's already known. It doesn't need to be written. It would be like doing a jigsaw – no, not that interesting. It would be like painting by numbers or something.

It's very hard to explain this because the entry point into writing and literature is story. That's the thing that excites us when we are eight years old and twelve and twenty. That's where we enter into this game. But we try and run away from it as fast as we can once we realise more important things are at stake. And story takes care of itself anyway, don't you think?

CHARLOTTE WOOD:

Maybe. Eventually . . .

LLOYD JONES:

Yeah, eventually. Things happen. Things just happen in the most mundane ways: 'Oh, it's raining. I have been caught without an umbrella.' That's an event. What will I do now?

CHARLOTTE WOOD:

And yet your narratives are still very compelling. With *Hand Me Down World*, for example, the narrative urgency is very strong from the beginning, with that question, is she going to get the baby back? At what point do you find this necessity, this question?

LLOYD JONES:

It's a curious mix, I think. You are absolutely right to describe it as an urgency because that's when things take off for me. It's an emotional state I get into, really, and it has to do with language – the excitement over the voice that I have uncovered, the voice will take me places. In *Hand Me Down World*, all those different voices, all those interior lives, that's interesting. As soon as I realised that would be the mode of delivering this particular narrative I was excited by it, because you find yourself coming up with endless possibilities of perspective on this person who is passing through the world. Nameless, faceless – well, not faceless, but without any identity other than that which is imposed on her by all these other people. That excited me.

Say with *Mister Pip* – I had that section about that bedroom, but it was moribund. I had just finished reading a part of that section out to a friend of mine on the phone. As I'm reading it out I'm realising, 'This is dead, this is dead' – you know, you can tell by the quality of the listening at the other end of the phone. It's – well, you'll know this, I'm sure – it's terribly, terribly deflating and disappointing. But it's also liberating, and I move quite quickly from one state to the other.

Anyway, so I'm on the phone to this person and I've been given tickets to the ballet and she is a former dancer and she says something like, 'I don't know what to wear tonight.' I said, 'Why don't you wear your roller skates?' and laughed. That was the end of that. I put the phone down – and immediately I wrote a sentence about a white man towing a black woman behind him in a cart. Now, where did that come from? Roller skates perhaps, possibly? Who knows, but it was the most interesting sentence I had written for a long time. Then somebody has to see this event, of the white man towing this black woman behind him. At that very moment, the voice of Matilda comes to me at the *same* moment Bougainville is flushed up from the depths. And so, suddenly, the civil war provides a kind of a tension to everything else that's being described. Also, that naive voice is playful, fun. It was liberating, after the constipated word drawings I was doing in the previous drafts.

CHARLOTTE WOOD:

That is fascinating, and to me it seems completely natural. I can easily understand how all of that happened – and yet it's so mysterious, it's almost inexplicable, isn't it?

LLOYD JONES:

In a way you don't really want to know, do you?

CHARLOTTE WOOD:

No, and it doesn't matter, I suppose. You end up sort of making up a story about how you wrote the book afterwards, don't you? Can I go back to your earlier writing life – you began writing in your twenties, I think. Do you remember what that first impulse was?

LLOYD JONES:

The first time I actually entertained the idea of becoming a writer? Well, there are a lot of ways of describing that and none of them, on their own, get to the nub of it. So I'll put a whole lot of things forward here. First of all, books weren't mysterious things in the household I grew up in. My mother knew where the gold was. She knew it was in the library, and we were all led to the doors of this magnificent library from an early age. That's the first thing – books were in my life.

CHARLOTTE WOOD:

But you weren't an especially bookish kid?

LLOYD JONES:

No, it was all sport for me. But still, compared to all my mates, I read and they didn't have books. But when I was nineteen – this is just one element of this whole thing – I got meningitis rather badly. Three people in New Zealand got it that year. The other two died.

CHARLOTTE WOOD:

Wow.

LLOYD JONES:

And in two weeks I went from being incredibly fit – very, very fit – to walking around on a cane and having to rest after fifty metres.

CHARLOTTE WOOD:

How terrifying.

LLOYD JONES:

Yeah, it is. You see how quickly life can just drain out of you. It's amazing really. I really do think that changed me in some way. Not in a very obvious way but . . . I became more interested, I suppose, in more ethereal things, like poetry. I really, really liked poetry. I didn't understand it, although I thought I should. I remember reading e e cummings around that time, and not being able to make head nor tail of it, but I liked the idea that I was reading it.

Then I started a postgraduate degree in politics. I was studying seventeenth-century English, the civil war . . . there were an awful lot of political treatises that you had to decipher. It was another language, you know. I was living in Auckland, and one moment I'm reading this stuff and the next moment I'm writing a poem. It was the very first thing I ever wrote, and it was about Rangitoto, the island. That was pretty exciting, really. Terrible poem of course, rubbish. I wrote other poems, you know – the sea dashing up the rocks, endless things about the sea. [*laughs*] I read a lot of Pablo Neruda around that time.

So that was just suddenly finding language as a toy, as a plaything. Making a mark on a sheet of paper the way a toddler in a highchair establishes his presence in the world by dragging a jammy finger down the wall. It was an act of self-assertion. Entertaining the idea of becoming a writer happens a bit later. But around that time I give up the postgraduate degree because I think, 'Well, this is more interesting.' So I go back to Wellington, get a job unloading aeroplanes. Most of the time I read novels, which used to really piss the other guys off, or one old boy in particular, who would sit behind his desk, grey jacket on, stack of pens in his pocket, looking out the window at the rain falling. And I would be reading a book, which annoyed him because it belittled his job in a funny sort of a way.

I read and read and read, and then I saved up for a fare to America.

From Los Angeles I got a month-long ticket on the Greyhound and I just journeyed.

You've got to imagine what New Zealand was like in the 1970s. There were no black people, for example; I had never seen a black person. And suddenly to arrive in this country that was so big and loud and noisy and extroverted . . . and in the newspapers they had these wonderful cultural pages – in those days the book culture there was second to none in the English language. Not now.

So, all that was exciting. Sitting on that bus looking out of the window at a landscape cinematically changing by the minute, and the person sitting next to me . . . you know, Americans talk. So there is a kind of a narration going on on my left-hand side, and a cinematic thing happening on the right. There are a lot of things happening, and you've got an option: you can write a letter, as you did in those days, or you can just start writing things down, as I did. And so, at that point, one finds one is living as a writer.

I end up in Schenectady in upstate New York, staying in this old derelict hotel – the State Hotel – filled with old people waiting to die, and Vietnam vets. Crazed, mad. And I'm on the top floor, writing my novel.

The novel was called *Eckstein* and it was about a photographer who can only look but can't really interact. And in a funny sort of way Eckstein is me, on that bus. It's kind of mapping out the emotional distance that this guy has in relation to things seen and heard. This was exciting: writing freehand, filling the wastepaper basket. At night, the Vietnam vets prowled the hallways. Often you would have to push one away in order to open the door.

I remember this woman who worked at the hotel, I thought she was a bit of an old bag – she was probably younger than me now – and she used to clear the paper basket. She looked at me one day and she said, 'Lloyd, honey, if you ever want to write a letter to somebody, you can write to me.' [*laughs*]

CHARLOTTE WOOD:

She thought you were writing letters and throwing them away?

LLOYD JONES:

She assumed I was writing letters, because what else would those words be? But in a way I should have followed her advice. I probably would have learned more about writing if I'd thought about what she said, thought about writing her a letter that she never saw, about what I was thinking and doing and seeing and hearing.

Anyway, at that point I'm telling myself – but not the world – 'I'm a writer.' I'm twenty-four. And then I thought, well how does one become a writer? There were no writing schools I was aware of and it probably wouldn't have suited me if there were. Temperamentally, I wouldn't have been right for it because I'm not a good student. I have to learn in my own way.

But at the start of that bus trip, quite randomly, I pick up a book in San Diego. It's called *Young Hemingway*, about his years up until the age of twenty. I could really relate, because here is somebody who has already lived the life that I'm living right now. I sort of read it like an instruction manual. He got a job as a newspaper man, on the *Toronto Star* or whatever it was. I thought, 'Ah, that's what I've got to do. I've got to get a job as a newspaper man.' So when I got back to New Zealand I became a reporter, which was a very, very good thing to do. And I wrote in the hours before I went to work.

CHARLOTTE WOOD:

In an interview you mentioned a Saul Bellow novel that changed what you were working on. What was it?

LLOYD JONES:

Oh yes, in Schenectady. Quite near the hotel was a very good bookshop. There is a great serendipity involved in just picking up the books that are right for you at that time. I wandered across there – this was when I was still convinced by my genius – and I just happened to pull out this book and I opened it up at random. It was *Humboldt's Gift*. And everything that was wrong about my book was right about this. It just had the smell of life on the page, and it had voice. People were bursting out of the pages. It had music. I wouldn't say it was deflating, it was exciting. On that same day I bought Susan Sontag's *On Photography*. And – I'm sure it's the case with you, that the big leaps you make are from the books you happen to pick up. It all seems like it was meant to be, in a curious sort of a way.

CHARLOTTE WOOD:

Yes! And you wonder what would have happened if you hadn't picked it up! It does seem so crucial, every time, that it was *that* book, doesn't it? I had a young writer contact me yesterday, he's nearing the end of his first novel and having a hard time, and he asked me what I thought he should read to help him finish it. It's an impossible question. What one needs is so personal, I could never advise him.

LLOYD JONES:

Yeah, that's where there's more mystery. He has to go into the library and wander around and have something catch his eye for some reason, and speak to him at that moment in time.

CHARLOTTE WOOD:

Yes, speak to him about *his* book, connect for him in a way that I would never be able to detect. So, the idea of voice seems to be crucial for you. You've talked a lot about voice being the key to writing.

LLOYD JONES:

I think so. It comes down to how you view language, and making a distinction between words as mere conveyers of information, and words as musical notes. It's a big, big difference.

With voice, language is particular to every individual. We all speak in a slightly different way and we use our words in a slightly different way. Those words lock us into the world in a particular way. That particular way is what contributes to literature. We don't all have the same experiences. We've got to find the voice that speaks of that unique experience. Inevitably then, if you take that view, voice is central – and it comes right back to that vitality you alluded to. That energy, that reason to tell. It all comes back to satisfying the question of voice.

CHARLOTTE WOOD:

It's very difficult to explain the concept of voice, isn't it? I think a lot of people see it in terms of the character's voice, not the voice of the book. How does one explain it?

LLOYD JONES:

Well, it's not the voice we speak with, it's the voice we think with. It's the interior life brought to the surface. Obviously the story has to be done through language, but it's not the voice we might whisper. It comes back to the advice of that woman in the hotel: 'Why don't you write to me?' Pico Iyer once said writing should have the intimacy of a letter. I think he is right. You should feel, as a reader, that you are being singularly addressed, you know, quietly.

CHARLOTTE WOOD:

Are you always writing to someone?

LLOYD JONES:

I should be. That's another way of getting that vitality into it, I think, the idea of a piece of writing being addressed. Otherwise, why else is it being told? Even if the reader is a phantom in your own mind, perhaps you have to adopt the position that you are telling someone.

After all, language is an act of persuasion. Who are we trying to persuade? The phantom reader. How can I make you see this hill the way I see it? I will use language to create the picture so you can only see it the way I see it – an act of persuasion.

CHARLOTTE WOOD:

Do you need a lot of confidence for that persuasion?

LLOYD JONES:

I guess so. That's an interesting point, because when my writing is at its crappiest – which no one ever sees – there is a degree of passivity sitting behind it. It's like there's no determination to make it believable, there's no inner belief in it. It may be that in those instances, if I did think in terms of addressing it to somebody, it would suddenly have that little raft of air under it.

CHARLOTTE WOOD:

In your master class you said something intriguing: that 'the writer's fidelity must not be to the eye'. The fidelity is not to what is seen.

LLOYD JONES:

Did I say that?

CHARLOTTE WOOD:

I thought it was very interesting, because it runs counter to so much of what one is taught – and I've taught it myself – which is to 'see it in your head, like a film'.

LLOYD JONES:

Yeah. Well, one of the discoveries I have made was that . . . initially I used to write fairly cinematically. So my sentences were loaded with detail, a lot of visual detail. I thought that's what was important: providing word pictures. It wasn't until I read people like Carver in the 80s, a lot of those guys – Tobias Wolff, Richard Ford, people like that – that I understood voice is the thing.

At that point I began to close my eyes, and write with a pen. Writing then became a kind of an aural thing, rather than a visual thing. Even now, like a lot of writers I suppose, I tend to write the first few pages in freehand. Because if I write straight onto a screen, I'm looking at what I'm writing, I'm not hearing it. It comes back to the voice thing. I've got to be . . . I'll be seduced by the sentence magically appearing on the screen and some other critical factor comes into play: Oh, is it any good? Oh no, I should go back and take that brick out and put a new one in here. That's not a way to proceed, no. So yeah, the fidelity, the fidelity has to be all the time to the voice.

CHARLOTTE WOOD:

What about the creation of character?

LLOYD JONES:

What about it? [*laughs*]

CHARLOTTE WOOD:

That comes to you through voice as well?

LLOYD JONES:

Yeah, it does, but character reveals itself in interaction. Character reveals itself in what that person sees, what they think, how they respond to the situation at hand. I mean, I don't think you need to fully kit out a character in the first page, say what they look like and give their backstory and history. None of that is interesting.

It's more interesting, I think, that every character starts off as a mystery and slowly reveals themselves. That's why we read. Why are we sitting in this café with this person who is miserable or has no money? What's going to happen to them next? We'll leave the café with them and see what happens. As you go on, it's through events, really, that character reveals itself. But I must say, I never really think about that.

It's a curious thing, because as a reader I actually quite like reading a bit of nineteenth-century description about what they're wearing, descriptions of faces – probably because I can't do that. If I could, I suspect I would. But I don't think it's terribly important. I think the situation, and how they respond, is important. The reader decides what they look like. The reader needs more credit for bringing completion to a story. Leave a bit of space around it.

That was the great lesson from Carver, who learned it from Hemingway, of course. The reader does an enormous amount of work, enjoyably, in those stories. That's why we find them such powerful experiences. Without having that work to do, if all the work is done on our behalf, all we can do is sit as we would in the cinema with imagery sort of washing over us. There is nothing left to be done. It becomes a sensory experience. It doesn't become a creative act – reading is a creative act, when you are given the opportunity.

CHARLOTTE WOOD:

Let's go back to *Mister Pip* for a bit. You referred to Matilda's voice as playful, and you've spoken before about the need for playfulness on the writer's part. But given the very sad subject matter you are dealing with, this can be a difficult concept to understand. Can you tell me about the role of playfulness for you?

LLOYD JONES:

I probably don't mean it in quite the sense you have taken it. I'm thinking about in terms of a readiness by the writer. A combination of playfulness and intense concentration – two impossible things to hold at the same time. It's a lightness in oneself, a sense that anything can go, anything can happen here. Don't predetermine anything. Be prepared to be surprised by what just sails out of you onto that page and go with it. That's what I mean by playfulness.

CHARLOTTE WOOD:

A kind of experimentalism?

LLOYD JONES:

That's what play is, isn't it? Just playing around, seeing what will happen, trying something out. I think that's when you flush something out that you couldn't otherwise arrive at. I couldn't possibly have sat down and said, 'Right, I'm going to write from the perspective of a Bougainvillean girl from the age of twelve to thirty-something. Now, who else will be in this? Oh yes, a charismatic white teacher.' No, it would never have happened. So, playfulness kind of takes you there.

CHARLOTTE WOOD:

It must have been exciting when you realised you had this young girl's life to write from. Were you daunted by that?

LLOYD JONES:

I remember one day going to a publisher's party in Wellington. I was driving down with a poet friend and he said, 'What are you working on?' I said, 'I'm writing this thing from the perspective of a twelve-year-old black girl.' Then I burst out laughing – because it just seemed so improbable. Yeah, it was exciting, and it hasn't happened that often. There have been a few moments where it just seems to happen magically.

Halfway through writing that book I had to go down to Central Otago to work on a documentary film. I was on the brink of saying no, I couldn't do it, because I couldn't give up this thing, it was happening in such an extraordinary way. Then I thought, 'Oh, I need the money.' So I went, and I found myself getting up very early in the mornings.

It was winter, six o'clock or something like that. I would be walking around, and the air down there is very dry and incredibly cold, very cold. And the book was just pulling me. It was like being spoken to. It was almost like I was just channelling this thing, you know? I somehow got into a zone, a very special place. I'm resisting saying things like, 'I was given the story', or 'It was a gift,' or any bullshit like that, because I also worked hard for it. But nonetheless, in this final form, it was a kind of a magical transaction.

CHARLOTTE WOOD:

Amazing. Have you ever had that again?

LLOYD JONES:

I've had moments. I haven't had it for the whole duration of a book. Most of the time, when a writing project is going well, as I said earlier, things will connect in ways that were just meant to be. You find yourself utterly amazed at how this thing is writing itself. You are just a kind of co-pilot. It's a curious thing.

CHARLOTTE WOOD:

Do you always recognise when things are connected? With the fresco of words in the bedroom, for example, and then the twelve-year-old Bougainvillean girl – did you think, 'Yes, these are part of the same thing'? Or did you think, 'Now I'm going to work on this girl and leave that bedroom thing aside'?

LLOYD JONES:

I was quite prepared to leave the room, because it hadn't worked. But then at a certain point in the writing, when Mr Watts is talking about his wife Grace being pregnant, it suddenly just became clear. 'Ah, of course. They will create the room for the unborn child.'

In a funny sort of a way, maybe at a subconscious level, perhaps the narrative was always driving towards such a point. Who can say, really? That's why, when we discard stuff, whole drafts of stuff, it's not a waste. We've uncovered material that will find its way into something at some later point.

CHARLOTTE WOOD:

Have you ever thrown a whole book away?

LLOYD JONES:

Oh God, yeah. Yeah. I mean, most of what I write is absolute crap.

CHARLOTTE WOOD:

You must write quickly, then. You've published a lot of books – do you mean you throw stuff away as you go, or you've written a whole book and then thought, 'No, that's no good'?

LLOYD JONES:

I have done that. I usually don't . . . you know, I wouldn't call it 'a book'. I would think, I've written hundreds of pages of something that has been forced onto the page. It's been hard labour. You always know, actually, when you wake up in the morning. I always write first thing in the morning, and if I lie there for a minute longer than I need to, I always know, 'This is a sign things aren't going too well are they, Lloyd? You'd better own up to that fact.' [*laughs*]

CHARLOTTE WOOD:

But I feel like that all the time! Do you push through that feeling, or is it a real signal that you've got to chuck stuff out?

LLOYD JONES:

Well, you just keep banging your head against the wall and you find out what's wrong one way or another. I do think sticking with it is terribly important. I don't think when the going gets tough that you can just walk away from it for a couple of weeks and think taking a leave of absence is somehow going to cure the problem. I really do think you've just got to keep at it, keep picking away at it. And at some point you will get some clarity.

It may come from a moment of acknowledging, 'No, this

is all wrong. This is completely wrong,' and just pushing it aside. And like I said earlier, often there is a little moment of discovery too – when you know exactly what's wrong with it. And then suddenly you are off on a different course.

CHARLOTTE WOOD:

Can we talk about your ease writing from the point of view of female characters? You seem to do it very naturally, which isn't always the case for other writers.

LLOYD JONES:

Well, I wouldn't describe it as an ease. But, first of all, I just make no distinction. Why should one? Literature deals with the particularities of an individual, and that individual is only known to us, the writer, and will only reveal him or herself as everything progresses in the writing.

This notion that men cannot, should not, write women characters is completely anti-literature. It's absurd. Anyone who believes that just doesn't understand literature. The whole ability to imagine the other goes right to the core of writing, really, and the value of literature.

I think we get caught up in the generalities. The media is very good at appealing to and dealing in generalities. That's what it does. But literature pulls us back from those group positions, tribal positions, to the perspective of the individual, which should be the most representative of humanity. Not groups and affiliations, and particularly not those who want to put fences around themselves and say, 'Do not come in here. You don't understand this.' What absolute horseshit!

Who actually ever understands another person, anyway?

In the case of *Mister Pip*, for example, someone will say, 'Oh, how did you manage to get into the skin of a fourteen-year-old black girl?' And I say, 'I didn't.' I got into the skin of a person who happened to be called Matilda and who happens to be a Bougainvillean girl. Does she exist? No, she doesn't.

She only exists on the page. And her existence, whether you believe it or not, depends on my ability to be persuasive, which comes back to my use of language.

It's not like I'm trying to depict someone who already exists out there. She doesn't. And I don't think people who advocate this discussion around who you can write about, white people writing about black people, men writing about women – I really, honestly don't think they actually understand what it's all about. I really don't. As you can tell from the tone of my voice, I find it intensely irritating.

CHARLOTTE WOOD:

I agree with you completely. Writers should be allowed to write from any perspective – but there are many who can't, who do it very badly. They can't fully imagine the other.

LLOYD JONES:

Well, in that case they suddenly think, 'Oh, I'm writing about a woman . . . I've gone from cats to dogs' or something like that, right? But that's a false boundary. It's completely artificial.

Why is it thought perfectly normal for a man to be able to get into the skin of an axe murderer, but not the skin of a woman? What makes us have some affinity with axe murderers that we don't with women?

The point is that identity lives on the page. That's where it all lives. It's not trying to draw down from life. The playground is on the page, in language. It makes things exist or it doesn't, and that's where it works. And this person called Sally, Helen or Angela, she's . . . the sum of her is just the detail that's provided on the page. It's not some imperfect facsimile of somebody called Angela or Sally, who already exists out here, that we are drawing some comparison between the two.

CHARLOTTE WOOD:

You've several times quoted a remark Samuel Beckett made

about James Joyce, that is very important to you. But I'm not sure I fully understand it. Beckett said, Joyce's writing 'is not about something, it is that something itself'. Can you talk about this a little more?

LLOYD JONES:

Yes. He's not writing about something – 'about' suggests an object. In other words, it thrusts you into the task of describing something that's already there. But the *something* is emerging from the actual writing. So it's not starting with any objective in mind, but an objective actually results from the act of writing. It's a subtle distinction.

CHARLOTTE WOOD:

Is it partly also about being inside the work rather than outside it, approaching it from a distance?

LLOYD JONES:

Yes, I think that's a good way of describing it. If you're writing about something, you can see it all clearly in your mind, but that's the antithesis of what we were talking about earlier. You can't see it clearly in your mind, but something is emerging. And as you're putting words down, more clarity is achieved. So you're writing something that's going to deliver you somewhere, rather than writing about something. You get it.

CHARLOTTE WOOD:

I think I get it. But it's an interesting thing. You could spend a long time pondering it, I think. Which makes it more interesting.

LLOYD JONES:

I found that anecdote enormously liberating, actually. It's something I did instinctively, but when I read that, I felt, 'That's it! That's exactly my own modus operandi.'

CHARLOTTE WOOD:

How do you know when your work in progress isn't just decorative – that it has the necessary urgency you spoke of earlier, that need to be told?

LLOYD JONES:

Well, I think the act of writing begins as an act of engagement with something, not necessarily something you can see, but with ideas. For example, my work is all about engagement with identity. If I look back at everything I've written that is of any use – it's always been a grappling with or an engagement with identity. That's always been the starting point. So, if that is what you're really grappling with, however decorative the surface might be, it's going to have some fairly rich underpinnings. Identity slides around. It's not fixed.

How do we know if something is more than simply decorative? Well, it's like a reef. You'll see it, just sticking out now and then. There's some undertow there. There is something on the surface that's kind of in communication with something else you can't see very clearly, but you feel. So it has a kind of richness.

And I think it offers a texture too, when you are really trying to work an idea out, you're not actually putting it on the page, but the language is dancing along on the surface, while it's also hinting at some other layer. I think that's when you've got something going. There is some dynamic there that's not one-dimensional, it's not just one layer of decorative stuff.

CHARLOTTE WOOD:

When did you figure out that identity was what all your work had been about?

LLOYD JONES:

When I wrote the memoir.

CHARLOTTE WOOD:

Oh, that recently? Do you think that having discovered that, it will now disappear from your work?

LLOYD JONES:

It already has. It is very strange actually, to have this kind of ball of irritability rolling around inside of you, and it's all about identity.

CHARLOTTE WOOD:

Do you work every day, and at the same time?

LLOYD JONES:

Mornings belong to me, as a rule. It's always been like that. And sometimes very early in the morning. I like what Toni Morrison had to say about the twilight hour and the twilight state of four in the morning, that she's neither asleep nor is she fully awake. It just seems like the door is open. The door to the subconscious is just a little bit more open than it would be at any other time of the day. You can hear more clearly, which is important if you subscribe to the notion of voice. I work not for very long, really. It depends where a project is at. In the writing of a first draft, I don't think you need long. An hour, two hours. But once you have it, once you've got that mound of clay, it's hard to drag yourself away from it. Then you can just play around for hours on end, eight hours, nine hours. That's a different stage.

CHARLOTTE WOOD:

How has the writing life fitted with making enough money to live on?

LLOYD JONES:

Well, that pattern of working was forced on me, in a way, because of the working day. I had to write around the margins, plus the children and family life and all that kind of thing. I've worked as a freelance writer for a long time. And *Mister Pip* obviously made a big difference.

Now, to be honest, I don't really care. I remember a guy I knew at Hutt Valley High School. He went to university and got a law degree, then he ended up on Wall Street and made a bit of money, and then lost a bit of money. Then he ended up in Israel as a Lubavitch Hasid, living in a very religious town in the north of Israel. He's married to a really gorgeous Yemeni woman, and has an army of kids, I think about six kids. I said to him, 'Tony, how the hell do you make your living?' He said, 'I don't know.' He said, 'God provides.'

And I thought, 'Fuck, that's terrific! I'm going to adopt that approach.' And so I pretty much have. Something always happens. Something rolls around, a project comes up, some money comes in, you write something that makes more money than you expected. It just happens. And so I tend to make sure I have a decent amount of time for the writing, because that's the thing.

And God provides. [*laughs*]

The Story That Matters

Tina Makereti

Beautiful writing alone is not enough. Not now. Look around you.
—@slamup, Maxine Beneba Clarke, 11 January 2017, from Melbourne

kaupapa

In creative writing classes, we often ask the question: What's at stake? What we are asking is why the reader should invest time and emotional energy in reading a particular piece of writing. Why does it matter? Why should we care? We usually mean what is at stake for the characters in a story or the speaker in a poem emotionally or intellectually, ethically or spiritually, rather than what is at stake for the world in a greater sense.

Kaupapa is a word that can encompass both purpose and the concept of a manifesto. It's worth thinking about. What are you here for? What graces brought you here? What will you leave behind? I'm not suggesting you develop a manifesto, but I am suggesting we think about the purpose of what we write.

We cannot force our work to have a greater purpose than finding out what's at stake for this or that character, or figuring out the mechanics of that one story, the kaupapa at the heart of this particular piece of writing. Creativity doesn't work that way. And yet, for many, having a greater purpose is the only way creativity works. How do I manage to invest time in my creative work when there are so many other (more lucrative or personally important) calls for my creative energy? Perhaps the closest thing I have to a kaupapa is the belief that because I have been given a voice (1. The genealogical, historical, cultural and creative capital to have stories to tell; 2. The ability to write; 3. The power to publish and speak publicly), I have an obligation to use it. And then, given the great soup of things there are to write about, certain stories will always rise to the top of my pot: the urgent, untold, underrepresented; the stories that make us look again at what we thought we knew about ourselves, our history and our cultures. Stories that shake us. I don't know if I have achieved it yet, but I do agree the telltale sign of a good story is that it stays with us long after we have finished reading – it destabilises us at the core just long enough to see the world afresh. There's nothing unusual about this. Yet I don't know how many of us write with any purpose other than producing some good writing.

on beauty

Sometimes I try to write one of those cool kinds of essays in which the writer does not make an argument. I always fail. I am always making arguments. Life is too short and desperate and filled with urgency not to be making passionate arguments. I don't have time to wallow in beauty without purpose, though luckily the short, desperate urgency of life is beautiful.

show up

I've come to think of writing, most days, as a matter of faith. Show up and stuff will happen. If we're doing it right, most days, we're not going to know what's going to happen. The best things happen without our plans. Even though I would like it to be doing something different, something more artful and less bossy, this essay is telling you to write with purpose. But it can't be forced. It won't be forced. Ideas and philosophies and politics don't make good stories, they make good research. Then we have to stand back and let story lead us. If there is purpose in our thoughts, our research, our conversations, our general perception of life, story will out us. What really matters to us will come through when we write, it will come through our stories. Or, it will arrive in the imagery of our poems.

on discomfort

It was my lunchbreak, and I was browsing the New Zealand books table at Unity Books. I noticed her before she noticed me, and I tapped her on the shoulder. We laughed and embraced, caught up a little. I hadn't expected to see her there. It was one of those moments that seems strangely serendipitous: I rarely have time in a lunchbreak to head to the bookstore; she is rarely in the city. This is someone I have a great deal of fondness and respect for, who I think of probably more as family than friend. But there's always that twinge of inadequacy and slight discomfort. She had been a key participant in research for *Where the Rēkohu Bone Sings*, and I therefore feel as if I owe her a debt I can never repay.

After we chatted for a while, that day in Unity Books, my friend invited me upstairs, to where an important meeting was being conducted. They were having lunch, I should come and say hello, she said. I won't go into what the meeting was about, except that it involved leaders of the Moriori people, and government representatives, researchers and lawyers, and that imi/iwi–government meetings of this kind happen regularly all over the country, but particularly in Wellington. I was happy to reconnect with other hunau, or wider family, and meet some I didn't know, but my discomfort was beside me, like a badly behaved dog who couldn't sit still, as each new person was introduced and my book and I were introduced to them with much generosity. To each of these new people, as well as the ones I already knew, I felt such a weight of responsibility. I had written a story that was more theirs than mine. I could only hope that I did it well enough. I had created what I consider to be a lifelong obligation.

But signs were positive. At one point, they described my book to officials and other participants at the meeting as a way of getting closer to their history, and understanding what life had been like for their people, and the kinds of experiences that are very common for them. This was the main reason I had wanted to write it, so it was quite something to see that happen. If my discomfort actually was a dog, he would have rolled on his back at this point, put his paws in the air, and waited for me to scratch his tummy. But he wouldn't have left. Everyone joked that they would go downstairs and immediately purchase the remaining copies at Unity, and wasn't it convenient that the bookshop was down there? *Yes*, I laughed, cringing inwardly and outwardly that this wasn't something I could just give them freely. My discomfort stayed with me to the very end, while people offered me much warmth and lunch, and I said *no-thank-you-I-must-get-back-to-work*, and we embraced and promised to meet again soon.

I don't expect the discomfort to ever go away. And this dog has at least four legs: the discomfort I've described above; the personal discomfort of any lingering dissatisfaction with the work itself; the perpetual discomfort of having a fairly public occupation; and the slightly different discomfort I feel around my other relations for shining light on dark history. When the book was published, I had several options. One, commonly employed, is to claim the holy creative right to write *as if no one is watching*, and to publish as if no one is watching too. I do believe in writing as if no one is watching, when needed. I also know the reality is that someone is always watching, and words have consequences, sometimes massive consequences, and maybe you have to be without words, or to know people without access to words, to understand the power that writers wield. So I also believe in acknowledging, at some stage, those who might be affected by one's writing, and taking responsibility for that.

Which makes me very uncomfortable.

Other options include asking for permission from every person who might conceivably be affected by a work, and developing very complex systems of denial. The first is practically impossible and has the almost certain outcome of preventing publication, and the second is tiresome and dishonest. You can also simply claim it and be proud. *Yes, I wrote this, and that's okay.* I know writers often make peace with being somewhere in between on the spectrum of these options. I choose to accept that my discomfort with what I have written will, to some extent, always be with me.

Discomfort is the companion to having voice and being given publication. My discomfort sits alongside anything I write that has associated risk. Anything worth saying generally has associated risk – it may offend, it may contain errors, it may cause controversy or bring unwanted attention to the writer. Chiefly, *someone might get hurt*. It might make things worse.

Writers almost always have a pet discomfort. Some people keep a room for their discomfort, or send it to a storage unit in another town; appease it with elaborate feedings or punish it with regular berating and time-outs; perhaps try to lull it into submission with extended Netflix marathons.

The point is, writing will inevitably require you to make a decision. I have chosen to try and live with my discomfort, to notice it when it arrives, say hello, and allow it to shadow me for the day. Often over a meal or a drink it fades, though it has been known to get vociferous at this point, sending me home to a sleepless night, waking me at three in the morning, socking me surreptitiously in the eye. But that doesn't happen often, because I've decided to make friends with it, and I know that when it shows up there's a good possibility I'm doing something worthwhile.

tell me I'm wrong

Observation: in a room of young middle-class Pākehā students
(e.g. the majority of university lectures) there are many
clever, witty, talented, politically astute and very pleasant
people. Some of them are beautiful writers. Educationally,
they have always been surrounded by writers, theorists and
educationalists with the same sociocultural capital as them.
Few of them have stories to tell. Yet.

In a class of Māori/Pasifika/immigrant students (not so
many middle-class, not so many young) there are many clever,
witty, talented, politically astute and very pleasant people.
Some of them are beautiful writers. Few of them have ever had
the opportunity to read writing from their own communities.
Few of them have ever had the opportunity to write from or
about their own communities. Yet, I struggle to remember a
single one that didn't have a compelling story to tell.

There is a bias in these generalisations, but I do not think
it invalidates the observation. And for every generalisation
there is an exception. Yet there is a palpable difference
between these different groups. There is *so much more at
stake* for the second group. That they are even in that room
is a small miracle. Do not let me take away from the small
miracles that happen in the lives of Pākehā students. I get
it, I do, but this is not meant to be a competition. Sit with
these classes and their stories for a while and you soon realise
the power that something like being able to read stories from
your own communities has. Your voice matters, the Māori
and Pasifika and immigrant students learn. This is often
shocking for them to internalise.

What is shocking for me is the immense pool of talent that
goes unnourished and unnoticed in Aotearoa. Unleash the
literary power of these communities and we would have the
international literati at our feet. Not that that matters, but
it would certainly boost the literary economy. What matters
more is that generations of people from certain communities
would grow up with enhanced senses of themselves, their

abilities and their voice. Publish their stories and ensure they are taught at every level of the education system, particularly secondary school, then come back and tell me that I'm wrong.

we need more flavour

Okay, so when I said there should be something at stake in stories, I meant a slightly different thing from the kinds of big stakes I'm discussing here. However, these two different senses of risk are connected, and if you have an intimate relationship with the second (the precariousness of life), you may have a stronger ability to express the first (the necessity of jeopardy/something at stake to add emotional weight to your writing). Exceptions, again. But this is why we get better at writing as we get older. We've been through more. The hard times shape us.

Some people don't get the luxury of waiting until they're older to experience the hard times.

Thus, I cannot imagine having the immense privilege of being able to write and choosing subjects with very little at stake in a wider sense. Here I baulk at naming the kind of writing I'm thinking of, but it is as bland as the mashed potato, mince and boiled veg meals we used to eat in the 1970s. Look, it's often beautifully done, but maybe what we need to ask is whether it extends the narrative. Does it show us anything new about ourselves? Does it cross boundaries or go to the edges? This writing may be literary or popular, and it may have ups and downs (i.e. things are at stake for the characters) but in the end it's all very comforting.

Don't get me wrong. Comfort is good. It's why I like TV. Sometimes all we need is something unchallenging. What I do take exception to is the focus on this kind of majority literature at the expense of other kinds of writing. And then, the lauding of it. We must challenge the tight focus of our teaching, publishing and awards more often, not just because they tend to cater to a single socioeconomic class and culture, but also because we need more flavour.

zero

So let me ask directly: Where are our immigrant stories? Our stories of poor communities? Our stories of growing communities of street people? Our queer stories? Our stories of people with disabilities? Our stories of Pasifika communities? And while you can probably name more than one Māori writer, the statistics on publication of Māori writing might continue to surprise, since they aren't even halfway to proportional. Yes – these stories and these writers exist, in small quantities, often in small presses. But how many stories from any of these communities might the average New Zealander encounter in the average year?

non-required reading

This essay asks you to write something that matters. But that something is up to you. Patricia Grace writes simply about the lives of ordinary people, ordinary lives she knows about. She makes no pretence of ever doing anything else. And yet her work is seen as culturally and politically, even spiritually and nationally, important and challenging because these are the lives of ordinary people that were largely invisible to the majority of the Pākehā population until people like Patricia, Witi and Hone started writing. Sometimes simply writing about your life and the lives of people like you can deeply matter.

Sometimes, though, you are writing in an echo chamber. Sometimes there are lots of writers like you, writing lots of stories like the one you are writing. Go to the edges of the room. Feel along the walls for cracks and crevices, draughts. Maybe windows to other rooms. Dig away at the ingrained dirt in the corner. There are so many stories unwritten. So many lives unnoticed. Be brave. Make yourself uncomfortable. Do the work required.

imagine I am whispering

This one is scary to write down: *I don't like Katherine*

Mansfield. I don't mean her work, or her personally. More, what she has come to represent. I just want to say there are other writers in New Zealand, possibly more interesting writers, worthy of as much attention. And while we fawn over a great writer of a certain time and place and class and colour, and a certain amount of privilege, who spent most of her career overseas, who are we ignoring in Aotearoa now (or even in her time)?

write only

I would never tell you to write only towards political, social, cultural or spiritual purpose. Write what you are compelled to write, and if you choose to write only for the sake of it, for the sake of art, understand that this, too, is choosing a political, social, cultural and spiritual position.

permission

We invited author Nic Low to come and speak to a hui of Māori writers in 2015. He talked about wanting to imbue his stories with kaupapa. He might have called it something like political purpose. He talked about how unpopular that is, how it's something we're 'not supposed to do'. The response from many in the room was relief and pleasure at encountering this point of view, and being given tacit permission to write about things that concern us directly. Nic's book, *Arms Race*, is full of funny, clever, scathing, dark and entertaining stories that range widely. He could have written about anything.

Nic talked about the thing he is writing now. It's his big story, he said. The story you know you're meant to write, but you don't know if you're ready for. Are you good enough? Do you possess the right skills and background? Have you spoken to the right people? Did you get the permission you need? It was something along these lines, what he said. We nodded. We all knew about those stories. Many of us discussed the ones we had tucked away. Mostly we felt inadequate to do them justice. Nic looked unsure, concerned, determined. You never feel adequate, but if the story is in front of you, he seemed to be saying, you've got to rise to it.

kaupapa

This essay was written in the wake of the Trump campaign and early presidency of 2016 and 2017, the refugee crises of Europe and Australia (not the fact of the refugee populations pouring into those places, but the way they are treated) and Aotearoa's own shame at not alleviating the suffering of just a few more refugee families. Prince Charles is among the many comparing this moment in history to the 1930s; somehow Nazism is something certain factions of society are not even ashamed of anymore. The news in New Zealand this morning is that we have destroyed our rivers to the extent that they are unlikely to recover, but it's also unlikely the agricultural economy will meet any real limits.

We live in a time of jeopardy. Some say we are already living our dystopia. When I was very young I understood that progress meant that things would only get better for each successive generation, but I have spent the last decade grappling with the realisation that the world my daughters encounter may not be as ethically, emotionally, spiritually or even physically safe as the world of prior generations. We have to stop it, I think: Just Stop Everything. We done fucked up, as my girl would say. Our children watch us with eyes haunted by their own futures.

And I sit here writing, for that is all I know how to do. It is the only thing I am good at.

Writers are sometimes hesitant to put their opinions forward. 'Who am I to speak?' they ask. 'Who are you not to?' is my question. Now is not the time for passivity or meekness. Write the hard thing. Write the unpopular thing. Write the challenging thing. Open your eyes. Write the thing you are scared of. Now is the time for you to step into the story that matters.

No Hugging, Some Learning

Writing and personal change

Damien Wilkins

It's a default setting for a great deal of commentary on fiction, and on theatre, film and television too, that dramatic narrative is dramatic because *we watch people change*. This morally eventful spectacle is thrilling and instructive. We can learn about our lives in Lower Hutt from watching King Lear crawl about in the English mud. But what to do with the opposing idea that this insistence on personal change leaves out other ways of being in the world?

Seinfeld, the TV show famously self-described as being 'about nothing', had the rule 'no hugging, no learning'. To escape an earnest, improving agenda helped the jokes; there was also an appeal for accuracy: isn't life less purposeful than we routinely hope? Isn't there something cheesy and automatic about change as the goal, as story generator? Does existence render down so readily into lessons? Do we all really long to change and continue changing? Are our lives as quickly swapped for fresh as pairs of socks, new as washed shirts? Aren't there other ways of talking about experience than with the worn and suspect vocabulary of relentless growth?

What I'm saying is that the notion of personal change – change which is improving – is both disreputable and unmoveable, tarnished and resolute, art's cheapest trick and its most generous gift. How then to save such a precious notion – this idea of transforming ourselves and the world

– how on one side to save it from expediency, kitsch and other abuses, and on the other side, how to shore up its vital promise against cynicism and world-weariness or even simply the accusation that it falsifies our experience of life?

Change, of course, can bring us painfully close to what is arbitrary and capricious about the universe, revelatory, too, of the power structures that underpin our lives. In Joseph Roth's 1932 masterpiece *The Radetzky March*, a book I'll come back to, there's a tiny scene of great emblematic force in which Emperor Franz Joseph is having his hair cut by the new imperial barber, a terrified corporal. The barber snips at the Emperor's hair and nervously jumps away before approaching again with the scissors. The Emperor, a failing old man, seeking internal proof of his own power, instantly promotes the jumpy barber with a word – 'You're a sergeant now,' he says – and goes off satisfied that he has 'made someone happy'. But in a flash we've been inside the barber's head and learned that he's already feigned arthritis a couple of times to try for an early discharge from service – he wants to rejoin his wife and child and the 'nice little business' he has. The Emperor's generosity is a private disaster. The scene is a marvellously funny inversion of good fortune, a sly critique of the notion of a personal journey motored by individual resources, and these frequent plays of misunderstanding in the novel add up to a kind of cosmic failure of imagination shared by the entire Austro-Hungarian Empire, which is about to be swept away by the approaching war.

What prevents Joseph Roth's vision from becoming overwhelmingly bleak is that such scenes are themselves instances of the author's own imaginative reach and sympathy, surely one of the saving paradoxes of art. Any insight into human circumstance might not do the characters any good but its residue for us readers is, at the very least, affective. This is what Richard Ford has called 'the consolation of form'. In another context but with sharp relevance, performance artist Linda Montano, commenting on the difficulty of documentation when it comes to ephemeral art practices, said in an interview, 'It seems the primary document is the change inside the performer and audience.' *The change inside us* – well, this is not a document we can easily reach out for, though I'd like it to hover over this essay. If we think of reading itself as a kind of performance, the books I'm going to talk about have clearly changed me, at least as I appear to myself. And most of these books have been novels. So what does the novel promise us about change?

Lennard J Davis in his book *Resisting Novels* suggests the novel, addicted to the concept of self-understanding, is 'psychotic', in that it 'sees thoughts as so powerful that simply thinking something is enough to cause it to happen'. Based on confidently established psychological portraits of characters, the classic realist novel, Davis argues, tells a story of self-reliance, middle-class industry and personal growth and thereby confirms its innate conservatism. Localising change to individual success stories, the novel reinscribes reactionary politics. With self-understanding as the key to change, ideological underpinnings are rendered mute, Davis suggests, and 'the chaos' of living comes to an end in these fictions simply by a change of thought and heart.

While I'm not convinced the mechanism in the novels we come back to again and again is as efficient as that, it does make me think that creative writing 'how to' books tend to push the same mute button, pull the same industrious lever. And while such books might suggest standards of believability and process around character change – What does your character want? What obstacles stand in the way? What are the setbacks suffered along the redemptive path? – it's very hard to shift the basic requirement that writing is fundamentally about observable transformation located *in someone we care about*. Most of these creative writing manuals could be subtitled 'Hugging and Learning'.

To anyone familiar with the novel's ancient progenitors, this change-mania can look odd. Mikhail Bakhtin argues that in Classical Greek romances we simply observe people to whom things happen – as in folktales. 'Fate' runs the game and the character's role is to endure with 'his *identity* absolutely unchanged'. In these prototype novels, Bakhtin says, '. . . people and things have gone *through* something . . . that did not change them but that did . . . affirm what they, and precisely they, were as individuals . . . The hammer of events shatters nothing and forges nothing – it merely tries the durability of an already tested product.'

Thomas G Pavel in his recent study *The Lives of the Novel* usefully augments Bakhtin's reading of these Greek novels when he suggests that the tracing of characters' moment-by-moment inner feelings would have to wait until Samuel Richardson in the 18th century but that the Greek writers still signalled the existence of an 'inner, inviolate space' as readers register the protagonists' fortitude against the random events of the world. Pavel writes that Greek novels 'try to show how human beings experience the present independently of previous or subsequent events – in short how they are *surprised by life*.'

Of course, to be surprised can figure as an indictment – 'Haven't you learned anything?' we ask ourselves and others; it can be an admission of ignorance, innocence, embarrassing – but I think it's a beautiful phrase: surprised by life. A kind of creed for me, too, as a novelist, since it doesn't do away with human agency but places it in the field of influences and events and sets personal change at an operable scale, cognisant of contingency but also alert to openings, rather than imaging it either as repressive aesthetic norm – this is how stories should be – or as psychosis: novels are mad.

Now it's not my focus to think about the history of the idea of personal change but it's good to remember the idea has a history.

One of the more extraordinary books to have come out of the IIML's MA programme in recent times is Aorewa McLeod's autobiographical fiction *Who Was That Woman, Anyway?*

Snapshots of a Lesbian Life, published in 2012. I remember the shock in the workshop room as we discussed Aorewa's writing which she cheerfully told us was all true, except people's real names had been altered and some chronology rearranged. Impossible to shake the disturbing descriptions of her time as a student nurse-aide in the late 1950s in a children's ward – McLeod identifies most of these children as suffering severe birth defects. Her job was to feed these distressed children who usually had decaying teeth or bare upper gums, while being assured by the nurses that 'You must remember, they don't feel pain the way we do'; or her description of attending a public meeting in the 1980s where a senior National Party MP guest speaker suggested that all AIDS sufferers should be put on an island in the Hauraki Gulf, and I don't think he was talking about Waiheke. Telling such stories has many purposes but one of them is that it's a good way of measuring change. It's worth noting too that in measuring we weren't awarding ourselves a medal for progress, nor was the author – the best writing doesn't console exactly in this way.

What I felt reading Aorewa McLeod was how close we are to back then, how recently we were wrong. How easily we might return there too. Because it wasn't smugness we felt but a chastening sense of fright that collectively we'd forgotten significant parts of our history – that is, if we knew them in the first place. And this kind of prodding has a progressive agenda, since to consider our gains vulnerable and contingent might be one way of continuing to work for their security.

The other shocking, invigorating aspect of McLeod's book, *pace* Lennard J Davis and his resistance to the false consolations of self-understanding in the novel as a form, is that the central character in *Who Was That Woman, Anyway?*, the author's stand-in, *processes* very little of her experience on our behalf. She records – and often records her inexperience and surprise – and she is present in the writing, but there's a striking lack of reflection beyond this type of admission of naiveté and jolt. Personally I find this convincing, exciting even – such a detailed and illuminating range of experiences but so little direct commentary; other readers might react more coolly. The question in the book's title – *Who Was That Woman, Anyway?* – for these readers, imports an interrogative mode that isn't delivered on. We never find out who 'she' was because she never tells us. But what if she, the author, *doesn't know* who she, her fictional stand-in, is or was?

The personality as mystery, the life-path as forked and puzzling, feels unpromising, even off-putting, a bit perverse. The injunction to know thyself can be a totalising one and challenges to it look anti-social. Yet McLeod's book, in canvassing a near lifetime's worth of experiences from outside the mainstream culture, is all about the social. One steady pulse in the story told across the decades is that of the group – how groups of gay women found each other, how they behaved. The nurses in those 1950s wards, trained in, adepts at, or simply survivors of a dissociative environment, are also women who dance to 'Whole Lotta Shakin' Goin' On', own exotic underwear, play drinking games and have sex with each other. Ngaio, the central character, is thrilled by all of this and up for it; but she also often assumes a background role, even in the major events of her life. Far from being an artistic failure – 'We need more of you in here, please,' an editor might say – the self-portrait that emerges communicates that part of experience which does feel beyond our powers of analysis, the hard-to-narrate headlongness of many of our key moments, the times that feel less real once we surrender their aliveness to reliable hindsight.

Now another word for this quality is 'passivity', and passivity in characters is still a negative touchstone for reviewers and readers, and also for teachers of creative writing who tend to internalise this so completely as to elide it with that other easy-to-spot fault: the passive sentence construction. The premium on *being* active and *writing* active can often seem as reflexive as the PE teacher asking for ten more push-ups from unresponsive kids. It's as if we are telling writers and their characters to 'keep busy', much as we exhort our slightly depressed friend or our grieving self. The alternative to not keeping busy doesn't bear thinking about. Though maybe it does.

I want to add I'm not unaware that passivity's link to subjugation, victimisation and invisibility, especially in the depiction of women's lives, is culturally momentous. I'm always on the hunt for successful literary portraits of this quality. For while studies in passivity are hardly aspirational in any straightforward sense – we do not often long to be that figure who fails to act – they yet belong in the full accounting of human behaviour. Besides, bullying as well as resistance can take many forms and passivity's recalcitrance – its 'I'd prefer not to' – may yield surprising resourcefulness and, indeed, story, once the PE teacher in all of us calms down and the Bartleby in all of us gains a voice.

This essay, then, is sketching an attempt to hold two ideas together that seem contradictory. The first is that I've always tended to believe, along with my mother who assures her middle-aged children that we are all exactly the same in our deepest selves as we were when were babies, that people *don't* change. Not really. And – this is part of the same belief though not necessarily shared by my mother – that writing fuelled by an automatic association of potency and personal transformation isn't the only story worth telling. After all, even Vladimir and Estragon, in the play where, as the critic famously said, nothing happens twice, have, like those old Greeks, *gone through something*.

The second idea is that change is everywhere and that progressive thought, indeed our basic wellbeing, let alone art, relies on some underlying optimism about reinvention, recasting, redistribution. Work that sees disillusion as the only honest endpoint can feel as formulaic as its cheery opposite. 'Nothing to be done,' says Estragon to open *Waiting for Godot*, and then Beckett quietly goes about revolutionising the theatre. 'The essential doesn't change,' says Vladimir later, and suddenly Pozzo and Lucky burst onto stage. Here, to call literary form a 'consolation' feels way too mild; more like a detonation.

As a fiction writer, that's the double knot across my shoulders, which of course is the part of the body where writing comes from. So let me hunch for a short time over one small book in particular to see how far I can get with this problem.

The World Regained by Dennis McEldowney is a memoir which appeared in 1957 and was republished most recently in 2001 by Auckland University Press, where McEldowney worked for twenty years as editor, retiring in 1986. My sense is that he's best known as a publisher, though he wrote other autobiographical books and a couple of biographical works. *The World Regained* was his first – a book commissioned by a publisher to expand an original series of radio broadcasts McEldowney made concerning his astonishing story as one of the so-called 'blue babies'. He was diagnosed with Fallot's tetralogy, a congenital heart condition for which there was no effective treatment and from adolescence to the age of twenty-four he existed in his bedroom – 'this little boxed-up universe', he calls it – until he underwent what was, for the time, radical heart surgery. On its surface the book is calm, polite, transparent and helpful. Witty too, a great entertainment with its parade of blink-and-you-miss-them character studies.

Here's Dennis in hospital for X-rays (this is in the early 1950s): 'I stood behind the screen and was fed with spoonfuls of barium while the radiologist watched my insides moving before him. When I grew tired – I couldn't stand for more than a minute or two at a time – I sat to recover my breath in the wheelchair while he talked to me of television, which, no doubt because he was in the same line of business, he evidently thought would be a good thing.' The dry deployment of that 'evidently' makes the prose crackle. Or how about the indelible image of the physiotherapist who visits the men's ward where patients incapacitated by rheumatic fever watch as she does handsprings on the end of one of the beds – 'a display of surplus energy,' McEldowney writes, 'I thought a little callous.'

I said helpful and calm, but it is also an odd piece of work, gently polemical and increasingly digressive: a medical memoir which dispenses with that material after a while and looks elsewhere. I'll come to that elsewhere soon.

Below is one of my favourite New Zealand author photos.

This is from 1935, a newspaper picture of school kids at Sumner Beach, Christchurch, and no prizes for finding the author – there he is, looking the wrong way, thoroughly wrapped up and almost apoplectic with joy.

I love the way the boy's hands are splayed in the fashion that can only be produced by utter delight or terror or some mix of the two, as if an electric current is passing through the body. The fact that he's turned away from the photographer also speaks not of shyness but of self-transport – the boy is so overcome he doesn't know where to turn. He's rigid and, I would guess from the face, screaming. The other thing to love, of course, is the jersey he wears, while all the other kids of 1935 are in their togs. This was probably what I always wanted to wear when I was learning to swim in the unheated pool of Waiwhetu Primary School in Lower Hutt.

This beautiful, gently comic image appears in that reprint of *The World Regained*.

In teaching creative writing it took me a while – longer than it should have – to understand that the question of technique ('How do I make this book?') is also a question of value ('What do I believe about the world?'). Another way of saying this is that in writing a sentence you're also making a self and putting into circulation a set of images of the place you move around in, or would like to move around in. To think of literature as a kind of moral provocation brings another question into view: 'Who owns the images with which mine is in disagreement?' This question fuels *The World Regained*, which begins as the story of one life and grows into wider and thrilling commentary: there's a fundamental sense in McEldowney that present descriptions don't ring true and that we require new ways of talking about and dramatising where we find ourselves.

In the Introduction he wrote to the 2001 reprint, McEldowney alerts us to the fact that this personal story qualifies him to make broader statements. He bemoans the bad press the 1950s receives, especially from New Zealand writers: 'I had special reasons for finding the decade so exciting, but I never got over the suspicion that it would also have been exciting to anyone of a mind to be excited.' Are we back then in the world of those PE teachers barking their orders? 'Be excited!' Not really.

Certainly his story is about an appetite for experience denied, and the recognition that things won't come easily: 'I began to learn to live in the world,' McEldowney writes in the immediate aftermath of a successful operation, 'and I quickly

found the world did not lie open to me. It had to be conquered.'
That the conquering involves having a bath for the first time
as an adult (he buys a yellow rubber duck), or making a pot
of tea ('The number of things there were to remember!'), or
going for a walk, all lovingly detailed, suggests something
of the scale here. Courage is measured in tiny, involving
moments of dailyness. Change can be terrorising too, as
he discovers having existed for so long under ceilings: the
feel of the sky above his head is too overpowering and it
takes McEldowney eighteen months to shake off its phobic
intensity. Terror but also delight, which again works through
a marvellous minor: 'It seemed incredible when I found
the first. A *hole* in my sock! I said to myself, not believing
it, a hole in my *sock*! a hole in *my* sock!' But McEldowney's
book is also concerned to a remarkable degree with a kind of
debateability. First of all, the realist's question: 'What sort of
world is it that I'm in?' Secondly, the idealist's: 'What's the
best response to this world?' I mean the memoir doesn't just
suggest implicitly we reconsider some routine notions we
have; it doesn't simply prompt in the way any act of thinking
prompts us; *it makes its very scenes the site of an ongoing
interrogation of assumptions*. Action is frequently made up
of this kind of questioning.

Describing the invalid's shut-in life in an upstairs
bedroom, McEldowney opposes the untested observations of
well-meaning visitors: 'People who visited admired my view,
but supposed I must get tired of looking at the same scene
day after day. I didn't know what they meant; the scene gave
me no chance to get tired of it, it never remained precisely
the same an hour at a time, certainly not for a day or a month
or a year.' In a beguiling act of revenge on them and us, he
makes himself the centre of what's real, while anyone from
outside is vaporous and fabular: 'Visitors arrived through the
door to my room, appeared like a genie from a bottle, and
removed themselves back into the bottle when they left.' It's
a very different approach from, say, Aorewa McLeod's hide-

and-seek narrative. 'There are more remarkable discoveries to be made in a modern matter-of-fact New Zealand city,' he reproaches, 'than will ever be known by citizens who can never make the discoveries because they knew them all along.' McEldowney's form of explicit argumentativeness – felt even more keenly perhaps because it's cased in prose with impeccable manners – makes us feel there's other labour to be done, apart from telling us about the time when he moved from his bedroom out into the world. But what labour?

I hesitate to use the word biculturalism up front but not because it wasn't available when this book was written. *The World Regained* includes the fullish appearance of a single Māori, a sixteen-year-old fellow patient from the East Coast, 'immensely curious about everything around him, firing off rapid questions in an English very different from the accent used by more sophisticated Maoris who lived nearer the city . . .'

'The other patients,' McEldowney writes, 'had him teach them rude words in Maori. He was most of the time the most cheerful character in the ward.' This is New Zealand at a time when a nurse asks her patient: 'Are you English . . . or just Christchurch?' Still, reading is itself part of the bicultural project and registering absences is part of the story. Indeed, lying in a hospital bed, McEldowney does precisely this sort of national accounting, finding in the ward a Scotsman, a Samoan, an Indian, an Irishman, a Jugoslav, an Australian and a South African; and, having set us up for the punchline, 'even a few New Zealanders.'

The following sentence reveals the tender spot of the born-in-New Zealand Pākehā: 'There was a petty officer from the navy who said he was a New Zealander but spoke like a Yorkshireman.'

It's not just this sort of sensitivity which pushes my reading here. To approach biculturalism via a side-door we could say that *The World Regained* is in many ways about architecture, built spaces. A young man looks down on a world he can't reach.

At first windows are everything, then doors. Beds too, despite the absence of an erotic axis. (This memoir, through propriety, stares down sexual desire as narrative hook. In the reprint's Introduction, McEldowney mentions 'adolescent agonies'.) It's a book about optimum structures for living. It's about – key word, I think – *accommodation*, in the sense of finding somewhere to live but also in the sense of making a space for something or someone else. *Being accommodating.* It doesn't seem like a particularly robust virtue – to be accommodating carries little of the whole-heartedness of 'to be welcoming' – yet moving in the realm of grown-up literature perhaps we shouldn't expect such singularity; the generosity of good writing lies in its limitless qualifying of what we sometimes as citizens want stated and solved once and for all.

Anyway, let the word 'biculturalism' sit somewhere in the back of our minds as we go along with our theme of change for perhaps this preliminary reason: the demand for a dramatic narrative *in which we watch people change* squeezes the bicultural story at two points: first we register the 'at last' and also the 'what now' of Māori for whom the long wait has the dimensions of disaster and for whom this phase of Treaty settlement or post-settlement – elastic, disputatious, hopeful – has the quality of an open question ('finally Pakeha are recognising hurt, wrong and grievance and this moment can't be hurried so let's see what can be achieved'); secondly and dispiritingly we feel and hear the 'When will it end?' of Pākehā for whom the story isn't dramatic enough. Ongoingness seems like so much hard work and the longview hostile to our oddly self-cancelling desire for the change-of-all-changes, the one that brings an end to change. 'Haven't we heard enough from them?' Who gets to decide when we've had enough change is of course a matter of the highest importance.

One of *The World Regained*'s lessons is ongoingness; firstly because the author wasn't supposed to have any – McEldowney hadn't been expected to live much beyond his childhood years. As it turned out, he lived until his late 70s and died in 2003. But secondly because having re-entered the world, he found he had an argument with that world. I think this makes the book a classic in our literature, by which I simply mean it's eternally ripe for reprint'.

But as well as championing the book, I'm also using this work of non-fiction to think, paradoxically perhaps, about fiction and especially its burden or task, its dreary unreal requirement or its invigorating glory or some mix of the two – depending on where you sit – of showing the shifting of personality.

McEldowney's book is a true account of the years and events it traverses, so you could say its author is free of one constraint – the pressure to make stuff up, to make a pattern – and saddled with another: the pattern or lack of pattern which real life makes. He's stuck with his story, which happens to be his life. Crucially, he's in a position – and this is something he takes advantage of – to think about what art expects of life; to measure actual feelings against preferred expressive modes. As part of his ongoing argument with the dominant 50s discourse of disillusion he observes at one point that 'it never occurred to me to question why it should happen to *me*, the question which fiction-writers suppose to preoccupy such as I was.' So he's warning me that as a novelist I would get this same material wrong. He goes on, 'when I was enabled to change my state in life, I changed it, and was content.' A little later he clarifies and qualifies: moving from his bedroom to the world is gain and loss but gain is ascendant; there's more *of* and *in* the new life: 'I had to learn to make my view of life from a synthesis of many happenings rather than an analysis of a few.' 'And if I retained certain habits from my earlier days, among them a liking for doses of solitude, that merely showed I was one continuing person. I couldn't claim to have been made into someone else by my experiences; the heart operation wrought no fundamental change of heart; there was no point in time to which I could look back and discern a change from someone who was not I to someone who was. I remained I, all along the way.'

Probably in the end this is what draws me back to the book again and again – its surprising forays into a kind of domestic theorising about writing and especially this issue of change; its corrective to sentimental formularised readings of experience while keeping in place a vivid hopefulness, a winning combination not only because it communicates a vision of activism but because it's so hard-won.

The World Regained is also a wayward sort of writing manual. It doesn't shirk from the appeal of its life-and-death event – McEldowney's heart condition – indeed it has a built-in change focus, but its gathering force is oddly dispersed as the author 'gets better'; the dispersal might be its most compelling message. He devotes a chapter to attending the 1951 Writers' Conference in his hometown Christchurch where he hears James K Baxter's address and indulges in what he calls 'lion-hunting'. The young McEldowney is completely star-struck and reports that it's one of his happiest days to be in the company of New Zealand literati and the attendant critics and academics. He says this and means it but he also tells us they're wrong. 'I admire these writers and I know they write the truth. Yet heresy keeps breaking through . . . I cannot find life miserable . . .'

Here I'd like to switch hemispheres and decades again and go back to Joseph Roth for one of my favourite 'writer moments' in all fiction. As I said, *The Radetzky March* is set around a time of momentous change: the coming of World War I and the dissolution of the Austro-Hungarian Empire. There's a minor character, one Dr Demant, who is the medical officer in Lieutenant Trotta's regiment. Demant wears spectacles that are so thick that at one point Roth writes, 'he had no eyes anymore only glasses'. Dr Demant gets involved in a duel with Count Tattenbach, the regimental cad, over Demant's wife. The pair face off in a clearing. I'm quoting from Michael Hofmann's translation.

It was already morning, but the sun had not yet risen. The fir trees stood slender, upright and quite still, bearing the snow on their boughs with pride. In the distance cocks crowed back and forth. Tattenbach was talking to his seconds at the top of his voice. The consultant, Dr Mangel, walked back and forth between the two parties. 'Gentlemen!' said a voice. At that moment, Dr Demant took off his spectacles, a little awkwardly as he always did, and laid them carefully on a broad tree-stump. Strange to relate, he could still see the way quite clearly, the place where he was made to stand, the distance between that and the Count, and Tattenbach himself. He waited. Up until the very last moment he was waiting for the fog. But everything remained clear, as if the regimental doctor had never been short-sighted. A voice counted: 'One!' The regimental doctor raised his pistol. He felt brave and free, yes, for the first time in his life, even a little exuberant. He aimed as he had done once as a one-year volunteer at target practice (even then he'd been a wretched shot). I'm not short-sighted at all, he thought, I'll never need my glasses again. In medical terms it was a mystery. The regimental doctor promised to look into ophthalmology. At the very moment in which the name of a famous specialist swam into his mind, the voice counted 'Two!' The doctor could still see clearly. An anxious bird of a type he could not identify began to twitter, and from faraway he heard the sound of a trumpet. It was just then that the dragoons reached the exercise grounds.

And then we swing away from the duel to be with Lieutenant Trotta for several paragraphs – he's been worried about this duel and he's now convinced that everything is all right, not having heard any shots from the woods, good, he thinks, they've not gone through with it, and he rides along thinking positive thoughts. Positive thoughts in Joseph Roth are almost always the prequel to negative outcomes. Simply by thinking things, those things are ruled out. A few paragraphs later we learn that both Tattenbach and Dr Demant have died in the duel.

The business with Demant's glasses is strikingly odd. Why does he take them off in the first place – as if he's going to be involved in some close combat rather than a duel at twenty paces, or as if he's going to sleep? *I think he takes off his glasses to save them!* Such a brilliant insight of Roth's into the doomed man's state of mind; it reminds me of the great moment in Orwell's essay 'A Hanging' when the writer notices the condemned prisoner step aside to avoid a puddle on his way to the scaffold, not wanting to get his feet wet – for Orwell this is when he understands it's a human being about to die. 'I saw the mystery, the unspeakable wrongness, of cutting a life short when it is in full tide.' I feel the same shiver for Dr Demant. But Roth takes it one step further . . . the doctor believes he can, or he can actually, see better without his glasses!

Why do I think the doctor is a writer figure? Joseph Roth suffered terrible eye problems. In one of his final letters, he writes, 'my eyes are full of blood'. An eye inflammation stops him from writing and he interprets it like this: 'Eye is just expression of spiritual depression.' For Roth, eyes aren't windows, they're mirrors, harshly symptomatic. Writing of a later problem, he states, 'Like my eye inflammation back then, it's just another physical expression of the catastrophic situation . . .' His eyes prevent him working: 'Unfortunately I wear glasses now. . . . Apparently I have an astigmatism. Because of my eyes I won't be able to get going on the novel for another 2–3 weeks.' The biographical data is irresistible with regard to Dr Demant. Eyes matter in Roth, as does the recognition that he travels from actual to symbolic without pause. I'm not pausing much either. Demant's vivid, painfully brief moment of hubris is hardly the thing that kills him, though the language of self-understanding ('He felt brave and free, yes, for the first time in his life'), typically for Joseph Roth, can only be deployed ironically. One more thing. I see Demant as a writer because, despite his foolishness, he actually successfully fires the weapon. That's Roth's sly, unaccountable gift to Demant, and to himself – that he gets his man. This is not 'change or die' but change *and* die – done of course in deathless prose. Not the consolation but the gunshot of literary form.

Not quite half way through the novel, Lieutenant Trotta (the last in that line) is told by his commanding officer that the Fatherland 'no longer exists' – 'The fact is,' he says, 'we're all dead!' For Trotta, who doesn't quite believe nor understand how this could be true, the verdict nevertheless has what I'll call a novelising effect: 'All the processes of nature,' he feels, 'and all the events of ordinary daily life were touched by a menacing and unfathomable significance.' One becomes a writer at the unpredictable moment when everything seems alive with import. And there's nothing like reduced options to sharpen one's sense of urgency and possibility. The best writers I've seen come through the IIML's workshops are all suffering from this problem: the gift of too much significance.

This point about a nonexistent world is vital as we rejoin McEldowney. *The World Regained* has an almost sci-fi relationship to its contemporary setting. 'Neighbours' houses,' the regained and regaining person writes in earnest appreciation of the discovery once he gets to leave his bedroom observatory, 'did have backs to them. They didn't end in a jagged edge of lath-and-plaster like a cinema mock-up.' McEldowney, released into our upright, inhabited streets after years of enforced isolation, is an alien. He stares and makes notes. 'I used my eyes shamelessly,' he writes.

In a crucial scene, he attends the orchestra, and studies the audience, first observing their separateness: 'The young man in the seat next to mine who read the murders in *Truth* between items'; 'the office girls who sneaked sandwiches from boxes on their knees while they listened.' But then he's struck by something: he starts to feel their collective force as measured against his former solitary bedroom radio listening: 'the audience, every one of whose enjoyment of the music added to everyone else's, increasing it collectively.' Through this form of astonished accounting something strange happens: the concept of 'New Zealand' becomes testable, provisional, curious – an 'outside' that feels invented, and as such, available for change. Instability can be a synonym for suffering but also a boon for characters and readers alike as fixed coordinates morph into speculative placeholders.

In the book's most extraordinary chapter, McEldowney walks us around Christchurch streets, alternating between aversion to the busyness of those streets, their shrieking and their eating (he seems to have a thing about workers lunching on fried sole and mashed potatoes and a slice of lemon 'every noon for years on end') – 'I could not wonder the mental hospitals were full'; moving from this sort of rejection to different notes of humility and wonder in the face of the uncategorisable and complex and various ways of living, which are only defeating in the sense that they defeat McEldowney's proud sense that he *should* know what is going on inside other people. The idea that he might *never* know is, finally, savoured not for its sourness but for its plenty. Listening, actively eavesdropping on passersby, he sometimes, fortuitously, receives 'an unrehearsed revelation of what people were like.' He hears a girl saying to another girl, 'And all this happened because of a mistake in a telegram.' Yet these hints can't substitute for the strangeness he feels looking at others and the growing imperative to move beyond observation. 'It was not the looking and the listening, it was the amount I now began to be involved with people, that measured my entry into the world.'

From being the person others could not guess right about, he is now the one who gets others wrong. This sort of error measures the depth of our involvement. Getting others wrong turns out to be our necessary task, an index of humiliation most likely, but also a sign of health and, dare I say it, progress.

The World Regained repurposes the automatic narration of personal transformation in fruitful ways. It feels epic in the sense that its relationship to change is mediated through interpreting a wider world, which we see as it is *getting made and coming into being* rather than as a given. *The Radetzky March* is similarly scaled, though its dynamism, created in the early 30s in a Europe that Joseph Roth had already diagnosed as sick beyond help, is heading in the opposite direction – its soldiers are already ghosts of the longed-for battle that will eradicate the lingering present. The Austro-Hungarian given is already gone. In one of Roth's most crushing sentences, Lieutenant Trotta is 'like a man who had lost not only his home but his nostalgia for his home, his homesickness'. In a sense, 'New Zealand' – in its 1950s incarnation – is an idea ripe or rotten for revision. The implication, as well as the affective power of McEldowney's confessions, arguments and dramatisations, is that any status quo – naturally our present one included – requires continual scrutiny and vigilance. How strange and fitting that the revisionary hero turns out to be a bookish man with a congenitally defective heart, a person initially disqualified from our lives of engagement; a sickly tourist who examines our habits and asks annoying questions. This figure sees disillusion as a deficient response to a difficult and frequently defeating world – a world that regains him as much as is regained by him. Because here's the thing: this book is not really about watching people change, hugging and learning; this book, like all the best books, *is in itself a world of change*.

There are many beguiling entry-points to this shifting world, but consider, finally, the funny and strange uplift we get from the moment in *The World Regained* when the twenty-four-year-old author is admitted into Greenlane Hospital for his life-saving operation and is met by the nurses from Ward 3 who stare at their new patient. There seems to be a problem – but what is it? Then it makes sense. Of course they'd been expecting a blue *baby*, the ward had been prepared for an infant – they don't know what to do with this oversized sufferer. All their routines account for children, not this full-grown specimen. The physiotherapist, in particular, has a new challenge since she uses a toy cat to aid rehabilitation and usually instructs her patients, 'push pussy in, push pussy out.'

The delicious comedy of the scene is also hopefully robust enough to bear my last attempt at establishing the metaphorical purchase of this enchanting, urgent work. The nurses' incomprehension, followed by their adjustment, perfectly images how as readers, and by extension, as citizens, we must always be ready to move, be ready to accommodate each other, be ready collectively, in the collaborative way any audience is ready, to increase our enjoyment – joy carrying a powerful and explicit value in Dennis McEldowney's worldview – be ready, here it comes, to change. It also vividly enacts yet another moment in which we are surprised not only by literature but also by life.

What to Write About

Gary Henderson

In 1991 I attended Interplay, the International Young Playwrights Festival, in Warragul, near Melbourne. One night I found myself leaning on a bar chatting to a Czech playwright, who asked, 'What do you write about in New Zealand? I mean' – he shrugged – 'nothing happens.'

Under his piercing West Slavic stare, I felt immediately on the back foot and stammered something about us being a young country still unsure of our identity, and so mostly we wrote about ourselves. Sort of. Kind of thing.

He nodded, and shrugged dismissively, the way one does to a comfortable, middle-class pretender, when one comes from a country that has been repeatedly invaded, annexed, split, reconstituted, and was about to dissolve into two countries the following year. And when your president is a playwright.

Strictly speaking, President Václav Havel was at that time a *former* playwright, having been a banned playwright, political activist, jailbird, ex-jailbird, and then, in 1991, president, soon to become, the following year, ex-president, and six months later, president again.

Understandable, then, that the puzzled Czech writer at the bar could look at New Zealand and conclude that 'nothing happens'. It was as if he couldn't fathom why we voluntarily burdened ourselves with the vexing business of writing plays instead of getting on with relaxing at the beach.

If you deconstruct his question you find, as usual, some assumptions. The biggest is the assumption about what constitutes 'happening'. If your country's history – and even some of your own – is a story of continual and often dangerous political instability then you may have a view of what 'happening' means, and the things affecting your life that, as an artist, you can authentically address. It may also be difficult for you to imagine what there is for an artist to address in a relatively safe, stable country where, by your own definition, 'nothing happens'.

So, there is an assumption made about what is worth writing about. There is an assumption made about the purpose of a play. And in my rather flippant interpretation of his attitude, there is an assumption made about what is worth doing with your life.

What should you write about? What is the purpose of a play? Are there better things you could be doing with your life? These questions are so intertwined that an attempt to address any one of them inevitably crosses them all. So . . . easy ones first.

What should we, you and me, here and now, write about? Well, what's available to us to write about? What affects your life? I believe that any person has the right to tell any story. We do not forfeit that right because of our gender, race, age, nationality, culture, sexuality, wealth or any other aspect of our being. To try and deny anyone the right to tell any story is censorship of the most repugnant kind – censorship of the imagination. And I'd like to return to that notion shortly.

You have the right to tell any story, provided – and this is not a negation – that you establish an authentic connection with your material. It's a moral obligation you have as a writer. If you don't do it, you're a fake. Your work will be derivative; copied from some other play you saw, or something you watched on TV once.

You should be able to articulate, at least to yourself, your authority for telling this story, for making this statement, for addressing this question – however you like to express it. When that voice in your head, or even a real person, demands of you, 'Who are you to say that?' – you should be able to tell them.

Here's what I mean by establishing an authentic connection with the material. I teach playwriting and I always ask my students a series of questions about their plays, especially when they are embarking on a second draft, although they can be helpful at any stage. The questions are quite mechanical, but I find them useful for cutting to the heart of the students' stories.

First question: What happens in your play? They must answer this in a paragraph. Most students, on their first attempt, write the blurb for the back of a DVD cover. They don't tell me what happens in their play. They tell me something to pique my curiosity. Which is exactly the position I'm already in. I'm curious about what happens in their play. I want to know how it starts, how it develops, how it ends. Once they get it, they find they have encapsulated their plot in one paragraph – simple and uncluttered.

Second question: What is your play really about? They must answer this with a single word. It's hard, and I'm quite strict about it. The first time I pose these questions, it's an exercise; they're not going to be committed to their answers, so it takes the pressure off a bit, but it doesn't make it any easier. The single-word demand forces them to look for the big subject their play is addressing. Once they settle on a word, that's what I describe as their play's theme. Jealousy. Family. Betrayal. Solitude. Obsession. Loyalty.

You can almost feel the satisfaction in the room once they've come up with their word. 'Phew. Now I know what I'm writing about. Away I go . . .' In fact, most of us tend to stop there.

But the third question is the really useful one when you're prying apart your work: What are you saying about that thing? The students must answer this with a concise, provocative statement. The shorter the statement and the stronger the language, the better.

'Jealousy will kill you.'
'Families are dangerous.'
'Solitude will save the world.'

Everyone has a name for this kind of statement. Somewhere along the line I started calling it your myth. It's a human truth that you believe, or know, and which is going to inform your play, and your audience.

Once you have a statement you think lies at the heart of your play, ask yourself, 'How do I know this? Why do I believe this?' Your honest answer to this question is your authentic connection with the material.

I never ask anyone to reveal their answer to this. It doesn't need to be profound, or deeply private, but it might be. Like the Sonia song says, 'everybody has a war'. Maybe you know this thing because you've lived it, and it drew you to the brink of suicide. Or maybe you know this thing because you researched it. Or maybe you know this thing because you observed it happen to someone else. This last one raises a few issues, which I'll address only so far as to say that I'm talking about the human truth of the situation. I am not talking about the factual, blow-by-blow reproduction of someone else's life on stage. The line is blurry, and you have only your integrity to guide you.

If you have, or can establish, an authentic connection with the material, then you have the right to tell that story. I choose these words quite carefully. I don't believe it's obligatory to have this connection when you start work, but you must have it at the point you consider your play finished.

All of this is instinctive to an experienced writer, although it never hurts to make it clear. In practice, our instinct is nearly always to write about something we know about. The trick is to recognise what you really do know. For example some writers, especially beginning writers, believe they know about something because they've seen lots of TV dramas about it.

One other thing. When I assert that 'anyone has the right to tell any story', I choose to express it this way because it sounds neat and concise and a bit provocative. It might be more accurate to say that I believe anyone has the right to *attempt* to tell any story; and your ability to establish an authentic connection with your material is the only thing that affects which stories you should rightly tell.

It's about now I should acknowledge how pompous it is for me to tell you what rights you do or don't have. I don't have that power. You have to claim those rights. But in reality – real New Zealand reality – you can write about anything you damn well like. And perform it. No one's going to stop you. Are they?

It's true that there is no formal process specifically for the censorship of theatre in New Zealand. We have a film censor, an Office of Film and Literature Classification (who also deal with PlayStation, Xbox and other video games) and a Broadcasting Standards Authority. But our lawmakers see no need to censor, or classify, live theatre. So when I say you have the right to tell such-and-such a story . . . big deal. Of course you do. What's stopping you?

Well, lots of things. Writer, director and actor Danny Mulheron said once that if he ever finds himself saying, 'Oh god, I can't say that!' then he knows he has to.

Where does that censoring voice in your head come from? Let's assume it's not a craft thing. It's not judicious editing – it's you feeling that there is some thought you're not allowed to express. Maybe it's your own horror at yourself for even having that thought in the first place. What conditioning went on in your upbringing that now tries to muzzle you? What conditioning is all around us, right now, so pervasive that we've normalised it, which has you believing, 'Oh god, I can't say that.'

There have been examples in our country of public commentary straying so far from the promoted narrative that its author has been vilified or publicly dismissed. It happens regularly to scientists, researchers, investigative journalists and other whistle-blowers . . . but never to playwrights. Either we never challenge the national narrative vigorously enough, or we do but we just don't matter.

When I see a play that's advertised as 'outrageous', I know it won't be. I've never been to a piece of theatre in this country that outraged me. The word 'outrageous' has been hijacked and watered down to mean 'deliciously naughty'.

Everything hard, cutting or edgy in New Zealand theatre is fashionably so. True outrageousness is unfashionable. That's the right we should claim: the right to be unfashionably outrageous.

However, in 2017 Wellington reviewer Madelaine Empson somewhat controversially refused to review the performance she attended of *Manifesto 2083*, a play about Norwegian mass murderer Anders Breivik. Empson wrote, 'I refuse to review *Manifesto 2083* because it is a deeply offensive and problematic show. I will not be giving Anders Breivik any more of the airtime that he so desperately craves and does not deserve.'[1] She drew both criticism and support for her stance, with equal passion on both sides of the argument. It was never an argument about the quality of the play, perhaps not even about what it was saying, but about what it was doing. For me it was doing exactly what theatre should be doing. I'd seen the play the previous year. It was brilliant, and left me deeply unsettled.

So which stories *should* you tell? As I said, that's inextricably bound up with what you believe the purpose of a play is, and what is worth doing with your life. Brilliant New Zealand playwright Ken Duncum wrote a play called *Blue Sky Boys*, about an imagined night in 1964 when the Everly Brothers, at the darkest point in their career, played the Savage Club in Wellington the same night the Beatles played the Town Hall. There is a moment when Don Everly explains to the young ring-in drummer that he believes his purpose on the planet is 'to take my whole life, everything I know, and squeeze it down into a little two-minute song about a boy and a girl. Because it just seems to me – that's a worthwhile thing to do.'

What do you think is a worthwhile thing to do? Work it out. Write it down. Then find the courage to do it. It can be a humble goal, or something lofty. I tend to go for lofty. I want my play to add to the sum total of human understanding about what it means to be human. Whether it's a knockabout, door-slamming farce, or an intensely moving drama, that's what I want from my writing. Because I happen to think that's a worthwhile thing to do.

I read (and later found to be true) that on the opening night of *Death of a Salesman*, after the play ended, Arthur Miller saw an old man leaving the theatre, not looking too happy. It turned out he was Bernard Gimbel of Gimbels, the department store, and the next day, having seen *Death of a Salesman*, he ordered that no one would ever be fired from Gimbels just because they were too old. Imagine that.

On the other hand, maybe you just want to give people a good night out. Relax them and refresh them, set them up for the coming week. You're not alone. In a *Guardian* article from 2007, British writer and director Anthony Neilson says, 'We are entertainers. What we do is not as important to society as brain surgery, or even refuse collection. But when the brain surgeon and the refuse collector finish work, they come to us and it is our job to entertain them – not necessarily just to distract them, but to stimulate, to refresh, to engage them. That's our place in the scheme of things, and it's a responsibility we should take seriously.'[2] It doesn't matter whether you just want to make them laugh, or whether you want to profoundly alter their understanding of life – if you believe it's a worthwhile thing to do, take the responsibility seriously.

Then there's the question we all need to ask ourselves, and we probably have done: Is this the best way to spend my life?

Is my writing really going to have any effect on anyone, or am I just in love with the notion of myself as a writer? If I really do want to add to the sum total of human understanding about what it means to be human, is writing plays the best way to do that?

In the mid-80s I was studying theatre and film at Victoria University of Wellington. Brecht was very fashionable among us then. One day some of us were preparing for a performance of bits and pieces from various Brecht plays; a compilation of good political theatre. We were gonna show them. Just after 5.30, we remembered it was local body election day, and we had less than half an hour to get to a polling booth and vote. The irony was so obvious we felt ridiculous. We ran – and made it.

How long did it take you to write your last play? Don't count the thinking you did while you were weeding the garden or walking to work, count the hours you actually spent writing words on the page. Fifty? A hundred? Would have had more effect on the world spending those hours working at the city mission, or volunteering at the Citizens Advice Bureau? I'm not suggesting you stop writing and take up charity work. But I am asking you to address the question.

So what should you write about? You write about something you have an authentic connection with. You constantly remind yourself what you want your writing to do. You find the courage and claim the right to say the things you must not say. And you never forget that it is a worthwhile thing to do.

1   Madelaine Empson. Review. *Regional News*. Issue 50, 21 February 2017.
2   Anthony Nielson. 'Don't Be So Boring'. *The Guardian*. 21 March 2007. Accessed 11 May 2017. Web.

Thinking from the Middle

Stella Duffy

This year I will be fifty-four. I have fifteen published novels, maybe sixty short stories, and fourteen devised and written plays, with another in development. When my first book came out in 1994, I had already had a couple of short stories published, as well as devised and written theatre for over a decade, but it took me years to call myself a 'writer'. It took at least three novels with my name on the spine. The term 'writer' or 'artist' was for other people. People who didn't grow up in Tokoroa. People whose parents knew writers or artists or actors or agents or musicians or singers or poets or playwrights. People who knew – really knew – that it was possible for them to be anything they wanted.

That wasn't in my life and it wasn't likely to be. Then, when I was fifteen, Theatre Corporate brought a touring *Hamlet* to my high school – and no, lovers of the canon, lovers of Shakespeare, it was not the writing that changed my life. It had nothing to do with the excellence or otherwise of the production. What made all the difference was that *someone like me* was in the cast. Johnny Givins was the big brother of my friend from primary school; his dad worked at Kinleith Mill like my mum and dad did. *Someone like me* was being an artist. And that changed my life – I still didn't know how I personally would get there, but I now knew that people like me could work in the arts.

This piece, then, is for people like me. It's for those of us who feel deep in our guts that we have a story we want to tell – hopefully more than one – but we don't yet believe we can do it. It's for those of us who are having a crisis of confidence in the middle of an otherwise perfectly (or adequately, or barely) successful career. It's for those of us who don't wake up every morning full of the joys of creativity with time and space and energy and health to get on and do the work. It's for those of us who know that lovely as it can be to make our own work, it also takes courage and fearlessness, it also takes being brave when bravery is in short supply. It's for those of us who know that pieces like this can take themselves – and us – far too seriously indeed.

It's a pick and mix of what I know as a middle-aged, mid-list author. Some stories will be relevant now, some might be relevant later; as with any suggestions about how to write or what to make or how to create, take what sings to you and ignore the rest. (Unless the bit you're ignoring is the bit that says you just have to do the work – don't ignore that. That's the one thing that is not subjective. You *do* have to do the work.)

You just have to do the work

You do. No one else is going to write your story. Talking about your story is not going to get your story written. Telling your story to your friends, your children, your mother, your therapist, the dog, is not going to get it written. You do have to write the words.

Write the words then make them better

I probably know about two hundred published writers. I don't know anyone who thinks they got it right the first time. Some, maybe sixty to seventy per cent, don't plot very heavily; they work out much of their plot in the first draft, and then work and rework. Some plot massively and don't write until they know everything that happens, and in the order it happens.

Some do a mix of both. Pretty much everyone will tell you it also changes depending on what you're writing. There is no one way – there is not even your own one way. There are many writers who will tell you they thought they had a method and then on their third or thirtieth novel that method failed them and they had to find a new way. Every story needs its own method, or at least, its own version of a method.

Your voice versus the story's voice

Yes, many of us have a style we often fall into – that can be comforting for a reader, it can be comforting for a writer – but don't be fooled into thinking that this is the only way you can or must write. Each piece of work also has its own voice. It can be humbling and valuable to get out of the way as a writer and work to find the story's voice instead of your own.

You don't have time

Yeah, you do.

Chekhov, Dostoyevsky and Trollope had full-time jobs (and wives, yes, I know). Beryl Bainbridge was a solo parent who got up an hour before the kids woke so she could write. Toni Morrison was an editor before she wrote fiction. Frida Kahlo worked in pain, with pain. Einstein worked in the patent office. Aphra Behn was a spy. Sue Townsend and Monica Ali wrote when the kids were in bed. Maya Angelou had loads of jobs before and while starting to write, becoming a writer who knew about so much because she'd done so much.

These people are not magic; they are not superhumans. They chose to make work. Of course you have time to make work. You might have to do it in bite-sized chunks, you might have to give up something else (sleep, beer, smoking, holidays, social media) to do it. You might have to be more disciplined than you already are, but you do have time. Get on with it.

How to write in bite-sized chunks

Five hundred words a day is doable for most people – not perfect words, just the *next* 500. If you write 500 words a day, five days a week, fifty weeks of the year (yay, holiday!), you'll have written a first draft of a novel in a year. Then spend the same time making it better. And again. Done. That's the book you've been going on about *but not writing* for the past three years. Now send it out and start the next one.

A writing career does not follow a defined path

My (ex-) publisher turned down my seventh book. I thought it was my best; they didn't. Luckily they hadn't given me any money for it, but they didn't want it. I was gutted, mortified and shamed, as well as without a publisher. It happens. It happens much more than most writers are prepared to admit. Two things to say about that:

If we writers were more honest about how little most of us earn, certain falsehoods about writing and publishing would die overnight.

Publishing is a business and not every book will suit every publisher.

As it turned out, I eventually went to Virago with that book, *State of Happiness*. It became the first book I had longlisted for a major prize (the Orange Prize for Fiction) and it remains (in my opinion) one of my best books. So, a happy ending followed the awful upsetting bit, because I kept going.

Good things and bad things are both useful for a writing life

I've had wonderful things happen in my life and kept writing. I've had cancer twice and chemo-induced infertility and failed IVFs and many close family and friend deaths and kept writing. (There's no sick pay or compassionate leave or holiday pay when you're freelance.) Sometimes it's hard to write when the brilliant things are happening. Sometimes it's hard to write when the awful things are happening. I think it is always easier to write, to create, when it's what we do anyway, what we do around or in spite of pain, alongside or because of joy. If we always write then we can become practised in writing whatever is going on. That's not to say it's easy, but in a freelance life, with a career terribly dependent on the whims of the market, it's good to carve out something regular. Writing *anyway* is something regular.

Shame is useful

None of us is as brilliant as we want to be, that doesn't mean we can't try, keep on and work at it. Shame can be a good indicator of something happening. The piece of work you're creating now may not be as good as your last, or the one before that; a writing career is not a steady progression of improvement. Sometimes we feel the wind at our back and everything works out easily and the piece flows. Other times it is a hard slog – neither way guarantees a good piece of work. But shame, that odd feeling in the lower depths of your stomach, close to the groin, almost sexual, almost pleasurable – that's a great place. Where your shame is, there is your edge. Where there's an edge, there is juice. Jumping over the edge can be the hardest and the most liberating thing to do. It may not result in great work immediately: when we take a new turn, make a new leap, it can take us a while to find our way, but there is magic there. Embrace the shame of not being as good as you want to be – it has learning in it.

n.b. Check out where your characters feel shame too. Not ashamed – that's generally about incident – but shame itself, the emotion in the core. It will give you some useful information.

Writing is political

If you are writing a novel, screenplay or play in which all the characters are white, middle-class,[1] privileged, able-bodied and mostly male, you are not writing the truth of the world.

It is totally fine for you to do this if this is the story you want to tell – but make sure you know you're doing it. Don't accidentally feed the lie that the white, able-bodied, middle-class man is the norm and everyone else is a minority.

Writing is not hard work

Being a miner is hard work. Working twelve-hour days in a textiles sweatshop is hard work. When my dad retired he was a boilerman – if nothing went wrong with the boiler, he'd come home after his night shift having read a book overnight. If something did go wrong, he'd come home in the morning covered in small burns and taking salt tablets to replace salt lost in sweat after hours fixing the boiler. That was hard work. Writing is not a coalface, it is not a sweatshop, it is not hard work – but you do need to work hard at it.

You don't need a special place, silence, music, this desk, that pen, that laptop, this paper to write

Make up as many superstitions as you like, but know that they are barriers you're putting in your own way. Do the work.

Not everything is a book

The reason your story or novel is stalled might be because it's actually a film or a script, or vice versa. Have a play with it and find out.

It might also be because this is not the story you really need to write now. Go deep, be honest, check out that shame place inside you. It might be that you need to write something else right now.

It is also possible that your idea is not the great idea you think it is. All of us have a bad book (or several) in us. Sometimes we publish them anyway, sometimes we abandon them, sometimes we come back years later and make them better.

It's okay to let things go – make sure you're not letting it go because you're being lazy or fearful, but if it's neither of those, and if learning some new skills won't help, let it go. Get on with something else. Nothing is wasted. What you learn in letting something go is huge.

And finally . . .

Relax. It's going to be fine. Or, it won't be fine. Either way all you can do now is the work.

You had the idea and when you had the idea it was the most beautiful thing you had ever seen heard smelled touched tasted felt. The idea would not leave you alone and so, knowing that your tools were faulty, knowing that creating the entirely glorious is impossible, you started the work. You kept on with the work. You kept on when you didn't know how to do it, and you learned in the doing. You kept on when you couldn't see the next word, let alone the next page. And yes, some days you kept on when it was all joy and every word was perfect and each phrase held a note that only you and a million other people would ever hear, and it was easy. What you now know is that day of ease is paid for by all the other days, those many more days when you were only as good as the worst you could be – and you did the work anyway.

You kept on, and you brought yourself to a place where it was done.

And then you turned around and worked on it some more. You ripped it apart and remade it, you sucked it dry and breathed new life into it. You did all of this by yourself, sometimes in silence, and sometimes with the music of raging insecurity at your back.

And eventually – *eventually* – it was finished.

It was not as good as the vision you had at the start. It did not have the glory of your original idea. It could never have that shimmering perfection because we are our own imperfect tools, and all we have to work with are the words through our mouths, our guts, our racking, coughing chests, our running legs, our pumping fists, our deep shame and our too-brief moments of bliss.

And because all that we have to create our work is just this flesh, this body through which we write, this flawed implement to turn an idea into reality, that reality will never be perfect.

You already knew that, and you did it anyway.

Because that's how it is: we aim for the perfect, we create the imperfect.

And then we give it away – and start again.

---

1   Yes, I'm writing this from London, but I grew up in Tokoroa. Aotearoa has a class system too.

Write Where You Are

Pip Adam, William Brandt, Rajorshi Chakraborti, Gigi Fenster

Interviewed by Emily Perkins

Write Where You Are is a collective made up of authors Pip Adam, William Brandt, Rajorshi Chakraborti and Gigi Fenster. Together, their work is focused on increasing the accessibility of creative writing in communities and to individuals who face barriers to participation in the arts. Since 2014, they have been visiting two prisons in the Wellington region, Arohata Women's Prison and Rimutaka Men's Prison, and offering creative writing classes in environments such as Remand, the Drug Treatment Unit (DTU), and Unit 9 (Te Whare Manaakitanga – the Special Treatment Unit at Rimutaka Prison).

There is a tradition in Aotearoa of arts practitioners working with prison inmates: the painter Colin McCahon visited long-term prisoners in Mt Eden Jail, giving advice about their paintings.[1] *Verbatim*, a play by William Brandt and Miranda Harcourt, made powerful theatre out of interviews with prisoners As Brandt writes:

> For a prison inmate, creative writing offers a number of possible benefits. These range from a constructive way to pass time to new skills and increased employability, personal growth and insight.[2]
> Creative writing also has the potential to become

a life-long practice, carried back into the community after release. All you need is a pen, some paper and a desire to engage in the writing process.

Write Where You Are is inspired in part by the work of Michael Crowley, a British writer and youth justice worker who conducted workshops in Wellington. Crowley's book on this work is *Behind the Lines: Creative Writing with Offenders and People at Risk* (Waterside Press, 2012).

This interview was conducted over two sessions, and has been shaped and edited for clarity. During the interviews the camaraderie, openness and mutual support of the collective members was plain to see: they finished each other's sentences, asked after each other's experiences, and there was a lot of laughter.

EMILY PERKINS:

What led you to develop the Write Where You Are collective?

WILLIAM BRANDT:

I had worked on a play called *Verbatim* that saw me visiting a lot of prisons. It was very different from this work in that I was kind of extracting, mining the prisons for life stories, doing interviews, then transcribing them. That was a long time ago but it made a huge impression on me. Then in 2014 I got invited to a workshop that was being organised by Arts Access Aotearoa, run by Michael Crowley, and Pip was there too, so we connected. I felt like I'd been waiting to do something with prisons and I liked the idea of teaching in there rather than just going in and sort of taking something away.

RAJORSHI CHAKRABORTI:

Before moving to Wellington I lectured in literature and creative writing at Edinburgh University, and then here I was a stay-home parent trying to find time to write. When

William and I caught up for coffee he mentioned teaching in prisons, and I had missed teaching alongside writing, and the opportunity to teach in a completely new location with its own possibilities was very appealing. And so I asked William if they wouldn't mind another person on board and they were very welcoming.

GIGI FENSTER:

I was looking to do some volunteering, and that was maybe a shift from South Africa. There, volunteering in prison might have not been the first place one would go to make a difference. In New Zealand, it feels like something one can usefully do without forgoing other urgent needs. I was looking into that and I heard the Howard League on the radio talking about literacy. So I applied to them to do literacy and then they said, actually, we need someone to do creative writing, when they heard about my background.

EMILY PERKINS:

Was this at Rimutaka?

GIGI FENSTER:

Yeah. I subsequently found out they'd had one specific prisoner in a specific unit who had asked for creative writing.

PIP ADAM:

I'd been visiting prisons for about twenty years, mainly alcohol and drug units. And I'd always been quite dubious about the therapeutic potential of art. But then I went to the Michael Crowley talk, and he brought some evidence-based research that through imagining yourself into someone else's experience, which is what you do in a lot of art and especially creative writing, you can build empathy. And I thought that held a little bit of weight.

EMILY PERKINS:

When you came into that space, did you think about what it was going to be like to teach there – just the physicality of it?

RAJORSHI CHAKRABORTI:

I'd never been into a prison before. Both Gigi, my usual teaching partner, and I are New Zealanders who are not from New Zealand originally. Gigi's taught at prison for a whole year more than I have, but there are probably two very different backdrops we have in our minds, in her case perhaps the South African prison system. In my case the Indian prison system was one frame of reference, and the other is what we are constantly exposed to in the form of American prisons, in documentaries or TV shows. If you've not been in a prison in the country you live in, you get a lot of ideas of what the inside of a prison is like from documentaries, which are often shot in America. And of course there are issues about prison life and culture here that are worth questioning and being concerned about – the growing number of prisons, who is being incarcerated for what reasons, I'm not at all romanticising any of that. But within that, the fact that we're allowed in, and the degree of transparency and interaction without the feeling of anyone listening in – there is something about it that is genuinely reassuring. Lots of things facilitate this feeling: these people have first of all chosen to be in the writing classes. They've been in that therapy unit for a long time, so when we come to them they have explored many things about themselves and probably are in quite a self-aware, healthful place within that context, as much as it's possible to be. Compared to everything I've read about Indian prisons and everything we've been exposed to about US prisons, I actually feel rather proud of this aspect of being a Kiwi.

EMILY PERKINS:

Have you articulated the potential outcomes of this work in a collective way?

WILLIAM BRANDT:

We're all agreed that we're not therapists, and that's probably a principle that we adhere to.

PIP ADAM:

The therapeutic side of it comes second for me, because the real reason I wanted to facilitate workshops in prisons was that I felt this real missing voice in New Zealand literature. As education becomes more expensive and that sort of thing, I really wasn't finding a lot of writers who had had experiences similar to mine, and I liked the idea that there was a way of increasing the range of voices. I liked the idea that possibly submissions for [literary journal] *Sport* could come from inside the prison, or this voice could be represented in a different way.

GIGI FENSTER:

I'm also doubtful about the therapeutic value and if there is therapeutic value whether we're the people to be giving it. Crowley is trained, I think, as a social worker, so he has that background. We're lucky in Unit 9 in that we work with therapists, and while creative writing in itself may be therapeutic, we're not giving therapy.

PIP ADAM:

One of the things is that the motivation to write, in me, is often to sort things out that I don't understand. I might see something and think, 'Why is that person behaving like that,' and that might spark a short story. I think that whether someone's writing about dragons or time machines or whatever, creative writing does have the facility to do that. And sometimes that creative writing process somehow *meets* the therapeutic process, and joyfully.

GIGI FENSTER:

I think of this one guy – for therapy they had to write about how they see their future, and he wrote about his future with gazillions of dollars and beautiful babes in bikinis, and sports cars, etc. If that was in a creative writing environment we could have been able to ask questions like, 'How does this character get that?' 'What does he do?' 'If you read a book where he won the lottery and got gazillions, what would you think of that?' and test that, maybe.

EMILY PERKINS:

You're suggesting that looking at a problem through the lens of fiction, that's a way of also thinking about problems of life.

WILLIAM BRANDT:

Yeah, problems of life. But there's also the danger of *fantasy*, as opposed to imaginative investigation. And fantasy is when what you're writing becomes this closed loop that you're feeding something in yourself with. Just for the pleasure of doing it. Like, you know, pornographic writing. Wanting to summon that world so the writer could be in it.

PIP ADAM:

Even the process of stopping and thinking about outcomes, for a lot of people, that's one of the things fiction can do. It can make you stop and say, 'If I do X, I can think that through to the end, and if I do Y, I can think that through to the end.' And there are some people for whom that facility is not well developed. I mean, I used to be like that. So that practice is good. And also a lovely thing about characters is that you start to see consequences as well, in a different way. I think that fiction can give you that, whether you're reading or writing. A thing about prison is that they've got fantastic libraries.

RAJORSHI CHAKRABORTI:

I think our classes are tiny drops in their oceans of coping with time, coping with the way life has turned out for them, what they might or might not have done, none of which we know anything about. But then I attended my first presentation, and those who chose to had developed the writing, and read it out and presented it, alongside music, poetry, and more than one haka that they had practised entirely in their own time with their own initiative. I realised that in some small way our classes had sparked off wonderful work that emerged from within them, and some wellspring of motivation that was in them. So alongside feeling this humility about the limits of what we can achieve and the limits of what we know about the people facing us, and what their lives are in that context that we only visit for two hours, what we do in that time did also spark off some wonderful responses.

EMILY PERKINS:

The courses are eight or ten weeks, once a week, is that right?

GIGI FENSTER:

We're looking at something more ongoing, because some of the guys were saying they'd like that.

RAJORSHI CHAKRABORTI:

It's often like starting a car engine in a cold country on a cold morning, where the next week, just to warm up again and remember how nice it had been the previous week, takes about fifteen or twenty minutes. I know it's not possible within the constraints of budget and other things, but if we met two or three times a week, we could all go deeper, and a lot more would emerge.

WILLIAM BRANDT:

The eight- or ten-week course is supposed to build, so we start with low-level concepts like the word and the sentence and grammar, even.

PIP ADAM:

Yep, we do a lot of grammar . . .

GIGI FENSTER:

Metaphor . . .

PIP ADAM:

Tense. You know, something as simple as tense and point of view.

RAJORSHI CHAKRABORTI:

Turning bits of life into story is my approach, whereas Gigi actually remembers to introduce ideas that are essential to making it happen, such as 'What it is to write in first person' and 'What is a metaphor', so we complement each other.

EMILY PERKINS:

Are you delivering a talk or a presentation, or setting exercises?

GIGI FENSTER:

There's so much shifting according to the group. We might go in thinking we're going to do exercises, then discover actually they want a lesson on figurative versus . . . you know, and then give a lesson. Or go in with a whole lesson and then discover actually they're not interested, they'd rather do exercises.

PIP ADAM:

But the way it looks on paper [*laughter*] is that we'll give a five- or ten-minute talk – and it's a real give and take, because we've had participants who are English teachers, we've had PhDs, so often these people take the class, often they know more about grammar than I do. So it's, say, a big chat about tense, and we might have some examples, and then we'd do some writing exercises. But there are days when people don't want to sit and listen and there are days where people have got really interested in point of view, say, and want to talk for the whole forty-five minutes about that. So the flexibility's huge.

EMILY PERKINS:

What are their responses to the reading materials you bring in?

RAJORSHI CHAKRABORTI:

It forces us to be very economical and to bring in extracts that evoke what we want to begin discussing very quickly. For example in one of the classes, we were talking about metaphor and figurative speech, but then we wanted to take it further and say that sometimes a metaphor can be extended where an artist builds an entire story out of it. What starts out as a metaphor, they decide to treat extremely literally, and that becomes the springboard for a story which is both utterly real and yet happening on another plane. So we did the opening paragraph of *The Metamorphosis*, and people really responded to that: he's not saying 'he's feeling like a beetle', he *is* the beetle. And then we get into the nuts and bolts of what it is for a first-time beetle to try and turn around, and get back on its legs . . . The other one that received a wonderful response was the South Auckland Poets Collective. We showed a YouTube clip where these six guys performed brilliantly on a stage, and they talked about what it is to be a man and what their values were, and that was actually our first class, just to begin a conversation about poetry, about performing, and about how poetry emanates from experience.

EMILY PERKINS:

So you're reading the room, reading the students –

WILLIAM BRANDT:

Yeah, we're asking them, what would you like to do, or would you like us to do this. But you've got to come in with plenty of options. [*laughter*] You have to have something to offer, eh, you can't expect . . .

RAJORSHI CHAKRABORTI:

Sometimes when you think 'Should we introduce a certain concept?' One of the things that outsiders, unfortunately, ask is, 'Are they up to the reading?' or 'Are they up to the writing?' Well first of all, it's self-selecting. So these are people who have a basic level of confidence in their reading and writing abilities. And the other thing is to assume nothing, because some of them are reading and writing at a very advanced level. We're always trying to bring the conversation back to a place so everyone, no matter what their background or how much reading or writing they've done, can find a way to participate and remain interested.

PIP ADAM:

And that's where the peer teaching is absolutely vital, eh? Because we can split up but also we can bounce ideas off each other, like if I come up dry William can say, 'Oh, shall we do this?'

WILLIAM BRANDT:

Sometimes people in the class will peel off, just want to do something by themselves . . .

EMILY PERKINS:

They'll go to another place in the room and write?

PIP ADAM:

Yeah.

EMILY PERKINS:

So if you've got different people coming in and out, how do you do the work of establishing the environment, the trust that we all talk about as creative writing teachers?

GIGI FENSTER:

In Unit 9, these guys have done a lot of group therapy by the time they come, and so they've done a lot of work on how to give feedback to each other, how to be responsive – we can also have guys from different gangs in the same group – they've done a lot of work, so it's very easy. It's not an issue.

PIP ADAM:

It is like coming into someone else's whare, eh, but it's minute by minute as well. Sometimes there'll be dynamics, and we'll look at each other and think, We're not workshopping today, or, This person's feeling vulnerable. It does feel like you're building it ten minutes at a time, like, For the next ten minutes we're going to do this, and I think, We can handle that, and after two minutes it might not work.

WILLIAM BRANDT:

It's predetermined, the culture or the atmosphere of the room is set for us, and we have to move into it and operate within it. We do have a couple of things that we always say, and the strongest one is that 'No one has to do anything.' No one has to read their work out loud, no one has to write. If they want to just sit in the room that's fine.

PIP ADAM:

They might want to draw, or read.

WILLIAM BRANDT:

So probably the only rule is that there are no rules.

PIP ADAM:

And the other one is that 'Nothing's wrong.' One of the things I love most about the work is that it never again seems normal to ask someone to read out their writing, you know what I mean? In a university-based workshop, you think, of course we read it out, and we're all fine with that – but going in there, every week reminds me that actually we pour ourselves onto the page and it's actually a huge thing to share this with other people.

WILLIAM BRANDT:

In DTU we thought, They're a bit more signed up to the programme because they're going through this intensive course, and so we tried to push a little bit harder with giving feedback. We got them into groups, tables of about four people, and said, 'Okay, so now read your work out and swap ideas.' And I was at one of these tables saying, 'How's it going?' and they were just like, 'Why would I want someone else to talk about my work to me? What the hell?' And I thought, That's a very good question!

PIP ADAM:

As a teacher, you're always going back to those core beliefs. Like, 'Oh. Because that's how we . . . Oh my god, why are we doing this?'!

GIGI FENSTER:

And this thing of 'Nothing's wrong': I've become nervous of giving too many instructions or making an exercise too specific because I see that they get anxious about getting it wrong, and so it's all quite general, things that you can't possibly 'get wrong'. On one occasion, I think flash fiction, we tried to give a whole lot of information about the form – you have the story before the story, for example – and it really put the guys off. It was too much instruction, too much to fulfil, too much possibility of going wrong.

PIP ADAM:

These often are people who have been told they're wrong all their lives. And, this looks like a classroom, no matter how freaky and hippie we think we are, it looks like a classroom

– we look like teachers – and god, for most of them, school wasn't great.

EMILY PERKINS:

What are the tools they're given for writing? Have they got pen and paper?

RAJORSHI CHAKRABORTI:

The couple of classes I attended in Arohata, they had to leave their notebooks at the end of class every week and they were put away in a cupboard in that classroom.[3] But in Rimutaka they were allowed to keep their notebooks with them. Everything has a different meaning in that prison context and one of the most moving things is how meaningful their notebooks – their simple notebooks – are to them. Like for those whose books were kept away in the cupboard, when they were handed back the students would reacquaint themselves with them, like this is what I put in it last week, and even when they're not participating directly, they're kind of sitting up actually decorating their notebooks, or making them theirs. Whereas a notebook is just something we take for granted. In the case of these notebooks, they were a space and a territory that was theirs, and they really expected that even if they weren't holding onto them, their privacy and sanctity would be respected.

EMILY PERKINS:

There are words that get used a lot in a creative writing room, like 'freedom' and 'constraints' and 'vulnerability' – there is a kind of agreed expectation of vulnerability – and those words must have a different weight inside the prison environment. Are you reaching for different metaphors for your teaching?

GIGI FENSTER:

So many of them write about themselves, they write about their own experience so much.

PIP ADAM:

It's simple things, like we had an exercise once that talked about a cellphone, and there were women in there who hadn't been outside in the time of cellphones. We had [an exercise with] a pet once, and this woman was like, 'I've been in here since I was eighteen, I've never had a pet, what would I know about pets?' So I guess, that's not what you're asking but – often the vulnerability they're demonstrating – it's understanding the different gauges of what that means in there.

WILLIAM BRANDT:

The vulnerability is really present, isn't it?

GIGI FENSTER:

It's so naked, it's . . .

WILLIAM BRANDT:

. . . If they write about pets, then . . .

PIP ADAM:

. . . there's tears . . .

WILLIAM BRANDT:

. . . every time. Because they write about pets that they haven't seen.

PIP ADAM:

And pets that they may not see again.

WILLIAM BRANDT:

And that time we said, 'Draw a picture of a face,' and one of them drew her baby, which she had given birth to and then not seen again, basically. And so she was falling to pieces, and – that's just there all the time. You never know when someone is going to break down because they've written something that, you know . . .

PIP ADAM:

That idea of 'freedom' is really interesting. When your whole life is . . . You know, even – not being able to be bare-footed when you want to be, just those simple little things . . . When you say to someone, 'You know you can do whatever you like in your writing'. . . I think it might be easier for a group of people living in this world [outside], to move with that idea of freedom –

GIGI FENSTER:

Ugh, that idea of, 'Prison's all in your mind.'

PIP ADAM:

Oh, god I hate it when people say, 'I've been to prison in my mind, I was a prisoner in my mind.'

GIGI FENSTER:

'Free your mind.' Well, actually . . .

PIP ADAM:

We've set an exercise where we'll expect someone to talk about a ravine or a wide open space, and they'll talk about their Converse shoes or they'll talk about, you know, the toast they ate for breakfast. And one time someone asked us, 'Is this prison near the sea?' because a lot of them arrive and don't know where they are, and we said, 'No it's miles from the sea,' and she said, 'I'm sure I can hear the sea at night.'

GIGI FENSTER:

In Unit 9 they do so much work on vulnerability that it's become a characteristic they speak freely about: 'I'm not like my dad, I'm really vulnerable now.' And when Norm Hewitt came he spoke a lot about that with the guys. So I've found them really open about writing with each other, and exposing themselves. Where I think it got tricky is when it went out to the world, and that was different.

EMILY PERKINS:

What do you mean?

GIGI FENSTER:

[A Wellington literary event where prisoners' work was presented to the public] was really a bad experience for one of the guys. What happened was that they all wanted their work to go. They agreed and consented, the therapist agreed, and one of the therapists got permission to video it, and show it to them, and the prisoner just hated it. He was so angry and upset about it. He said it sent him to his dark place. And I think that was a lot about the exposure, and seeing everybody listening to his deepest, darkest things while drinking beers and then clapping and going off to their homes.

WILLIAM BRANDT:

I reckon this comes back to the assumption we make, and that university students in a creative writing class all make, which is that you write to be read, and you want to be read, and you represent yourself. And that is just not necessarily part of the equation. For lots of the people in our [prison] classes, they're not interested in that, eh?

PIP ADAM:

A lot of it's for a very specific audience. Like, a woman will write a story for a daughter, or for a sister. That was what was so huge about that small publication that we did. I suddenly realised that's what *I'd* want. *I* write to be read, and all of a sudden it's like, 'Nah!' Like, why would you ask someone else for feedback on your work?! 'I like, it, it makes a good noise inside of me, why would I give it to anyone else?'

EMILY PERKINS:

The private, in-house presentation of readings is different though?

GIGI FENSTER:

That presentation at the end is really awesome. So they are publishing in a way; they're presenting to their cohort.

PIP ADAM:

And the control there is totally the writer's, because you can see who's in the room and make the decision to present your work, whereas once it's on paper it's a little bit different.

RAJORSHI CHAKRABORTI:

Another wonderful thing about that presentation, I came away with a new view of my inner hierarchy of 'what's literature'. It's like tennis, when you say, Singles is the greatest, then there's doubles, then maybe mixed doubles. Before, my hierarchy, unfortunately, would be individually created written work, then oral work, then group work. Because group work by definition involves some level of groupthink and dilution of complexity, was my traditional way of looking at it. Individually created written work, it was my assumption, is where the most reflection and complexity would have gone in. But actually that was challenged by these guys, in the 'Heart/Mind, Stone/River' exercise.[4] First of all they came up with many things, but then we wanted to introduce them to how much editing forms a poem. We asked them to cut up strips and then said, Let's look at all the different effects we can create just by different sequencing of these lines. So we created a collective poem. Then, at the presentation my respect was greatly enhanced for work that is meant to be read out – when they read out some of their very personal pieces, with this haunting, very biblical, powerful oratory, those traditions, like they really *read*, and also for work that is collectively created. We each contributed a little bit, but the final thing is only because we all came together with something that no individual could have created.

WILLIAM BRANDT:

You meet individuals in prison and you can imagine them as writers, but there are others who get plenty of value out of it, and whose work you find interesting, but they're not, in that sense, necessarily writers, although they can contact it. But I think that creative act of focusing on an activity and interrogating yourself and then seeing the result in front of you is – that's what I really love about those classes – is that's all it requires to be valid.

PIP ADAM:

It makes you feel kind of humble.

RAJORSHI CHAKRABORTI:

This experience has been creative teaching *learning*. We come in with an awareness of the stark disparities of our context. Our day is kind of unimaginable to them, to a large extent, and their day is unimaginable to us. And what keeps it more so are the limits of what we talk about. They only share their stories in glimpses. There are several elephants in the room. We don't ask, Hey man, how does it feel to wake up in your fifth year in prison on a given morning, which is something that's a burning question – how does it feel? Likewise, we don't share, 'A really funny thing happened with my kid this morning.' I could come into a classroom here [the IIML] and say that, because your students in a regular classroom become aware of roughly who's in your family and whatnot, but there all of these things are out of sight and off-limits. I find that a big constraint on just interacting with them as though we were human beings meeting in a room to discuss literature. It's not that.

EMILY PERKINS:

Do you approach what form you're teaching with the same sort of flexibility as the class structure?

GIGI FENSTER:

We had one guy who wrote a play. Other than that it's mainly poetry.

PIP ADAM:

We get some very strong prose stuff. With form, that's where reading *and* writing are so important. We bring in a different form, they decide whether they like it, it becomes a possibility for them. We often copy other people's work. There's often a surprise at plainspoken work – we give them a Patricia Grace story that's written in a very conversational tone, and for some people it's quite exciting to see that something can be written like that. Because – you know, fantasy's written in quite a high register. One woman came to me one day and she'd read the new Jack Reacher book and *Wuthering Heights* in the same week, you know, so there's this interesting idea of where the language sits. Form is a constraint that's helpful to order ideas, to say, 'We want this many syllables in each line,' or 'We only want a rhyme on every second one.' And musically, those rap rhythms – I sound like a white lady – but you know, a lot of that is really complex formally and lyrically and a lot of them can make that stuff happen almost automatically.

WILLIAM BRANDT:

Coming back to the structure of the course, we do that foundation in the first half of it and then we start talking about genre and form, and then we ask them to generate material as the basis of a draft, and to think about what form they'd like it to be, whether they'd like it to be a poem, or a piece of fiction or whatever.

PIP ADAM:

And we get creative non-fiction as well. Using your own memory can be good because imagination can be problematic sometimes. There's often these beautiful memory pieces. That amazing one by that guy . . .

GIGI FENSTER:

It was a piece about a really nice day and how he was with his kids and then he said, 'I have to leave you now to go to work.' And he said to me, 'In the original version I had to leave them to go to my pad. But I changed that for this audience.' So in his original version he was leaving his kids to go to his gang, but then he changed it, and that was interesting; there's a sort of correction in creativity, that's him thinking about what's appropriate for an audience and for his kids.

RAJORSHI CHAKRABORTI:

Very few of them use the class to write, say: 'a character unlike me doing something interesting that's worth shaping into a story'. It frequently for them goes into addressing and exploring the personal. So first person, where there isn't that much difference between the narrator and them, that's the form they take, they grab it and use it to write and achieve things. It's using storytelling to look at your own life, whether to marvel at it, feel bafflement, feel all of the things you feel – literature becomes the vessel to explore that. So we're trying to talk with detachment about writing that you can do very deep things with, but we try to talk about it as a set of abilities and a toolbox.

GIGI FENSTER:

This is really nice what you do, William and Pip – you generate a piece and then you say, 'What genre suits you best for this?' I like that.

PIP ADAM:

And sometimes people will write in more than one genre. I remember someone had one idea that they were trying to work out and they worked it out in poetry and then they worked it out in creative non-fiction and then they worked it out in fiction.

EMILY PERKINS:

How do you know if you've had a good connection with someone in terms of their writing?

RAJORSHI CHAKRABORTI:

Laughter is ever-present, in their banter and giving of feedback, and their private jokes. More emerges because of that laughter, so things are going well when people are comfortable laughing and talking, and for a while you can pretend to forget that at the end of this you will be prisoners, and I will go out. This is the mountain of things we don't talk about, you know. When I used to teach at university I cared about my students feeling comfortable, but alongside that there was another metric by which I measured a class's success, which is how idea-rich the conversation had been. How many thoughts, suggestions, possibilities, I had managed to plant in their heads and air in discussion, for them to go away with. In prison, that second criterion falls away. The priority is the sharing of each other's company. And in the course of that, what emerges. My metric at the end is kind of, learning happening by the by, because we've created a certain human atmosphere all together.

EMILY PERKINS:

Those human connections are unquantifiable, but I think often there's a long after-effect of those sorts of environments. I don't know if people imagine prison as a place of laughter –

PIP ADAM:

The person who runs all the programmes at Arohata says to us
that she can hear us laughing and she knows that the course
is going well, and it's not just in that class – often when you're
walking down the corridors you can hear people laughing. . .
Rachel O'Neill's idea is that humour has to operate in cultural
understanding, if you take humour outside of a culture or a
community, people don't get the humour, and I think part of
the community building that happens in there is that some
things are funny. One of the biggest jokes is when we do the
exercise Exquisite Corpse[5] – every time we do that. It's odd
because there's some kind of weird hive-mind that makes it
make sense, but someone will always like, repeat their line,
or play a trick – and people find that funny.

WILLIAM BRANDT:

They just love it.

PIP ADAM:

The work's often really clever, and funny as well. I think that
it is a community-building thing – and that's vulnerable, isn't
it – to laugh in a roomful of people and think, Oh, is everyone
else laughing, or to make a joke in a roomful of people is
quite a vulnerable thing. The laughter's a release. Often
we're doing silly – you know, William's grammar lesson 'Dog
bites man / Man bites dog' – often language is funny because
we're messing with it, and saying 'It's very important to have
your subject and object in the right place' and it's like 'Oh
grammar, hilarious.' [*laughter*] And they laugh at us a lot.

WILLIAM BRANDT:

The first DTU exercise we did, we did that sense one:
something you see, something you smell, something you
hear. And one of them wrote, 'I see a guy with a big beard.'
And everybody laughed at that. [William has a beard.] I
think they do find us quite entertaining.

PIP ADAM:

With creative writing you can allow a degree of lightness.

WILLIAM BRANDT:

Yeah, it's just walking into a room and . . .

PIP ADAM:

. . . Having a play.

EMILY PERKINS:

You've talked too about how some exercises can inadvertently trigger very personal feelings . . . what are some of the ways that you deal with that?

WILLIAM BRANDT:

I find that they sort it out, the class sorts it out. Sometimes there is a guard present, they might come and say, 'Would you like to take a break?' There are hugs.

PIP ADAM:

In prison there are such strong communities. And there's problematic stuff in those communities, just like there's problematic stuff in my communities. We would always mention to somebody that an upset had happened, so you know someone will keep an eye on them for the rest of the day. And in a therapeutic setting, like the DTU, sometimes that's seen as a breakthrough rather than a breakdown, which I feel a little bit uncomfortable about, but in DTU, there are five or six counsellors as well, and I remember someone saying, 'She wasn't able to get to that in therapy, and somehow she got to it in creative writing, and that was great, we were able to talk to her.' But if I know they haven't signed up for therapy, *they* then decide where they go. Some of them are very comfortable with going quite full on, but others are not.

That's what I think is so interesting about the shoe story. You know, a blue Converse shoe symbolises so much in that place, and stuff that most readers would not understand, but that was one of the most emotional pieces. Yet she was completely comfortable writing about that because primarily it was a close study of a quotidian object, not a head-on confrontation of the things that object stood for.

WILLIAM BRANDT:

What we typically do if someone cracks up is we just stop and we don't do anything. Because they're much more connected to each other than they are to us and it's not our place. I certainly feel bad because I feel like I unwittingly put this person in a situation they don't need to be in. You know the idea that you write to get in touch with your feelings, or that you *want* to go to those dark places, I don't feel like that's what it's about in there at all. It's just pointless, it's like hitting someone over the head.

PIP ADAM:

Although it's so often unwitting, like we did one on food once – 'Can you remember a meal that you enjoyed?' – and of course, what a fucking stupid idea, of course the meal was with *family* . . .

WILLIAM BRANDT:

In DTU someone has a 'breakthrough', and it can be useful, and the therapist will actually grab them and say, 'Let's go and talk about that,' and take them somewhere. But in Remand they can be emotionally in a difficult place but there are fewer opportunities for therapeutic intervention[6] so you do not want to just churn that stuff up for them. So ideally you have to set it up so they choose where to take it – but that's very difficult, because you don't know what's going to take them where.

EMILY PERKINS:

I'm struck by how much you are required to be totally in the moment and present, and also totally prepared.

GIGI FENSTER:

This is where two people teaching makes such a difference. I used to walk out of there shattered.

PIP ADAM:

And we've had it – at one point I triggered someone really badly, and someone was angry as fuck . . . I was able to step back and get out of the road, because I was not helping the situation at all, and William was there. And then sometimes I might get upset, or you [William] might get upset, and then it's so good having two people in the room.

EMILY PERKINS:

Are you talking about getting upset in the room, or after?

PIP ADAM:

Yeah, in the room. Every now and then the gravity just hits me and I'm like, 'This is a nineteen-year-old woman who's looking at being in here away from everything and everyone she loves for a long time.' Because, god, often you think, 'I'm teaching! Teaching teaching teaching,' and then it's like, 'Oh there's barbed wire out there, that's right.'

GIGI FENSTER:

When I was teaching on my own I'd always be in the car on the way home thinking 'Why did I do that?' and with two people you debrief all of that. You know, 'Why did I say that?' And they'll reassure me, 'It's okay that you said it, don't worry.'

EMILY PERKINS:

If you feel like 'I really wish I hadn't said that, done that,' is it ever hard to go back the next week?

GIGI FENSTER:

Yeah, when I was on my own. I did find it hard sometimes. But with two I don't.

WILLIAM BRANDT:

I had that run-in.

EMILY PERKINS:

You had a run-in?

PIP ADAM:

Yeah, because William, he's the most confrontational guy. You've gotta watch William.

GIGI FENSTER:

Actually you didn't have a run-in with him. He had a run-in with you.

WILLIAM BRANDT:

It's actually an interesting case study. This is something Michael Crowley talked about. Sometimes he gets people writing something that he feels is unhealthy. The example he gave was this young guy who was writing about a gun, and I think he was in jail for shooting someone, and he was writing about the gun in a kind of eroticised, cool-guy mode, you know: the gun was heavy in his hands, there were 'three men in the clip' was how it went. And Crowley said to him, Look, you're free to write that, but I don't want to be involved, I don't want anything to do with that. It comes back to that idea of a fantasy, there's something sort of destructive about it. He's not necessarily making a judgement about the person, but he doesn't want to be involved. And so doing this class there was a guy who wrote stuff that I felt was violent and unhealthy. I feel like a hypocrite, because we're always saying, You can write whatever you like, and we're trying to create this free space, but what he was putting in the poem was stuff I felt uncomfortable about, and . . . I said, Look, I'm sorry but I feel uncomfortable about this, and I think that the therapeutic community would feel uncomfortable, and I can't include this, I'm sorry.

GIGI FENSTER:

You weren't stopping him from writing what he wanted to, all you were saying was, This is not going to go into a group poem that is going to be presented. Which I think is something very different. Maybe it's not a distinction he would have made –

WILLIAM BRANDT:

He was *so* deeply hurt. And he was sitting there going, 'I'm good. You know, I – I'm a good writer.' And I was saying, 'Yeah, you *are* a good writer' – he *was* a good writer – and I just felt really terrible. I still feel really bad about it.

GIGI FENSTER:

I think it was his impulse control. And that's what the other guys said. And he came to the presentation and he presented work. And so I think it was all fine in the end.

WILLIAM BRANDT:

It was kind of a happy ending because when I came to the presentation there he was and he looked me in the eye and we shook hands and he got up and read his piece and that was all great, but . . . And this is a unit for guys with violence problems, and you can't expect not to have things go wrong. The other thing about that guy, I told the psychologist about it and she said, 'Was he violent or did he threaten you?' And I said, 'No,' and she looked very pleased.

EMILY PERKINS:

Like, it was a blow to him and his sense of self, and he didn't
. . .

WILLIAM BRANDT:

. . . Yeah, he managed it in a civilised manner.

EMILY PERKINS:

Tell me about censorship – what does that mean in this context?

PIP ADAM:

Again, this work takes it back to first principles, it's kind of like, Does writing have the power to incite? That's my understanding of the need for censorship, this idea that writing can incite you to take actions, and one thing is that there's a complete language going on in there which we're often not privy to. So often with some of the writing they're just cracking up because we're going, 'Oh, that's sweet,' and [*laughter*] it's about a dog – and you know, dogs have such different meanings in there . . . and every now and then someone will just let you know. Yeah, I think if I understood half the meaning of the words being used, I'd be shocked. [*laughter*]

GIGI FENSTER:

There was one guy who wrote a really sexy piece . . . and then before we presented he said, 'I want to do the sexy piece but will you check it's okay?' The therapist said, 'It's fine.' And before he read it he gave a little introduction and said to the guys, 'Please just listen maturely to this.' [*laughter*]

PIP ADAM:

It was an exercise in senses.

GIGI FENSTER:

It was nice! It wasn't sexy in a sort of ugly way.

PIP ADAM:

There was polite clapping, and it was mature. I was looking at my shoes.

GIGI FENSTER:

If there'd been violence, or . . . I think the men we work with are just self-censoring. Or I'm naïve and we're not seeing it.

PIP ADAM:

I think there is a lot of self-censorship. Because language is so powerful in there. You can say the wrong thing in the wrong place and you're either in trouble with Corrections or you're in trouble with the people around you.

EMILY PERKINS:

How about what language means to them through the process of doing the course?

PIP ADAM:

In there, the people who can read, read avidly, and they read *everything*. And there's a huge letter-writing culture. They are very *au fait* with feelings on paper, events on paper. And the power of language through lyrics . . . when I talk about hip-hop culture I mean it as a deep and profound culture. There are women who write in graffiti-type script – those pillars of hip hop, these ways of being in the world, the elements of rap and R&B, it's such an important thing. And then on top of that – because unfortunately there's such a large representation of tangata whenua – quite a few women we met last year, their first language was te reo. One woman writes in te reo and then translates into English. There's this huge oral culture – I know that sounds really 'the oral culture' but people really hold their whakapapa orally in there because

they haven't got photos or family or marae around them . . .
I'm impressed constantly. Especially that thing of not being
judgemental. I remember that woman saying to me, 'Oh, Jack
Reacher's a bit like Heathcliff,' and I thought, 'He is!'

RAJORSHI CHAKRABORTI:

We're among a minority of volunteers in that system who
come from an utterly secular orientation. They are quite
often exposed to a rather biblical, sermonising, pulpit way
of speaking, a morally charged way of using language, with
those rhythms that we all recognise when we hear them.
Imagine an intersection of hip-hop rhyming schemes and
biblical oration. So that comes through as well, really
powerfully and beautifully.

GIGI FENSTER:

Because we are coming from a secular orientation, we can
be nonjudgemental. And we are not coming in with moral
expectations of the writers. Rather, we can focus on craft and
literary tools. If, for example, someone talks about 'being
fried', we can discuss metaphors for drunkenness rather than
sermonising on the evils of alcohol.

PIP ADAM:

And everything we give them, they're up for. We'll give them
the most complex poem, the most contemporary kind of
short story – you give them Kafka and they love it. We gave
them *Hamlet* and they loved it; we gave them Rachel O'Neill's
really oblique square prose poetry and they engaged with it
in a way that I think if you gave it to similarly aged people
who were outside, possibly they might not be so open. And,
obviously, sometimes they don't like some of the work but
you often get further because on the whole they read more
agnostically, their minds are really open – I feel so passionate
about it. I just love it in there.

WILLIAM BRANDT:

Gotta get back in there.

PIP ADAM:

We're the only ones trying to get in.

RAJORSHI CHAKRABORTI:

I'd be happy to go there many, many more Mondays. We were there for eight weeks and between then and our next course, I was very aware that Mondays are coming, one after the other, and the lives of the few people we briefly met are carrying on, and that's what I mean about the tiny drops of time we see, and the enormity of everything we don't know.

1   'The attraction of art'. *Stuff.* 14 October 2007. Accessed 8 May 2017. Web.
2   William Brandt. 'The road to teaching creative writing in prisons.' Arts Access Aotearoa. 25 May 2016. Accessed 8 May 2017. Web.
3   For operational and privacy reasons notebooks were retained by the tutors until the next class.
4   Rachel Bush in *The Exercise Book*. (2011). Eds. Bill Manhire, Ken Duncum, Chris Price and Damien Wilkins. Wellington: Victoria University Press.
5   In this exercise, developed by the Surrealists, a line of a story or poem is written on a page which is then folded over before the next line is added by the next member of the group, and so on, until the page is complete. It is then unfolded and the story or poem is revealed.
6   Arohata has a range of programmes for women on remand including tikanga, obtaining a driver's licence, and creative writing. Art and craft programmes were added in February 2017.

Provocations

Victor Rodger

Ideas Are Easy

Heretic is a play by a white Australian. It's about a white American anthropologist and a white Australian anthropologist who clash over their respective research on Samoan people.

Heretic is the single most influential play I saw as a burgeoning writer. While I could certainly appreciate the intellectual argument going on in the foreground, my eye and my heart were drawn to the two or three Samoan characters running round in the b(l)ackground; the ones who weren't given anything approaching a character arc, let alone anything approaching three dimensions or a character. What was their story, I wondered?

It seems like I've been answering that question, metaphorically at least, for the last twenty years.

Writing for me is a political act. It's an act of representation. Initially it was an act of representing my very particular point of view: that of someone who was of mixed Samoan and palagi descent who didn't know their way around the Samoan world and learned the hard way. But it has developed into a broader desire to put Pasefika characters and actors front and centre, a desire to resist the dominant narrative.

The actual act of writing for me has been a mixed bag. Ideas: they're the easiest bit. I had one when I was recently by my sick aunt's bedside; I had another while I was writing these very words this morning in Honolulu, inspired by the names of my friend's diabetes medication: Victoza and Tresiba. Inspiration is literally everywhere. But taking those ideas from page one, scene one, all the way through to 'ua uma, the end – well, that's a different matter.

I wrote the core of *My Name Is Gary Cooper* in a week but when someone asked me what I was trying to say I got stumped for five years until I knew how to answer the question and then rattled off the rest of the play in another week; conversely I wrote *Club Paradiso* in two days.

As for my writing process? Gah, you tell me and we'll both know. Seriously, that's something I still don't understand. Case in point: in 2014 I listened to a read-through of my autobiographical first play, *Sons*, exactly twenty years after I wrote the very first draft. I won't lie, I was impressed: impressed that the play remained emotionally true after all these years; impressed that the dialogue didn't make me want to throw myself out of a window (as the very first read-through had in 1994); and especially impressed with the way that I captured my father's voice. At the same time as I was busy being impressed with myself, however, I kept thinking: *I literally have no idea how I wrote that.* Still don't.

One thing I do know for sure though is that, as the Public Image Ltd song goes, anger is energy, and it can be a great driver for any writer.

Ten years ago I spoke to a group of community college students in Queens about the spurs of my work. It wasn't until I prepared my talk that I realised most of my plays were born out of anger, even if they went on to become comedies; born out of a desire to express a specific point of view or explore a certain situation that hadn't been heard or represented in the theatrical canon.

Why theatre? I suspect it has something to do with theatre being the first form I engaged with. I tried to write *Sons* as a novel and got no further than two pages in; ditto when I tried it as a screenplay. But for some reason it came to life as a play. Theatre continues to be my first language when it comes to writing, and the one I am most comfortable with.

What follows are the eight seeds behind my eight plays.

Speak Your Truth (but Don't Be a Slave to It): *Sons* (1995; rewritten 1998)

They tell you to write what you know, because it increases your chances of being able to write characters and situations and time and place well. But they don't always tell you that sometimes you need to let go of the truth in order to follow the story – in other words, write what you *don't* know. I learned to do that when I wrote my first play, *Sons*: to absolutely speak my truth while at the same time not remaining a slave to the actual events the story was based on.

There's a long backstory to *Sons* but the direct catalyst for the play was an out-of-the-blue phone call in the late 80s from the one Samoan auntie I knew growing up. She was upset. Her accent made it difficult to understand everything she was saying, but I understood enough to realise that something had happened to my father. That he might, in fact, be dying.

At the time I didn't have a relationship with my father. I'd never lived with him. I spent a large chunk of my childhood hating on him; by the late 80s I considered myself ambivalent as far as he was concerned.

Only maybe I wasn't as ambivalent as I thought because after that phone call from my auntie I decided to go and see him. If he was dying, I reasoned, it seemed like the right thing to do. He was my father, after all . . .

That meeting threw me for a loop: the man I'd hated in my head was actually charming and charismatic. By the end of our afternoon together I wanted nothing more than for him to acknowledge me as his son to his other children who weren't aware of my existence, and to be welcomed into the family fold.

It didn't quite work out like that.

My decision to re-establish contact with my father (and more so my decision to get to know my half-siblings without revealing my identity) set off a chain of events that were dramatic, confusing and painful – not just for myself but for many others in both of our families.

The way events unfolded after that meeting took so many twists and turns I remember literally thinking to myself: This is more *The Young and the Restless* than *The Young and the Restless*.

And so I wrote *Sons* as a way to make sense of that very confusing time; to make sense of my father. Even to make sense of myself. (Watching a revived version of the play in 2014 was like watching an hour and a half of live therapy.)

But I also wrote it because at the time I was going through that difficult period, there wasn't a book or a play or a film that reflected my specific point of view, i.e. that of a mixed-race Samoan man who had been raised by his white mother who was trying – and often failing – to negotiate his Samoan father and, by extension, the Samoan culture itself.

And so, to paraphrase the late African American science fiction writer, Octavia E Butler, I wrote myself into existence.

Represent: *Cunning Stunts* (1997)

In my second year at Toi Whakaari: New Zealand Drama School I sat in the audience of a play about a highly respected white man of power in Africa who came unstuck because of his penchant for male company.

There was one actor of colour in the cast. He played several minor roles. I felt sorry for him because he didn't have much to *do*.

This was swirling around in my mind later that year when I wrote *Cunning Stunts*. At its core I simply wanted to create some mixed-race characters and bring them to the fore (an extension of *Sons*, in a way), presenting them as racially specific without making race their defining characteristic. But I also wanted them to in some ways echo where I sit on the spectrum of what it is to be Samoan, which is different from the majority of Samoans but still part of the whole.

And so three of the main characters were the very gay afakasi Samoan Remick, the very droll afakasi Tongan Fla and the very sexually fluid afakasi Māori Marti. The story I attached to them? A decidedly shallow little sex comedy about a woman who discovers her boyfriend has been unfaithful with her three best friends.

Cunning Stunts is a play I often omit from my CV, but the one thing I will say is that all the characters of colour all got to be front and centre, and unlike the poor actor in the play that inspired it, they certainly got to do something, even if it was just sleep with the same man.

'You Look Like a Savage': *Ranterstantrum* (2002)

So there I was at a Wellington dinner party, innocently eating the last of my lamb shank with my hands and really getting down to business, when a white Australian at the table said, 'I hope you don't mind me saying this but you look like a savage.'

When someone from a country that categorised Aborigines as flora and fauna until 1967 says to a Polynesian that he looks like a savage, you bet they'll mind. They might even be inspired to write a play.

That incident was one of the chief triggers for *Rantertstantrum*, my difficult third play (so difficult I didn't finish it until the Monday before it premiered). The other two triggers:

(1) arriving home one night to discover the glass front door shattered and what looked like blood splattered everywhere (only to discover it was red wine);

(2) working with a palagi woman who had reportedly been assaulted by Samoan assailants.

All three incidents combined in an attempt to describe what it can be like as the only person of colour at a dinner party or at a gallery opening (which often used to be the case, especially in the late 80s in my native Christchurch), where people would often expect you to be a spokesperson for an entire race.

In *Ranterstantrum* a Samoan man gets mistaken for a rapist at a dinner party. For me it's a (very) black comedy. Admittedly it doesn't make everyone chuckle. People kept asking me during the fraught rehearsal period, 'What are you saying?' I looked at them like a deer in the headlights. I wasn't exactly sure (and indeed that question has stumped me a few times). But the director Colin McColl calmly navigated the play towards opening night.

Ranterstantrum is probably the closest I've come to the dreaded D word – didactic – but I think it remains a provocative and timely exploration of the still thorny subject of race and race relations.

Stirring It Up in the White World: *My Name Is Gary Cooper* (2007)

I spent a large chunk of the 70s and 80s devouring movie magazines like Rona Barrett's *Gossip* and *Photoplay*, reading about stars like Raquel Welch and Erik Estrada. So it seemed somewhat inevitable that one day I would create a play that drew on my almost encyclopedic knowledge of Hollywood trivia. That play was *My Name Is Gary Cooper*.

If you say the name Gary Cooper to anyone under forty, these days you're likely to get a 'Gary who?' look. Back in the day Gary Cooper was a big star, arguably best known for his Oscar-winning turn as the beleaguered sheriff Will Kane in *High Noon*. But in Samoa people still know his name because he flew there in the early 50s to film the movie *Return to Paradise*. They have what is known as 'Return to Paradise beach' in Lefaga and the Gary Cooper suite at Aggie Grey's Hotel.

The seed for *My Name Is Gary Cooper* was planted at a barbecue in Auckland in the early 2000s when one of my mates said he'd seen a documentary about the making of *Return to Paradise* in 1952. Apparently the documentary featured several Samoan men, named for the star, saying in their thick Samoan accents: 'Hello, my name is Gary Cooper.' Shortly after that barbecue there happened to be a screening of *Return to Paradise* at the Hollywood Cinema in Avondale, the last of the old-school movie theatres left in Auckland.

Return to Paradise is similar to a lot of those old Hollywood movies from the 50s set in the South Pacific: a white protagonist enters the brown world and stirs things up. What if, I wondered after watching the film, a brown character entered the white world for a change and stirred things up? What would that look like? The answer was *My Name Is Gary Cooper*, which begins at that screening of *Return to Paradise* at the Hollywood Cinema, and then ping-pongs between 1973 Los Angeles and 1952 Samoa.

In many ways it's the flip side of *Sons*: in *Sons* the afakasi protagonist wants to become part of his father's family; in *Gary Cooper* the afakasi protagonist wants to destroy his father's family.

Finally I managed to marry all that movie star trivia I gleaned as a child with my desire to see Pacific characters at the heart of the action.

What if: *At the Wake* (2012)

Deadlines. Oh God, let's talk about deadlines.

Not so long ago I had a deadline for a script. It was 2am. Actors were arriving at 10 that morning to read the script in front of the producer. I was still in bed, stressed out of my mind because the script was far from finished. And yet *nothing could make me get out of bed, open my laptop and start typing*. I began to feel a sharp pain in the middle of my chest from the anxiety. Is this how I'm going to go out, I wondered, clutching my chest. A heart attack?

No, as it turned out. It was just the stress of procrastinating.

Eventually I forced myself out of bed, opened my laptop and did indeed make that 10am deadline – but it was stressful.

So to do away with all the stress I feel with commissions

and deadlines, I set out to write a play just for myself for a change, to see if I could still write without the stress of a looming deadline.

At the Wake is in many ways a spiritual sequel to *Sons*. It started life as an aborted short story about a white grandmother who rounds on her mixed race grandson for wanting to wear an 'ie faitaga (a formal lavalava) to his mother's funeral.

But the real provocation for the play came from me asking two of the most important words any writer can ask: *What if?* Specifically: What if I was in the same room as my Samoan father and my Scottish grandmother, since we never were in real life? What would that look like? I decided the only way this would have happened was if my very much still breathing mother had passed away and my father had come to pay his respects.

My actual grandmother would have been horrified by much of this play, especially by the grandmother character, Joan, a hard-drinking, foul-mouthed woman prone to recounting her past sexual exploits without the slightest provocation, who bears virtually no resemblance at all to my real, god-fearing grandmother. However the two of them do have one profound thing in common: a fierce love for their grandsons.

Spectrum: *Black Faggot* (2013)

Destiny Church's 'Enough is Enough' march against the Civil Union Bill in 2004 featured fathers marching with their sons. Watching the march I knew in my heart that at the very *least* one of those kids would be gay and most likely feeling wretched about his sexuality. So in 2006 I wrote what would become the five or six cornerstone monologues of *Black Faggot*, and then stalled. But in 2012, when there was a lot of negative chatter within the Pacific community about the impending Marriage Equality Bill, I was newly inspired to finally finish the play.

With *Black Faggot* I wanted to present a broad spectrum

of gay Samoan men, since they had often been presented as nothing more than objects of mirth within Samoan theatre. I went for it. Cum on the wallpaper. Pretending to know how to eat pussy. Graphic descriptions of sex with a Tongan stranger. I thought I'd pushed it. As it stands, *Black Faggot* is my most successful work to date and especially embraced by straight, white middle-class audiences around the world.

Go figure.

Bringing the Dead to Life: *Girl on a Corner* (2015)

Shalimar Seiuli was an American Samoan fa'afafine working as a prostitute in Los Angeles. Early one morning in 1997 she was discovered by a police officer in a car with the actor Eddie Murphy. Eddie claimed he was simply giving Shalimar a lift home out of the kindness of his own heart. Shalimar told the *National Enquirer* a very different story. Shalimar had her fifteen minutes of fame but the next year she was dead. She fell five storeys from the roof of her apartment. She was only twenty-one.

I remember being struck by the Eddie Murphy scandal in the 90s because of the Samoan connection through Shalimar. But it wasn't until 2014, when I happened across an in-depth article about the scandal, that I was inspired to write Shalimar's story from her point of view.

I was moved: moved that a young fa'afafine from American Samoa died so young and never got a chance to fulfil her dreams, whatever they may have been.

With Shalimar long dead, I had to make a lot of the play up, but the directors rightly billed it as a fairytale. In my version she gets her happily ever after, although not in the way she would have liked.

The Heart of Darkness: *Club Paradiso* (2015)

Robbie Magasiva is perhaps New Zealand's most successful Samoan actor. We've now worked on five plays together since playing brothers in my play *Sons* (1998). I've known Robbie so long I've forgotten that people who only know him from watching him in film or on TV or in a play still get starstruck when they meet him on the street. I'll watch him deal with fawning fans and be like, 'Oh my gosh, he's *just* an actor. He just says *my* words.' But the thing is, Robbie always does my words justice, which is why I've written four roles with him specifically in mind.

In 2015 I asked him what kind of role he would like to play that he hadn't yet. He thought about it and then said, 'I've never played evil.' From that provocation came *Club Paradiso*.

I wrote the play over two days in Los Angeles while I played *Who's Afraid of Virginia Woolf*, *Jesus Christ Superstar* and *Tommy* on loop in my office.

The play is pitch black.

It's the first time that I had to keep asking myself: can I actually bring myself to type out the thought I just had in my head? And I'm glad I did.

The play featured an all-Polynesian cast of seven. Not everybody liked it: some thought it was predictable. Others took issue with the way it portrayed brown bodies on stage.

Me? I think it's possibly the best thing I've ever written. It gave the entire cast a chance to really strut their stuff, to reach. In terms of the spectrum of what exists for Pacific casts, I stand behind it and am proud of it. And Robbie was outstanding. Almost twenty years ago, in 1998, he was one of those Samoans running round in the background of that influential production of *Heretic*.

Deepest Blue by Accident

Bill Manhire

Just Desserts

The accidents that wave most vigorously are the typos, often called literals in some quarters. My own best example comes in 'A Nice Garden', a short story that originally appeared in the *Listener*. A woman is having a nervous breakdown. She has a small, demanding baby, and a complacent, self-absorbed husband. Her days are an endless round of domestic chores. One day she collapses. She spends her afternoon more and more frenetically tearing out shrubs and plants from the hillside section behind her house. That evening, as her husband is falling asleep, she says – 'loudly and distinctly' – 'I made a dessert and I feel at peace.'

+

Strange Type

I wrote: in the dark cavern of our birth.
The printer had it tavern, which seems better:
But herein lies the subject of our mirth,
Since on the next page death appears as dearth.
So it may be that God's word was distraction,
Which to our strange type appears destruction,
Which is bitter.
—Malcolm Lowry

+

Responsibilities

Don't blame the *Listener* editor, or the printer. Years ago the publisher Methuen asked me to edit a couple of collections of short stories from the magazine. In the second volume I found myself choosing a 1968 story by Marie Bullock. She was best known to *Listener* readers as MB, a regular contributor of chirpy domestic tales from the point of view of a happily harassed housewife and mother. The story I settled on was (I thought) much more interesting: an early account of suburban neurosis and mental collapse. At the very end, the protagonist is tearing down the curtains inside her house. 'Her high happy laughter rang out above the cursings of her husband and the baby's screams.'

Marie Bullock had been anxious about her story, and I remember reading the proof very carefully. When it left my hands, 'A Nice Garden' was word perfect, letter perfect. Then the book was published. *Oops.* Not long after fielding a phone call from the furious author, I learned that it had been an in-house copyeditor at Methuen, idly glancing over the page proofs a few hours before they were to be sent back to the printer, who spotted a woman chatting to her husband, mentioning a desert she had made, and thought, 'That can't be right' – and helpfully inserted the extra 's'.

+

Two Literals

There's a poem by Louis Simpson
where he mentions a Soviet dictator.
But – one of those infuriating things – there's a misprint.
A letter has fallen out.

Thus Josef Stain makes his way into history,
accurately enough.

The novelist Jim Crace also tells a story

about a young compositor. Somewhere in London,
labouring over a poem called *Paradise Lost*,
he grows more and more puzzled
by the name of a character he's not otherwise seen.

Presumably a man with absolutely no Christian
  background.
An apprentice; maybe a migrant.
Anyway, he makes a small adjustment . . .

Thus, high on a throne of royal state, *etc*
Stan exalted sits.

I don't believe this, but I like it.

Stan and Stain. Terrifying.

+

My favourite literal belongs to W H Auden, who once penned
the line, 'And the poets have names for the sea'. The proof
came back from the printer as 'And the ports have names for
the sea'. Auden kept the error. As he wrote to a friend, 'The
mistake seems better than the original idea.'

+

Auden also co-translated Old Norse poetry, and his versions
first appeared a few years before his death in 1973. It's hard
to imagine him being happy about the printer's error in a
posthumous publication of his rendering of *Völuspá* ('The
Sybil's Prophecy') which offers the closing image of a flying
monster: 'The dark dragon from Darkfell / Bears on his
opinions the bodies of men.' Auden's original version had
'pinions', and if he had lived he would surely have reinstated
them.

But what a wonderful mistake!

+

You could probably make a small anthology of poems that play with the idea of printing errors. Google tells me in a matter of seconds that Paul Muldoon and Charles Simic have both published poems called 'Errata'.

> For 'Antrim' read 'Armagh'.
> For 'mother' read 'other'.
> For 'harm' read 'farm'.
> For 'feather' read 'father' . . .
> —Paul Muldoon

> Where it says snow
> read teeth-marks of a virgin
> Where it says knife read
> you passed through my bones
> like a police-whistle . . .
> —Charles Simic

+

Then there is John Dennison's reworking of an Eileen Duggan errata slip, which appears in his 2015 collection *Otherwise*.

Errata

after Eileen Duggan, New Zealand Poems, 1st edn, 1940

For their death *read* your death;
for I had always *read* I always;
for nothing that *read* nothing can;
for moon *read* mourn;
for limb *read* lamb;
for cuckoo *read* cockerel;
for thundered *read* thundering;
for quiet *read* quake;
for the hills' river *read* the hill's riven;
for Oh *read* Or;
for and if atonement *read* and is atonement;
for there *read* here;
for as *read* so;

for no *read* yes.
These, and other errors, are due to war conditions.

+

In fact, John Dennison's poem, as he acknowledges, is partly a found poem. Several of his errata are among those cited in the original Eileen Duggan note.

·ERRATA

Page 12 line 10 *for* your death *read* their death.

" 19 " 15 *for* weevile *read* weevils.

" 19 " 24 *for* axel *read* axle.

" 20 " 6 *for* precepts *read* percepts.

" 30 " 8 *for* On *read* Oh.

" 32 " 11 *for* moon *read* morn.

" 34 " 2 *for* as *read* so.

" 36 " 9 *for* lamps *read* lambs.

" 37 " 6 *for* I have always *read* I always.

" 38 " 12 *for* on *read* upon.

" 46 " 9 *for* Baukawa *read* Raukawa.

" 46 " 11 *for* Oh for *read* On far.

" 50 " 1 *for* cockoo *read* cuckoo.

" 51 " 7 *for* hills' great river *read* the hills' great riven.

" 51 " 24 *for* thundered *read* thundering.

" 53 " 15 *for* nothing that you *read* nothing you.

" 54 " 15 *for* and atonement *read* and of atonement.

" 58 " 7 *for* there *read* here.

These, and other errors in typography and punctuation, are due to war conditions.

+

I suppose found poems are mistakes.
I suppose puns are mistakes.
The best metaphors are definitely mistakes.

+

Hello Douglas, My Old Friend

Wikipedia tells us that the American writer Sylvia Wright first coined the useful term *mondegreen* in 1954, after mishearing the Scottish ballad 'The Bonnie Earl o' Moray'.

The poem opens:

Ye Highlands and ye Lowlands,
Oh, where hae ye been?
They hae slain the Earl o' Moray,
And laid him on the green.

Sylvia Wright heard:

Ye Highlands and ye Lowlands,
Oh, where hae ye been?
They hae slain the Earl o' Moray,
And Lady Mondegreen.

+

In naming this project after a mistake, we don't mean to say that we want your error-riddled, hastily shot-off drivel, but we do want the work that isn't afraid of being wrong. We want something that we can't quite recognize, but which feels uncannily familiar. We want to get spooked by it or laugh or maybe both. All of that.
—http://themondegreen.org

+

Visual Mondegreens

There used to be a café in Willis Street called Fat Albert's. It put its shingle out on the footpath every day – just the name in a semi-circle of evenly spaced uppercase letters:

FATALBERTS

I always walked on by. The thought of meeting Fatal Bert was just too troubling.

And once, driving on the island of Islay, I glimpsed a loosely spaced sign that seemed to say WHITEST ONE. In fact, it must have said WHITE STONE. It was probably the name of a distillery.

I made a small poem out of that mistake – as a present for the person I was travelling with:

A Gift

I will place this paper in your hand
against the times you are alone:
my white one – my whitest one –
my pale, white stone.

+

Stumbling

You never set out to discover something new. You stumble upon it and you have the luck to recognise that what you've found is something very interesting.

Duncan Haldane, co-winner of the 2016 Nobel Prize for Physics

+

The most exciting phrase to hear in science, the one that heralds new discoveries, is not 'Eureka!' but 'That's funny.'
—Isaac Asimov

+

- Penicillin
- Background radiation
- Viagra

+

Unpredictable Turns

The excitement of writing a poem is not the following of a plan but the discovery of a subject. And I like to think of those discoveries as inspiration, an inspiration that doesn't precede the making of the poem, but is summoned into being by the poet's engagement with language – fooling around, and then being critical, and then fooling around again. Beginning poets need to learn how to be stupid. That is, they must find a way to embrace a kind of vacancy – we might call it day-dreaming – that results in the acceptance of interesting language no matter where it might lead.
—Lawrence Raab, 'Poetry and Stupidity', *Plume* 69, 2016

So poetry requires patience, some kind of obsessive quality or a willingness to submit to unpredictable turns. A poem that you thought was going to be about your grandfather in particular circumstances, maybe sitting on the porch with a dog, in the process of tinkering with the poem, all sorts of things come out. Once you have words on the page, they make love to one another. They pair. They do strange things. Then, to your great surprise, through the various drafts of the poem you realize that the only way to make this poem work is to get rid of your grandfather. Sorry, grandpa.
—Charles Simic, *Boston Globe*, February 2015

+

The Imp of Storytelling

Poets mostly open their arms to the unpredictable turn. Novelists can be less certain. Nabokov asserted that his characters are galley slaves. Yet we have all heard novelists describing how characters can develop a life of their own.

Jim Crace, talking to the *Guardian* about his novel *Quarantine*:

> But books – if they are going well – have the habit of
> . . . insisting on unforeseen agendas of their own. I can
> remember very well the afternoon that *Quarantine*
> abandoned me and my intended satire of Thatcherism
> and went off on a tangent. It was the passage when
> Jesus was meant to make a brief guest appearance.
> He'd be allowed half a sentence at the most, and only
> to give my chosen setting its historical provenance.
> I wrote, 'He was a traveller called Jesus, from the
> cooler farming valleys in the north . . .' But that half-
> line expanded into a paragraph, and that paragraph
> bloated into a chapter, and that chapter offered up
> a host of possibilities. By tea-time, the traveller had
> seemed to cure – with a miracle? – a satanic man
> called Musa. Jesus was unignorable now. He would
> become a major character.
>
> 'Ah, that's because the Holy Ghost was standing
> at your shoulder while you wrote,' I was subsequently
> assured by a fellow guest (a priest) on a radio show.
>
> No, not the Holy Ghost, I said, but the Imp of
> Storytelling, celebrated for its mischievousness,
> its cunning, and its generosity. It had caused me,
> an atheist, intent on writing a novel broadly about
> contemporary earthly matters, to produce a book of
> strangely scriptural intensity, a novel which (mostly)
> underscored people's faith in gods rather than
> undermined it.

+

Fiction in the Fowler Centre

Four visiting fiction writers touched briefly on the respective virtues of control and accident during a panel at Wellington's Writers and Readers Week in 1996. Carol Shields, Kate

Grenville, E Annie Proulx and Keri Hulme were gathered in front of a huge crowd to discuss, among other things, characters and characterisation. Keri Hulme was talking about her second novel, *Bait*, which remains unpublished. It had kept growing, she said, had in fact turned into two novels. She carried the manuscript around in her backpack. But one thing that was holding up completion was the fact that two characters needed to die. She kept on trying, but they kept on finding ways to resist their fate. What could she do?

E Annie Proulx, in a loud stage whisper: 'Give them to me for the weekend.'

+

The Forest Primeval

In her autobiography Janet Frame describes how, living at Frank Sargeson's and 'anxious to appear working', she would spend some mornings simply typing familiar phrases – '"The quick brown fox jumps over the lazy dog" . . . and my old favourite for unproductive moments, "This is the forest primeval, the murmuring pines and the hemlock speak and in accents disconsolate answer the wail of the forest"'.

Those words are from the opening lines of *Evangeline* by Henry Wadsworth Longfellow (1807–82), a poet whose work she had once chosen for a fifth-form class prize. There is a poem that starts this way in *The Pocket Mirror*, and among Frame's papers versions of the phrase appear a number of times – working to make those unproductive moments come alive. At such moments she was clearly typing as fast as she could: punctuation and keyboard accuracy were not important considerations, and the lines speed by. On one sheet the forest primeval quickly gives way to a memory of her father's love of 'Just a Song at Twilight', then to her sense of 'a

combination of delights'; then there is a memory of
Stratford . . . followed by thoughts about walking
'into the hinterland' – 'the palisade or the stars/or the
mountains or the self', 'the great beyond/the back of
beyond'.

And then, after some longer lines that seem to
contain the first stirrings of 'The Recent Dead', she
types out these words:

This is a poem for autumn.
And for the hinterland.
For inklings, and the gravity star.
How many lines to the row
surrounded by wooden furniture
I sit
with music
and tears
perhaps I will set down
poem after poem
to celebrate the movement of air
in light
into bodies
out of bodies
within lives, nothing but the movement of air, the
   great exchange.

There is still some improvisation here – 'How many
lines to the row' – but suddenly the words are shaping
themselves into a poem.

Language is always as much subject as medium
in Frame's work. And it is clear that the energies of
words can lead to the surprise of meaning – 'enemy,
any moan, anemone' ('The Anemone') – and to
travels in unexplored territory. 'In writing,' she
once told Elizabeth Alley, 'the hope is always that
the imagination will come to rest in invisible places.'
Maybe free association was one of the ways in which

the imagination began its journey to such places. It is
noticeable how many of these poems take the shape
of a walk – sometimes a real walk in a real place,
sometimes a walk through a subject. The impulse is
always to ramble, alertly, rather than to march in step.
—from Bill Manhire, Introduction to Janet Frame
   (2006), *The Goose Bath*, Auckland: Random House
   New Zealand.

+

The First Rule for a Poet

Charles Simic tells a story about the Mexican poet Octavio
Paz going to visit the French surrealist poet André Breton in
Paris soon after World War II:

> He was admitted and told to wait because the poet
> was engaged. Indeed, from the living room where he
> was seated, he could see Breton writing furiously in
> his study. After a while he came out, and they greeted
> each other and set out to have lunch in a nearby
> restaurant.
>
> 'What were you working on, maître?' Paz inquired
> as they were strolling to their destination.
>
> 'I was doing some automatic writing,' Breton
> replied.
>
> 'But,' Paz exclaimed in astonishment, 'I saw you
> erase repeatedly!'
>
> [Ah, said Breton] – 'It wasn't automatic enough.'
> —'The Little Venus of the Eskimos', 1993

Even the surrealists cheated! As Simic goes on to say,
you need to open yourself to chance in order to admit the
unknown. But you have to be prepared to fiddle the books
a little, so that the unknown will at least be interesting. The
conscious mind eventually has to do its work of selection and
arrangement – and this process, which can sound mundane,
is also a significant imaginative act.

+

In the field of observation, chance favours only the
prepared mind.
—Louis Pasteur

+

I have quite a boring and technical writing process,
which is probably not of interest to anyone else in
the world, but it's hard not to talk about this without
mentioning my best friend, Gregory Kan, who also
put out a book this year called *This Paper Boat*. I
met him when I was in a writing course and we did
the Iowa Writing Course together, which is one at the
IIML; we became really close friends after that.

In that course he kind of introduced me to text
randomisation and cut-up techniques. To get a lot of
the images in the book, a lot of them started off from
generative exercise-y things, like, Greg built a really
amazing text randomiser that will garble sentences
and things like that. I don't want to say I just put it
into a machine and it came out that way, I have done a
lot of work around it to pick the good things out.

There is a lot of sifting that goes into it . . .
—Hera Lindsay Bird, *The Wireless*, 2016

+

The more constraints one imposes, the more one frees
one's self.
—Igor Stravinsky

Art lives from constraints and dies from freedom.
—Leonardo da Vinci

The greatest enemy of art is the absence of limitation.
—Orson Welles

+

http://glassleaves.herokuapp.com

+

Rhyme can be an aid to invention rather than a bar to
it. It is an aid because it forces us into corners where
we have to act and take the best available course
out. In the process of seeking it, we bump up against
possibilities we would not have chosen were we in
control of the process.
—George Szirtes, 'Formal Wear: Notes on Rhyme,
Meter, Stanza & Pattern', *Poetry*, February 2006

+

Bernadette Mayer's Writing Experiments:
http://www.writing.upenn.edu/library/Mayer-Bernadette_
Experiments.html

+

• Surface translation
• Google Translate
• Writing between the lines

+

Someone once asked the poet John Ashbery why he went
through a phase of writing sestinas. Well, he said, you
know how exhilarating it is, when you're riding a bicycle
downhill, and you get to the stage where you don't know
whether it's your feet pushing the pedals or the pedals
pushing your feet . . .

+

I used to make creative writing students write haiku with a
single added requirement: that they use only words from the
racing page of the newspaper. All the best words are on the
racing page.

+

Paul Griffiths on *let me tell you* – a novel he wrote using only the 483 words spoken by Ophelia in *Hamlet*:

> I began with the idea of taking all the words spoken in *Hamlet* and rearranging them into a new text. However, it didn't take me very long to realize that while initially I could say almost anything with this stock of words, unless I took huge care in monitoring what I was using, I could easily end up with a highly resistant residue of archaisms and prepositions.
>
> I therefore decided to use not all the words in the play, once each, but all the words spoken by one character, with no restriction as to number of uses. Now if you choose Hamlet as your character, his vocabulary is so vast there's virtually no constraint – and I needed an active constraint to make the book work. If you choose Francisco, there's the opposite problem, of being able to say only a very little. Ophelia has enough words to express herself on all sorts of matters, but also few enough that she is constantly bumping up against the unsayable.
>
> The constraint also allowed her to give readers the experience of reading words they have read before but are reading now in a new context. Because her mad scenes introduce a language that is unusual and therefore memorable, the reader easily recognizes, for example, where 'rosemary' comes from.
>
> At the same time, I wanted the book to do what novels generally do: tell a story. Ophelia has one of the play's most powerful lines: 'Lord, we know what we are, but know not what we may be.' My attempt was to give her something of what she may be.
>
> Also, and again quite aside from the constraint, here was a character who invites questions, a character who has very little opportunity to speak for herself in the play, and may now do so . . .

—*Music & Literature* No. 7, 2016

+

Understanding the Vocative

Some years ago the poet and classical scholar Alex Scobie signed up for the creative writing workshop at Victoria University. He had had to take early retirement from his academic position because of a degenerative eye disease. But it was 1993, technology was on the move, and Alex had got hold of a very early version of a scanning machine. As I recall, it was like a photocopier: you put a page of text face down, and a machine-voice spoke the words aloud. Alex had started working his way through nineteenth-century English poetry . . .

Does the machine make mistakes? I ask him. Maybe there'll be slips of the tongue, misreadings, bits of Wordsworth or Keats gone wrong, that might be interesting to work with in your own poems?

'Well,' says Alex in a rather disapproving voice, 'you can choose between six rather disappointing American accents.'

He pauses for effect.

'And it does not understand the vocative.'

How do you mean, does not understand the vocative?

'Ah,' says Alex, 'let me explain. If a line of poetry says

O moon, O stars, O mystery of life

the machine will always say . . .'

– he pauses again –

'zero moon, zero stars, zero mystery of life.'

+

Happy Accidents

Red Horse

The red crayon makes us
happiest, selected out with care
and making the outline of a horse
when once it's there complete

a rare delightful business;
then colouring the horse in
red as well, occasionally
going over the edge
but mostly filling up the space
without dismay or panic
and reaching in the box
eyes closed for something more or less
surprising for the sky and finding
deepest blue by accident.

I Go to My Sister-Artists and Talk

Tusiata Avia

This piece was originally presented as one of the seven talks that made up Conchus Conversations: Pacific Women's Theatre Summit at Circa Theatre, Wellington, on 26 February 2017, an initiative of The Conch. The summit was a powerful, moving gathering of senior to emerging Pacific women theatre practitioners and creatives. The women who took part in this spoke their truth, pain, triumph and brilliance to an audience who laughed and wept and left feeling profoundly shifted.

This is dedicated to the extraordinary creative Pacific trailblazer, Dr Teresia Teaiwa (1968–2017).

+

I would like to share with you my experience as a creative practitioner and as a Pacific woman, and talk about how these two things are inextricably linked; how they are woven as closely together as Siamese twins joined at the heart. And how I believe this is true for all of us.

I feel as if I occupy an odd space in theatre; I am a fringe-dweller. Mostly, I'm a writer. I'm a poet and a performer – a performer mostly of my own stuff. For a period of my life I found myself on the stage performing my one-woman show *Wild Dogs Under My Skirt*. Mostly, I felt as if I didn't really know what I was doing. I had no training, and very little experience.

In 2001 I arrived back in New Zealand after a decade overseas. I was in my thirties and had never been involved in the arts. If I knew then just how much I didn't know, I probably would not have embarked on writing and performing a one-woman show, which, incidentally, I ended up doing – on and off – from 2002 to 2008.

Like many people who seem to know what they're doing, I often feel like I don't – or at least I feel as if I'm on the very edge of what I know, which is not always a comfortable place to be. And like lots of people who seem to be in the thick of things, I often feel on the fringes.

For a large part of my life the fringes felt like a curse to me; it was a curse to be so far from what looked like the centre, the normal, the mainstream.

I came into the world this way, far away from the mainstream. I came into the world afakasi: mixed race, split focus, fruit salad, culture clash. I remember at my parents' custody hearing – when their marriage finally broke down – the magistrate announced the failure of this marriage was due to a 'culture clash'.

And like every afakasi whose Pacific language was not spoken at home, I had that experience of feeling too brown to be white, and too white to be brown. In Christchurch, where grew up, I was that 'big Māori girl'. In Samoa with my father's family, I was that 'too big palagi'.

From a young age I became an expert at trying to fit in. Imagine me as one of those full-figured Victorian ladies trying to stuff herself into a whale-bone corset. I spent a good deal of my life lacing myself into impossible shapes, pulling myself in so tight that my eyes nearly popped out of my head, so tight I could only take the shallowest of breaths.

I became an expert at trying to fit but it wasn't until my mid-thirties, when I entered a life in the arts, that I discovered what a gift my life had given me. Many gifts in life start off as painful ones. Not fitting in was great training. Not fitting in was a gift. It was a spiritual gift, it allowed me to walk between worlds, to become a boundary walker, a shapeshifter, it enabled me to inhabit a number of different worlds and write from inside those worlds in a voice that rang true.

I've always imagined writing is a bit like channelling. Mostly it's work and, like any other work, you've got to turn up, sit down and do it, whether you feel inspired or not. But sometimes – every now and then – it's like channelling, like receiving something from somewhere mysterious, somewhere unknown.

In those moments all I need to do is pick up the pen and let it come. And then, I sit back and read this *thing* that has appeared.

Sometimes a little bell chimes, alerting me that I am in the presence of this mystery – this *thing* I don't know, yet know that I know. I have to write it out for it to appear. I have to write it out to teach myself what it is.

It is the experience that I imagine a sculptor might have when faced with a block of marble, or wood or pounamu; she chips away until the thing of beauty inside the block reveals itself. I don't know what that thing of beauty might be until it is released from the block. Then I can stand back and take it in, then I can marvel: who knew there was a goddess in the stone?

What I have to say from here applies to everyone in their own context, but in particular I am speaking to Pacific women creatives.

Whether we are fully conscious of it or not, whether we create in response to where we have come from, or whether we create in reaction to it, or whether we are trying to ignore it altogether, we are always creating as Pacific women. How can we not?

Whether you were brought up in the village, learning songs and stories at your grandmother's knee, or whether you grew in the most colonised of English rose gardens, or in the most culturally sandblasted hood. Even if you never heard a single syllable of your Pacific languages – let alone the stories – you are still a Pacific woman.

There is something deep inside you – you can call it spirit or DNA – that *knows*. There are all kinds of things you can do to nurture this knowing, to keep this knowing in good company, to grow this knowing. You can also ignore this knowing (at a significant cost to your self), but there is nothing you can do to tear it up by the roots and destroy it. Nothing. You cannot un-be what you are. You can not un-know what you know. Even if you don't know it, yet.

This knowing. This creative and spiritual DNA is my creative source. Again and again it is my source. When I'm not looking for it, it is my source. When I'm telling myself that I need to write for a more 'mainstream' audience, it is my source. When I'm feeling beleaguered by those sly voices that tell me again – for the ten thousandth time – *again*, that my work is too brown, too niche, that again, I probably won't be programmed in the 'mainstream' event, it is *still* my wellspring.

When I write about the legends of Nafanua, the Samoan goddess of war – or of Taema and Tilafaiga, the Samoan conjoined twins – I have to spend hours combing through dusty books written by nineteenth-century male German anthropologists because I was brought up in Christchurch. I didn't learn these stories at my grandmother's knee, in my father's village, in Samoa. I may not know the plot-lines, but there is something inside me that *knows*, that recognises the spirit in these stories. There is something in these stories that matches the spirit in me.

Years ago, when I was writing my second book, *Bloodclot*, I received a friendly warning from a mentor to be careful when writing about Nafanua, the Samoan goddess of war, to be aware She has a gafa or whakapapa; that She has living descendants. This warning froze me for a while. I thought, Who am I to be writing about Nafanua? I looked at my piles of research and promptly stopped writing. But after a while, the answer to my question came: I am a Samoan woman and I can't claim physical whakapapa to Nafanua, but, as a Samoan woman, if I can't connect to this mighty goddess, this potent source of inspiration and guidance, if She can't be a guiding force for me – then who can? I don't claim physical whakapapa to Her, but I do claim spiritual and creative whakapapa. The goddess – and we all have our Pacific (and other) goddesses: Hina, Pele, Lilavatu, Hinenuitepō – belongs to us all. As Pacific women, we belong to Her.

This is the knowing. The thing we do not yet know that we know. The thing embedded within us that we are chipping away at to more fully reveal.

All artists have this. In fact, I believe all humans have this, but I'm here now, speaking to all creatives and in particular to my sister practitioners, to exhort you to trust what you know. And to trust what you do not yet know that you know.

It is the beautiful thing within you. Maybe it's looking like a block of wood right now, but the goddess waits to be freed. And only you can chip away until She is revealed.

Sometimes you'll need to do this chipping alone, but much of the time you will need the support of others. We need each other. In this current paradigm of competition, of contestable this and contestable that, it is easy to believe there is not enough to go around. It is easy to believe that we are not sisters and allies and midwives to each other's beautiful things, but that we are fighting each other tooth and nail to survive, that the failure of your beautiful thing's funding or award or good review means the greater possibility that my beautiful thing might have a chance at life.

This is a lie. Again: this is a lie.

There is a reason the Samoan deities Taema and Tilafaiga are conjoined twins. There is a very good reason that we come from eons of honouring the Va: the relational space between us. There is an excellent reason for the Samoan phrase Teu le Va – decorate the sacred space between us, beautify the sacred space we share. As Pacific women we are already good at doing this. Most of us are intuitively aware of the Va, whether we know it termed this way or not.

We mustn't be lured into seeing each other as competitors fighting for air and food and water. There is enough to go around! I'm not completely away with the Samoan fairies; I know there is only so much funding in the Creative New Zealand pot. But there is enough in the Va of our communities; there is enough in you, and in me, to nuture the beautiful thing, and to midwife for each other.

We have all given birth to someone or something. This is our nature. It is also our nature to help midwife for each other. It is only fear that stops us.

This is what fear sounds like. When I started to write this I became aware of you. I didn't know who you were at that point, so I made you up in my head. Soon you became a scary audience, an audience who would sit in judgement of me and just know, somehow, about my deficits.

Who was I to be telling *you*, scary, judgemental audience-in-my-head, about theatre? Surely you know more than I do? Surely you have been to drama school? Surely you have an arsenal of techniques, knowledge and secrets that I'm not privy to? And surely you will find me out? Find out I'm a fraud, an odd misfit who fell into theatre almost by accident, who occupies a fringe-dweller position and doesn't have the authority to speak to a scary audience about theatre!

Welcome to the voices in my head, the monstrous, fear-driven voices in my head. These voices have dogged me all my creative life, reminding me that I am not enough: not experienced enough, qualified enough, old enough, young enough, white enough, brown enough, thin enough, academic enough, street enough, theatre enough, literary enough, disciplined enough, relaxed enough, prolific enough, enough enough.

The voices have never gone away, but I have learned over the years how not to let them take me over completely. How do I do this? I go to my sister-artists and we talk. Honestly. I out myself and this usually gives others permission to out themselves too. It is a huge relief. We confess to each other and realise how much the same we are. We ignite courage in each other. We act as mother-confessors and absolve each other.

A host of high-level women creatives are tortured at every stage of their projects by their own monstrous, fear-driven voices: the international multiple award-winner who fears she is a has-been, the professor who fears she's not qualified, the celebrated writer who lies face down in the grass in despair, the senior practitioner who is busy in her own head writing bad reviews of her latest work before the reviewers beat her to it.

If you have never suffered these voices – you are extremely lucky and extremely rare. If you have, welcome! You and your voices are welcome here.

I share this with you to keep your monstrous, fear-driven voices company, to let you know we are teeming with them, struggling with them too. But I also point you back to the Samoan conjoined twins. We need each other. We need our sisters to help point us back to the knowing that lives inside our bodies. We need to honour the Va, to decorate it with our beautiful things, to beautify it with our sacred creations. We need to help midwife for each other. We need to speak our fears and struggles – to help soothe the fears and struggles of our sisters and inspire the great courage that also resides within them. And we need to make room for the goddess: the mighty Nafanua, Pele, Hinenuitepō.

+

When I presented this as a talk at the Conchus Summit, I was swamped by Pacific women creatives, young and old, whose experience I was articulating. As Pacific women creatives, we do not become overrun by these voices from out of the void. We are colonised from the moment we utter our first word.

Early on we learn our place in the hierarchy of Western society and then – whenever we enter it – our place in the creative industry. We will come up against racism (fancy and plain-packaged), we will be othered and underestimated, we will be relegated to the brown box or the diversity box and expected to stay there, we will be interpreted and misinterpreted by the mainstream. We spend our creative careers decolonising ourselves and our audiences.

I've experienced the goddess in many guises. The six Pacific women who now perform the new ensemble version of *Wild Dogs Under My Skirt* embody the goddess. The women who midwifed the show since its conception in 2002 – Mishelle Muagututia, Tanea Heke, Fiona Collins, Rachel House and, most recently, Anapela Polataivao – they are the goddess in action. I have to add here an honorary goddess, in the shape of Victor Rodger, producer of the new version of *Wild Dogs Under My Skirt* – we all know the goddess is a shapeshifter too!

As Pacific women practitioners, we continue the work of the women who have gone before us and who walk alongside us. For me, there are many who have inspired me, who have been the goddess for me: Sima Urale, Sia Figiel, Selina Tusitala Marsh, Nina Nawalowalo, Rachel House, Diana Fuemana, Fiona Collins, Lisa Taouma, Makerita Urale, Anapela Polataivao, Goretti Chadwick, Tanya Muagututia, Lindah Lepou, Rosanna Raymond, Patricia Grace, Teresia Teaiwa.

And we will be the goddess upon whose shoulders the women who come after us can stand.

Patricia Grace

An Interview with Briar Grace-Smith

PIP ADAM:

Patricia Grace is an Arts Foundation Icon who has won many national and international awards for her fiction, including the Neustadt International Prize for Literature, widely considered the most prestigious literary award after the Nobel.

Grace is of Ngāti Toa, Ngāti Raukawa and Te Āti Awa descent, and is affiliated with Ngāti Porou by marriage. Her recent novel, *Chappy*, was a finalist in the Ockham New Zealand Book Awards, and she's joined today by Briar Grace-Smith, an amazing writer in her own right, for a look into the career of this deeply subtle, moving and subversive writer.

BRIAR GRACE-SMITH:

Ngā mihi nui kia koutou i huihui mai nei ki te tautoko te kaupapa o te ra. Kia ora, everyone. Apart from all of the things that Pip has mentioned about Patricia's life and her writing life, for me she looms largest as my mother-in-law and my family member. I've talked to her so many times over the years, and mainly we've talked about babies who won't sleep and rebellious teenagers and chocolate cake recipes, so it's very hard not to look at her today and want to ask her about her recipe for vegetable soup. I'm struggling with that a little bit.

But one thing I wanted to ask, Patricia, because I've never known the answer, is about this thing called writing, and when you first thought this is what you wanted to do. And what was it in your life that brought this thing on, made you want to tell stories?

PATRICIA GRACE:

Oh, thank you, Briar. Rau Rangatira mā, tēnā koutou, tenei te mihi ki a koutou, ki a tātou katoa. Tēnā tātou katoa. I always liked the act of writing, and by the act of writing I mean actually putting words on paper, whether that was just copying words or writing something. Not so much writing stories, that came a little bit later, but I suppose I can say I was always keen on the written word. I always liked reading as well. I never, ever thought of actually being a writer. I didn't really know that that was something one could aspire to. I suppose it was because when we were children we were never introduced to writing that was familiar to us in our backgrounds in the country we lived in . . . We didn't have a lot of books in our household. I remember that I had a book of fairytales, and a book of poems. But that was about it when I was a little child. As my brother and I grew a bit older we became very fond of comics, and they were also not from this country. They were Ernie Entwhistle and people like that, Billy Bunter, orphans Todd and Annie.

At school we read from our Whitcombe & Tombs books: also stories from other countries. Lands of snow and robins and a lot of babbling brooks, and things like that. And even at secondary school, of course, the literature that was put in front of us was mainly from English writers, poets and so forth. Mostly male writers, already dead, in a far away country.

And I didn't know what real writing was either. What we were encouraged to do at school, when we were given little essays to write, were topics given from English textbooks, like 'A walk in the forest' or 'A day at the seaside'. And what we did really was regurgitate what we'd read. Even though I spent all my summers at the beach and in the bush, running around, it never really occurred to me to write about those. I wrote about seasides that had little stripy tents that I'd seen in the comics, where you went in and changed into your 'bathing costumes'. These were words I'd never heard spoken. Forest . . . I had heard the word 'forest', of course, but we always said 'the bush', and the forests that I read about in the comics, with babbling brooks and bluebells, were inhabited by woodcutters, witches and talking animals.

BRIAR GRACE-SMITH:

So when did you realise that you had your own voice, and your stories, and the way that you saw the world was important or valid?

PATRICIA GRACE:

It was very late on, really. While I was at teachers' college I came across the work of Frank Sargeson, and his was the Kiwi voice. I could hear that voice in his work. Katherine Mansfield, oh, I could see the New Zealand landscape, that little dog with the sandy feet, running along the beach. Slowly the penny dropped. And then I came across the work of Amelia Batistich, and there was another New Zealander with a different voice. I started to realise I had my own voice too, and that I would like to try that voice out.

BRIAR GRACE-SMITH:

So how did you go from there to getting published?

PATRICIA GRACE:

We were away teaching in a fairly remote area, and I joined up to the Penwomen's Club, based in Auckland. As a country member I couldn't go to their meetings, but I was able to take part in their competitions. They were monthly competitions, and I started writing for those. I started sending the results of those out to different farming papers and *Te Ao Hou* magazine and other places, and they came to the notice of a woman called Phoebe Meikle, who was an editor at Longman Paul. She wrote to me and asked if I had enough short stories for a collection. So that's where it all started.

BRIAR GRACE-SMITH:

I remember, I think when I was about thirteen or fourteen, my mother bought me the book *Mutuwhenua*, which was your first novel, and I had actually never experienced the kind of feeling or the affirmation I felt from reading that book before in my life. I loved it so much. We were on holiday up in Whangaruru, and I put the book down once I'd finished, and I left it for about a minute, and then I picked it back up and re-read it, because I related so much to the story of identity that was coursing through that story, and through the protagonist who was Māori (not Pākehā), and coming to terms with, and trying to understand, who she was. I was going through the exact same thing at that point, and it's pretty profound when something like that gets to you. You know, the power of writing, the power of how a story can kind of shift you and make you strong.

As a writer, and as a woman writer, and as a Māori writer, I guess we always are being political in some way. Politics is really just part of being. Are you conscious, when you're writing, that you are . . . Do you feel like you have a duty to inform change or is it just something that happens because of who you are? Or do you consciously go into a work thinking of something you'd like to say?

PATRICIA GRACE:

Oh no, I don't consciously go into a work thinking there's something that I want to say – it's more like there's a story I want to tell. What I am conscious of is that right from the word go, really, I've wanted to write about the ordinary, everyday lives of people, of Māori people in particular. I wasn't aware of the political nature of my work until reviews started coming out for *Potiki*, and I realised that even though I was still on this thing that I was going to write about, ordinary people in their ordinary lives, the issues to do with land and language, and being Māori, *were* the ordinary, everyday lives. So that was what I was conscious of doing.

There was one political act, I suppose, when I wrote *Potiki*. I decided not to have a glossary, and not to italicise Māori language words, the reason being that I realised that glossaries and italicised words were what you did to foreign languages, and I didn't want Māori to be treated as a foreign language in its own country. So I put this to my publishers, no problem, they agreed, and there was quite a lot of criticism around that. But, you know, we've stuck to that ever since.

BRIAR GRACE-SMITH:

It's interesting in *Potiki*, which is a story about the fight, or the battle, to retain whānau land, because some of you will be aware that recently Patricia and her whānau have been largely responsible for overturning – excuse me if I get it wrong – the Public Works Act that their land was under threat from, of being confiscated by the council – their family land in Waikanae, which had been gifted down to her through her tupuna Wi Parata – to be used as part of the expressway. And it's almost like *Potiki* in a way, even though these land struggles go on and on, with the telling of that event.

PATRICIA GRACE:

Yes, it was not so much the council, but the Land Transport Authority. We received the letter saying that the land, because I had refused to sell it, was being taken under the Public Works Act. We had to go to court twice over that, and surprisingly, even to me, we won our cases. And people were saying to me, 'Oh, so will you be writing a novel about this now?' And I said, 'I've already done that.'

BRIAR GRACE-SMITH:

I was on a panel recently, and [another Māori writer] vocalised that question, 'Why are Māori always writing about land and tangi?' and these various things. But it's because they're so much a part of our lives, and especially if you live, as Patricia lives, on her family land, on the pā there. And there are many, many tangi to go to every year, many funerals. So it's not surprising these stories come into the stories that we tell. Patricia, sometimes as a writer I grapple with this thing about not only being a writer, but a Māori writer, and sometimes feeling responsible for being the voice of your people, this thing of adding to a stereotype, or a cliché of a character. Do you ever, when you're penning a character, think, 'Hang on, has this been told before? Has this character been told before? Am I adding to a whole . . . ?'

PATRICIA GRACE:

Yes, I do feel concerned about that. On the one hand, trying to break down the stereotype, thinking that you don't want to add to stereotypes. And we get a lot of negative stereotyping as well. But then you're just wanting to write about ordinary people in their ordinary lives, in functional families, and on functional marae, for most of the time. And then wondering if by doing so you're creating new stereotypes. It is a concern, but somehow you just have to try and put those concerns away and write about what you want to write about.

BRIAR GRACE-SMITH:

Yeah, you can't afford to have the fear, can you?

PATRICIA GRACE:

No. So you just have to keep telling the story that you want to tell, in the best way that you know how, I guess.

BRIAR GRACE-SMITH:

You're telling your truths, I guess.

PATRICIA GRACE:

According to yourself, yes.

BRIAR GRACE-SMITH:

Many of your books, like *Cousins* and *Tu* and *Chappy*, are quite epic works, in that they traverse countries and also time zones.

They're huge, expansive stories, and I know because I've just been working on an adaptation, with Patricia, of the film of her book *Cousins*, which is just the most epic story ever. And I wonder how this weaving of things, or why this weaving of stories and characters, has become your way of telling stories? Not the only way, of course, but . . .

PATRICIA GRACE:

Well, it's my life, really. You belong to a whānau, you belong to a hapū, you belong to an iwi, and all those people are related to you through your ancestry. The relationships that I've been really interested in writing about are those family relationships. Cousins, you know, cousins are so important to us. They're our brothers and sisters. And I suppose finding a way of writing that is the challenge.

Finding a way of expressing all of those relationships. It's just like a big puzzle that you have to put together.

BRIAR GRACE-SMITH:

I know that you often write in different ways about the war, and that there are echoes about the war, or ramifications from the effect of war on different characters throughout generations within your stories. *Cousins* is one of them, and *Tu* is very much working in that area. Obviously, within your family, within your life, you felt the effects of war. Can you talk to me a little bit about that?

PATRICIA GRACE:

Yes, I was thinking about that the other day when someone asked a similar question. My father went away to war when I was about four years old, and I think came back when I was about seven. You know, I suppose it was a dreadful thing, losing your father away to war, but on the other hand, he was a sort of a hero, and I was a daughter of a hero, and there were special prayers for him at school. All our fathers had gone away to war, and we did miss them, and it was always a joy when we got little parcels and letters from far countries. But it never really occurred to me to write a story around that until I read his notebook. I know there was some of that, as you say, in *Cousins*, and most of that I had to do research for. I think as an adult I was finding out more about the horrors of the war than I thought about when I was a child, even though I did have nightmares when I was a child as well, about men walking around without any heads. So I suppose that was related to my father being away to war, even though he wasn't one of those without his head.

BRIAR GRACE-SMITH:

He also wrote to you, didn't he? Your dad wrote letters to you which you kept?

PATRICIA GRACE:

Yes. The only letter that I have is one that I wrote to him, so that's away in an archive somewhere. No, I think it's at my place, yes.

BRIAR GRACE-SMITH:

Being a writer is a strange kind of life. Really you spend a lot of your time in solitude, and by yourself, living with your own thoughts. And then suddenly you find yourself in your best pants, sitting in front of an audience, talking to them.

PATRICIA GRACE:

Yes.

BRIAR GRACE-SMITH:

I know that your husband, Kerehi Waiariki, as we knew him, was a huge support to you, not just in terms of, I guess, keeping it real for you.

PATRICIA GRACE:

Yes.

BRIAR GRACE-SMITH:

And I know he carried your bags a lot, and travelled with you.

PATRICIA GRACE:

Oh yes, but also there's quite a lot of research that has gone into some of the novels. He was always there, like my library, when it came to checking te reo. When it came to tikanga Māori, when it came to support, when it came to travel. Because he actually loved travel, and I didn't. I liked being there in the other countries, and meeting a lot of people, and seeing wonderful things, but I didn't really like travel. So yeah, he's missed in my life. Although he's still around, you know. I was thinking the other day, how he's almost just like a sprite, popping around here and there, and all over the place.

BRIAR GRACE-SMITH:

He was also a great storyteller himself. I remember going to his whānau land in Tuparoa, because it used to be that there was a whole busy port there, and a whole village where he grew up. And it seemed to me that he had a story for every mound, or every . . . He would go, 'Oh, that was where the old lady with the makutu eye, or the eye that could zap you, that was where she lived. We used to run past her house,' and it's no wonder, I imagine, that he inspired you a lot with his storytelling.

PATRICIA GRACE:

Oh yes, he was a great recounter.

BRIAR GRACE-SMITH:

That day we were at Tuparoa, Dick talked about the shop that had been there, and the character there, I think you were inspired by a little bit, before you wrote *Chappy*. Is this right?

PATRICIA GRACE:

Oh, yes. The reason I wrote *Chappy* was because Dick had told this story . . . Tuparoa is out of Ruatoria. It's on the coast from Ruatoria. So Ruatoria was the town. He told us about a Japanese shopkeeper who lived in Ruatoria, married to probably one of his relatives, a local woman anyway, and how well liked this person was in the community of Ruatoria. And I remembered that story for quite a long time; it stayed on my mind. One of the things he said was during the war the Japanese man was taken to Somes Island as an enemy alien, and was later deported. And what I was thinking about, and what he wasn't able to tell me, was how that Japanese man came to be there in Ruatoria. So I started research. I found the name of the man.

BRIAR GRACE-SMITH:

Did you?

PATRICIA GRACE:

Yes, but there was an embargo on information about him in Archives New Zealand. So I wanted to write the story, but not about that man, about *a* Japanese man, and I had to make up my own way of getting him to this country, and into that Māori community.

BRIAR GRACE-SMITH:

There's still a sense, in the way you talk about Chappy, that he evolves through other people's talk around him. It's quite wonderful, really. So he retains, throughout the book, a sense of mystery, doesn't he?

PATRICIA GRACE:

Yes. Well, I couldn't get into his psyche or into his head, you know. I knew his story had to be told from the point of view of other narrators. So I started off with one narrator, then came the second one, and then the third one. So, Chappy remains a little bit of a mystery, and I just did the best that I could. Because there again, I didn't want to stereotype.

BRIAR GRACE-SMITH:

An aspect that I love about your work, and that's part of *Chappy*, is there's a whole other level of story going on through a mythology that you create. And with this book there's the story of the baby that's stolen, maybe by the patupaiarehe, or the fairy people.

PATRICIA GRACE:

Yes.

BRIAR GRACE-SMITH:

How did that come for you, and how did it inform the writing? Because it feels to me like that whole thing of ghosts and creatures that come alive at night, like the patupaiarehe, that feeling is threaded throughout the whole novel in a way.

PATRICIA GRACE:

Yes. I think it's just going back to what I was saying before. You sort of want to write about what you know, and you want to write about the ordinary, everyday lives of ordinary people. And that includes your family, as I was saying before, your whānau, your hapū, your iwi. But it also includes your tupuna and your connection to the spiritual world, or people's connection.

BRIAR GRACE-SMITH:

Yeah.

PATRICIA GRACE:

And so anything goes, really. I'm thinking of *Cousins* now, with the unborn twin that speaks for Missy. When I first wrote *Cousins*, it was all in third person, and when I came to the end I thought that was a bit tedious, so I tried to think of ways of writing each woman's story in a different way. Also it helped to identify each one as being different. And I came upon this idea of using the unborn twin, who could see everything (it was 'eye of God', really), and could use that form of address, 'You, Missy,' talking to Missy, his twin sister. And who was able to tell Missy about what their mother was like before she was married. Being able to see everything and do everything. It was quite liberating to be able to do that.

BRIAR GRACE-SMITH:

I think that possibly living on the marae where you're from really informs that way you tell stories, because at once you have the kitchen up here, the wharekai where people are cooking food and preparing, and the everyday, mundane things of life. And downstairs, down the bottom, in the wharenui, these epic tales of life and death, feats of the ancestors – they're unfolding as well.

PATRICIA GRACE:

Yes. So, you know, it's just a way of including all those things that belong to everyday life.

BRIAR GRACE-SMITH:

They really lift the story up.

PATRICIA GRACE:

Yes.

BRIAR GRACE-SMITH:

This is jumping back a bit, but in the book *Tu*, you've described an event in Italy in World War II. And you describe the place that the men arrive at with such clarity, and it's so evocative, that I assumed on reading it that you'd been there. I didn't find until later that you hadn't been there, but you had researched . . .

PATRICIA GRACE:

Yeah, I did research. Part of the research was that I had letters from soldiers in the Māori Battalion, letters home. Wira Gardiner actually gave me his whole archive from when he'd researched for the book on the Māori Battalion. So I had those letters, which were much more valuable than the official history, because that was written after the war, and the letters were the personal thoughts and feelings of soldiers at the time. But I also came across a book . . . [*Cassino: Portrait of a Battle* by Fred Mandalany]. It was written about that time, about Monte Cassino. It was written by a journalist. It painted pictures. I found that very enlightening as well.

BRIAR GRACE-SMITH:

Right.

PATRICIA GRACE:

I had to get away with some things, like the colours of the mountains and stuff. But I enjoyed doing that. This journalistic book did give me some of that, and I had to broaden that out, I suppose. And nobody's come up to me yet and said, 'Those mountains don't look like that. They weren't those colours.'

BRIAR GRACE-SMITH:

[*To the audience.*] I've been grappling with the second draft of a novel, so I sometimes ask Patricia questions, or she'll realise I'm wanting to ask her a question, but I'm not actually asking because I don't want to take advantage of her. So yesterday she told me something which was really great. I said to her, 'I'm struggling with momentum, because novels are so huge.' I find it's so tough, and if I put it down for a week it takes me a long time to pick up the threads of the storytelling again. So I moaned to her about this yesterday, and . . .

PATRICIA GRACE:

What I said to Briar was – it's quite a good tip or trick, I suppose – when you finish your day's work, nearing the end of the day's work, to leave something in the middle of a paragraph, so that you only have to read that paragraph and then you can continue on, and hopefully you continue. Because it's quite difficult, say, to come to the end of a chapter and then get back in and start a new chapter.

So perhaps leaving something in the middle of a chapter, or even in the middle of a paragraph, or even the middle of a sentence, can really help out with writer's block, I suppose.

BRIAR GRACE-SMITH:

One last question. Patricia has written a draft screenplay of her book *Cousins*. And I'm amazed the way you can switch your brain around to writing visually so easily. But maybe the transition isn't as hard as I'm thinking it is, for a novelist?

PATRICIA GRACE:

It is very hard. *Cousins* has been in the pipeline for a long time, and I think I've written it a hundred times, so you got the result of all my apprenticeship, doing all those other drafts. I don't think it's very easy at all, really.

BRIAR GRACE-SMITH:

What was the biggest challenge for you?

PATRICIA GRACE:

The first scripts weren't done by me. But being true to the characters. I could imagine it would be easier to probably expand on a short story, rather than condense a novel. But on the other hand, I haven't got that sort of filmy vision. I think that you must have the visual things, and the aural things, to help, to make up for what you can't write.

BRIAR GRACE-SMITH:

Yeah. But I was really struck by your visual descriptions and the huge sense of character when I read the draft of your screenplay. The characters were there; they were very strong from the get-go. That must be part of . . . ?

PATRICIA GRACE:

Yes, the characters of *Cousins* are very strong in my mind, really, because they're based on . . . It's probably the most autobiographical novel, in a way.

[Briar invites questions from the audience.]

AUDIENCE MEMBER 1:

Can I ask a question? It's to do with the shape of the way in which you write. I heard you mentioning chapters. Recently I read a novel that had no chapters whatsoever. I wonder if you, in planning or progressing the story, think of the shape of how it's going to be presented in that kind of way?

PATRICIA GRACE:

Yes. I'm very clumsy when it comes to . . . I don't plan. I start, and then I keep on going. So, I might have an idea, like I did with *Chappy*. With *Potiki* I didn't really have much of an idea where it was going at all. But I suppose what's most important to me when I write are the characters, and I kind of follow them. So I might have a strong character, even if I haven't got a strong story idea. And so it's all trying to be true to that character, or those characters, usually several. But in the case of a short story it might be just one.

It's quite difficult to explain how I work. I don't have this sense of being at the beginning of a journey and going down the long road where I can hardly see the end. I have more a sense of being in the centre of something, placing myself in the middle of what it is, and you're in this circle, which means that everything is not distant, it's close. So that you can reach out to the circle for whatever you want, and whatever you need. If you need research, if you need ideas, if you need descriptions, then you bring them in close. That's about the best I can say about that really.

AUDIENCE MEMBER 2:

Kia ora. I remember Witi Ihimaera saying that if you're a Māori writer you really have to talk about the politics of difference in your work. You can't just write something that could be written by any other person. It's got to be related to Māori in some ways. And I wondered, as a sort of sub-question, do you have any role models of authors that have informed you or inspired you?

PATRICIA GRACE:

I think my real role models are my family – the aunts, uncles, all the relatives who really related so warmly to me and my cousins when we were kids. Who told, not so much big stories, but anecdotes about family, things about kēhua, ghost stories, and as children we told those to each other as well. And the way sometimes that the storytellers go right off track, and you think that they're never going to come back to what they started with. These are some of the devices that I've been able to use. Start there, go there and there and there and there, and make sure you come back to the middle. Or I've tried not to come back to the middle sometimes, you know. It's just a matter of what you want to experiment with as well. But I think the people around me, and the elders, are my inspiration I would say.

BRIAR GRACE-SMITH:

I'd just like to thank everyone for coming today, coming out to listen and support. And I'd like to thank you, Patricia, for sharing your stories with us. Kia ora.

PATRICIA GRACE:

Thank you, Briar. Thank you all for coming.

Mouth Music
Some proposals about listening

Chris Price

Where do poems come from? My sense is that I don't write
a poem so much as listen for it, as the thrush cocks its head
and listens for the worm pushing apart the earth under its
feet. But listening is also connected to looking. Where do I
look for these sounds? I am a writer who is also an occasional
percussionist and singer, and when I play percussion, the
answer to that question is simple: I look down and slightly
behind me, to the right. This is literally where my gaze
is directed for much of the time when playing with other
musicians, which leads me to believe that is where rhythm
lives. But although my gaze is always directed the same way,
really it is directed to a no-place, which is to say, inwardly.
Which is to say it is probably about switching off the eyes.

If I am singing, I need to be *inside* the song, not mechanically
repeating or reproducing it – the same thing is true of reading
a poem aloud – and the quickest way to get there is just to shut
my eyes. It's not a great way to relate to an audience, but it
does help you establish yourself in the song's landscape, from
where you can look out from time to time, to acknowledge and
connect with those who are listening as you sing it into being
just in time to take your next step forward. Being inside also
offers the possibility of varying the song: its tone, phrasing,

221

tempo, mood or emotional colour. Despite its fixed elements, the song may change or reinvent itself over time.

Robert Hass has a lovely essay on how a certain Wallace Stevens poem revealed different facets of itself to him over the course of his lifetime, as a young man, a mature man, and then an older one.[1] 'Let be be finale of seem' is the poem's hookline. For the purposes of my essay and this moment in *my* life I will take this statement as pointing towards the distinction between reproducing something, which is how we all begin, as children or artists, and inhabiting it. Of course in one sense it is Hass himself who changes, while the song remains the same. A poem may reinvent itself for the reader; it is perhaps less likely to do so for its author. But the song itself *can* change for its performer in the way that Stevens's poem changed for Hass. And of course it may change quite radically for the listener, when another singer and a new arrangement put a different spin on it, just as different guitarists will coax quite different sounds out of the same instrument.

The words may not alter, but if they are strong enough to make you care for them you will handle them afresh on each occasion they arise in you and find their way into the air. The kind of poetry I have in mind is a bodily art that relies on a score. There are poetries more interested in the visual or conceptual, and poetries more interested in speech than singing, but the type of poetry I am talking about is made of all the things song is made of: air moving through the column of the body, and being modified in signature ways by the body it moves through. These effects are not confined to lyric poetry – Gertrude Stein's work, for example, is also made of these things – but it is no accident that it is easier to remember the lyric of a song you have performed than to remember a poem you have read to yourself in silence, without moving your lips. Those of my own poems I have by heart (another bodily location) are lodged there because I have performed them with musical accompaniment, not as songs, but as words that continually seek their place in relation to the music by dint of listening.

+

When it comes to music, I speak as an amateur. I make no great claims about my skill set; I am trying to articulate axioms proved on the pulse. My ten thousand hours[2] have been spent on words, not notes; my musical chops are self-taught, and limited – and so I have to make the most of the few virtues available to me. My main virtue, as a percussionist, is the capacity to listen – which means, in part, an instinct for when to shut up and stay out of the way of the other (I am always tempted to say the *real*) musicians, since sometimes the most effective contribution to a piece of music is silence, or self-erasure (in this context not negative but positive space), and one of the tools of studio production is to take things away, and the one tool of erasure poetry is either white correcting fluid or black marker pen. The poet Mary Ruefle practises erasure as a daily discipline. In my mind I see her hovering over the printed text, thrush-like, listening for the poem and eliminating the competing noise of one word after another until she finds it.

It was only when I recorded for the first time that I learned to listen to myself, because when the recordings were played back, I discovered that I sometimes sang out of tune (the microphone is utterly unforgiving in this respect). The lesson in this painful experience is that singing with feeling isn't enough – whether live or in the studio, a part of you needs to be listening to the note in relation to all other notes at all times, checking its position in the landscape and making sure that it's in tune and in time with the other musicians and their instruments. Something similar goes on in the writing of the poem, regardless of whether it's interested in musicality or not: each part of it exists in some kind of relation to all the other parts. When you play live, you also need to be conscious of your volume in relationship to everything else going on in the band. If you are singing lead you are legitimately up front, volume-wise – people want to hear your words. If you're a backing vocalist, though, the blend is what matters: it's bad manners and bad music to dominate the lead vocalist or the other backing vocalists. Similarly, it's socially inept for a percussionist to be soloing over the top of a verse or someone else's lead break.

What's simply good etiquette in performing songs becomes absolutely critical in improvising. Laying down the groove is the rock drummer's job, but as a percussionist I need to cultivate a feeling for when to ride the groove set by the other musicians, when to let them lead, when to create openings that allow the others to detour from what the current groove dictates, and to listen out for moments when it might be appropriate to propose a detour myself, to liberate all of us from the straitjacket of a single overarching rhythm.

In improvisation, I can't always look down and to the right: my eyes must be open at least some of the time to both receive and give visual cues. Conversation requires looking as well as listening because the body, too, is talking.

+

Perpetual dissatisfaction with your craft may be the lot of the artist, but it's not necessary to master other skills in order for them to contribute to your primary work. Use what is most available to you, but don't be afraid of using what isn't. The poet and dancer Harmony Holiday (daughter of R&B musician Jimmy Holiday) says, 'The body should move, and the poem should move like the body. The body doesn't move in couplets, for me.'[3] I'm no dancer, but I am a fan of modern dance. Even in an audience – interesting that this word is rooted in hearing, not seeing – you can pick up something that may be of use. Thinking about how a poetic line trained in modern dance might behave creates a small detonation in me, a little 'Oh!' that tells me dance could still have something for this two-left-footer – a method of escape, a way of getting airborne.

'Here is why jazz players love the blues,' writes critic

Stephen Brown. 'It is the perfect box to break out of . . . This reveals the secret of jazz performance: First, construct a box. Second, break out of it. In so doing the musician enacts a moment of liberation. This may be a politically charged term, but surely everybody needs some liberating.'[4]

+

Catch the detonation before all the pieces land. Dancer Douglas Wright explodes backwards and upwards off the floor onto a chair behind him, as if he has found the secret of making not just tape but time reverse itself. You could use that.

+

For practical purposes, one of the main differences between improvisation in music and the improvising of a poem is that in true musical improv, you can't go back and fix your 'mistakes', make something 'better', remove passages of boredom, devise moments of surprise, or any one of the million things poets do that go by the name of revision. I think of the improvising musician as both auditor and editor, except that the improviser doesn't have the luxury of stepping outside time to think, to dwell on infelicities until the most felicitous version occurs to her, to figure out where and how the words have gone off track, and reverse up. When performing music, time can only go forward, developing on, diverging from or returning to what has gone before. You hold the piece's past in your memory while you play as the basis for inventing its future. There is an ongoing negotiation between fixity and flux. In live music, and especially in improvisation, the auditor/editor makes her fixes on the hoof or, on good days, on the wing.

It is harder to be interesting as a solo improviser, because you need a very high level of technical skill and fullness of humanity to work alone, with no one to bounce off. So the nature of the improv I am talking about is (at best) a high level

conversation between several musicians (four has always
been a good number – beyond that it's difficult to attend to
all parts of the music at once), in which part of the interest
lies in following the generation of ideas through a series of
twists, turns, plateaus and peaks. Inside an improvisation,
the sense of time is elastic. Sometimes the landscape remains
similar for long periods, then you climb into the mountains,
and emerge at a mountain lake. Sometimes you get stuck in
the snow at a roadside inn and have to explore the benefits
of whisky and conversation there. But improvisation in the
collective sense requires the ability to both lead and follow
– to share the lead around, or take the initiative from time
to time, to be happy as pack horse or postillion. Nobody
likes a stage hog. You also, collectively, need to see accidents
as potentially happy phenomena, rather than events that
threaten to dismantle or thwart your best intentions.

This process can also happen in collaborative conversations that aim to generate ideas. Someone brings an idea
that is improv(is)ed on by the collective mind into something
better, more focused or stimulating. Sometimes the original
idea is entirely left behind. It's a process that requires everyone
to have their ego under control, just like in a jam session,
which is not a place to insist on having things your way.

Free jazz maestro Ornette Coleman: 'For me, music has
no leader.'[5]

+

My guitarist partner likes to tell people that I am a control
freak – but that when we are improvising together I am
forced to surrender all control. When we are working with
a looper, he has complete compositional control, with the
ability to use every sound I make as raw material for in-the-
moment composition. He says this with a gleeful air, but the
point is that relinquishing control is a supreme pleasure. It
touches on meditation, and I sometimes wonder whether the
AA precept that the alcoholic must give themselves over to a

'higher power' is an alternative way of getting at this kind of absent presence.

+

Poetry is not usually a team sport or collaborative activity. But the similarity between group and solo improvisation, in music or poetry, is that there is no advance consensus about what is to be made. The point is that you are making it (up) as you go along. If improv were the same as working on a building, the building would likely be of no practical use, or even dangerous to inhabit, being held up by collective imagination rather than sound engineering and building skills – 'but beautiful', as Geoff Dyer says of the compositions of Thelonius Monk.

+

About 'mistakes': in improv, you may play a bum note from time to time. You can't take it back, and that can be mortifying, especially in a live recording, where it will continue to embarrass you for eternity. But to play that same note a second time, deliberately, to see where it might take you, is a way to 'honour thy error as a hidden intention'.[6]

This way of saying an old truth is one of Brian Eno's 'Oblique Strategies', and I take it to mean that there is no such thing, if you are sufficiently open, as a categorical error. Mistakes, too, are available for use. At their best they are moments of liberation. In the writing of a poem, this happens in private, but the effect can be preserved in the finished score, the words on the page. In live musical performance, an audience can often sense this moment of liberation for itself, in real time.

I don't know if it's one of Eno's axioms, but sometimes reversing a cherished strategy can be liberating, too. The New York trio Dawn of Midi has a traditional jazz line-up of piano, bass and drums. Their unlikely proposition is to play in a way that mimics the electronic music generated via sequencers using MIDI (musical instrument digital interface, a standard protocol developed in the early 80s for getting electronic instruments to talk to one another, and to allow one instrument to control another). Dawn of Midi's emulation of machines makes for a weirdly compelling live listening experience, defamiliarising the analogue breath of instruments made of wires and wood and the normal variations of human timing by attempting to reproduce the quantised music of sequencers.

+

A note on terminology: it's the more formally educated traditions (jazz, classical) that tend to talk about improvising. In the less educated traditions (folk, rock) it's called jamming. My personal definition of improvisation doesn't mean a bunch of people getting together to play a song that one or several or all of them know already, which is often what happens in a jam session. I don't even mean the kind of jazz that involves starting with a standard and messing with it, although that can get pretty wild and exciting. By improvising I mean starting with nothing and building something collectively, in the present moment.

+

Of course, nobody ever *really* starts with nothing.

+

So when I am writing a poem, alone (usually) in a room, I am also listening. But what am I listening for? What is that worm actually doing? It's easy to portray this listening as a slightly mystical business, so I have had to think about the answer, to think whether there even is an answer – and if the answer is mystical, whether I want to be a mystifier, since mystery may be a desirable emergent property of a poem, but is not in itself a construction material, or a technique that can be handed on to others.

What exactly am I listening for, then?

One answer is the faint gunfire of neurons, the crackle of distant memories, linkages, melodies, rhythms. Or, to shift to back to an earlier, visual metaphor, I am attempting to find my way through a landscape I have glimpsed momentarily by lightning, with my eyes closed. To write the poem is to essay a reconstruction of what that flash so fleetingly illuminated – a landscape, a community of connected ideas, events, facts and expressions, images, actions, utterances.

Another answer is that I am listening for or to the voices of other poets. Which is to say that, while not consciously reaching for a template or example, I am listening to what has stuck from what I have read. Occasionally though, an identifiable riff – perhaps a melodic phrase or rhythmic pattern that I (or others) might recognise as originating in someone else's song or composition – crops up in a poem, which is called (variously) allusion, appropriation, quotation, mimicry, found poetry, or theft. I am a product of my bibliography as well as my autobiography. (That statement itself echoes a remark made by another poet, Peter Gizzi.)[7] As a musician, I am a product of what used to be called my discography, here taken to mean not what I have recorded, but what I have listened to. I am in conversation with the past and the present. You could say I am jamming with both the dead and the living, whether they know it or not. The voices of other poets and musicians are talking to me, or through me. Sometimes, I find a way to talk back.

+

Robert Hass says that the line is 'a proposal about listening'.[8] The opening line of a poem is an earworm setting about its business, setting up the kind of thing you might be listening to or for, as a writer *or* as a reader. It calls into being a particular kind of poem, just as the opening bars of an improvisation call forth a particular set of responses, depending on the musical background of the improvisers. A shared musical background helps to get things going, because everyone speaks a version of the same inherited language, which is often called the tradition.

But in improvisation, a shared language may also stall and stale on its own habits and limits, which is one reason (although there are more pressing ones) why we should welcome immigrants with their different modes, rhythms, melodic and other conventions to detonate fresh seams in our own capacity to think and speak. The unsuccessful version of this is sometimes called cultural appropriation, which has about it a whiff of the coloniser or the mere impersonator. (Why be a fake Elvis when you can be the real you?) Improvisation itself can seem like a luxury denied to those whose tradition is under threat. At the same time, traditions too vigorously policed are like boxes: they can provoke a desire, among some of their inheritors, to jump out.

Whether the language of improvisation is shared or not, you are tossed something that you have to catch and either juggle or pass on to the next person in the circle whose hands are ready. The piece you make together may contain both the comforts of the familiar *and* the shock of the new. Improvisation admits of many modes: church-like hush, a robust sense of humour, an impish disruptiveness, the desire to throw all the toys out of the cot, the longing to recover order. Sometimes all of these in the same piece.

+

A common idea in much writing about creative expression is that the self vanishes when composition is in process. The current voguish name for this is 'flow'. I am not sure it is quite true that the self vanishes, I think it is more that when true listening happens, the self is not in the way of the other, but rather is operating in background mode, enabling reception as well as transmission. Haven't we all encountered people who operate entirely in broadcast mode, and seem to have no capacity to receive? It is not possible to win a war that way, nor is it possible to win peace. When a poem or an improvisation fails, it is often because reception has been lost. Part of becoming an improviser or a poet is learning how to keep the channels open.

+

There is another kind of listening going on, which I will risk calling 'listening to your life'. Which is not what you have consciously learned or done, but what you didn't know you knew until you saw it written down. Another word for what you are listening to or for is your character, something better defined (if at all) by your readers than by yourself. One of the most bruising but also the most useful aspects of being read and commented on (in writing workshops or in reviews) may be to learn the defects of character your writing unwittingly reveals. In *The Art of Fiction,* John Gardner suggests that these defects make themselves apparent at the level of the sentence, and he uses the more grand and nineteenth-century phrase 'faults of soul'.[9] He goes on to suggest, chillingly, that these are incorrigible.

I do not suggest that everyone suffers from such defects. Some writers barely understand what Gardner might mean because they have never had to face such defects in themselves. But I can say that his phrase strikes a deep and useful terror into my own defective heart, one that encourages me to listen out for these failures, although they can be very difficult to hear.

In the most general sense, I suspect that a 'fault of soul' may simply be a species of selective deafness, which is to say a failure of compassion. If you are not listening, whispers the world, how can I talk to you?

+

It so happens that call and response is one of my favourite musical devices. It occurs in the music of the Russian

Orthodox Church and other Catholic traditions, but I prefer the Russian for its alternative sense of harmony to the tradition I grew up in, and for the fact that, not speaking Russian, I engage with the form and feeling rather than the meaning of the words, which is helpful to an atheist. Call and response sounds to me like engagement between God and the congregation, mediated through the priest. (Leave aside for now the contradiction in an atheist who nonetheless talks about a conversation with God.) It is a stately and repetitive exchange, a deep groove whose frequencies are slow enough that it is hard to hear them as rhythmic, like whales speaking across miles of ocean, or the bass frequencies that we mainly 'hear' with our bodies.

Call and response is also a big part of various African musical traditions, from which it presumably filtered down into gospel. In African musics the groove is often far more vigorous and exhilarating. But both traditions seem to put the self in background mode, while joining it, temporarily, with other selves. That is, they generate temporary utopias; places where, it seems, we can all speak and be heard.[10]

These aren't utopias of the intellect, walled and structured places devised by the rational mind in an attempt to fence itself off from the ordinary miseries and failures of being human. Such utopias, when they try to fix themselves in place, often generate the opposite of what they supposedly aim for. Like the pop-up art and memory projects that helped Christchurch recover from its earthquake, temporary utopias are, at best, places of respite, like an inn that offers food, warmth and lodging on a long journey, but only as a staging point. They are forms of hospitality, one of the most necessary and beautiful forms of human behaviour. The host marvels at the tales of the traveller. The traveller is made, for a moment, to feel at home. Regardless of whether money changes hands, it is a gift economy, and as such these temporary utopias can be places where hope recharges its reason for being.

+

When money is at stake, it can seem that there is only one right thing to do, and an imperative to do it that overrides playfulness. When money is taken out of the equation, the number of possible 'right' things to do multiplies. Scientists call this blue sky research. Poetry, which has always earned more or less nothing, has always had a great deal of blue sky.

The philosopher Giorgio Agamben, reconsidering the nature of work in an extensive interview with the German weekly newspaper *Die Zeit*, asks whether human beings are really 'out of work' when they do not have a specific job (cobbler, architect, house painter) to do, or whether all human beings have an innate potential for activity beyond the work that has hitherto appeared to define them:

> A human being is a creature without a specific job, because no specific profession can be attributed to them. Consequently they are creatures of possibility, pure potential. The only genuinely human activity is that which renders current forms of work inoperative in order to open them up to new possibilities and uses.[11]

Agamben proposes poetry as a striking model for activity in an age when technology is rendering much traditional work redundant. 'What is poetry,' he asks, 'but a verbal operation that consists of neutralising the informative and communicative functions of language in order to open them up to a different use?'

An aside: regardless of whether you agree with Agamben's proposition or find it fanciful, it seems comically unthinkable that an interview such as this would be published in a weekend newspaper in New Zealand. Reading it over coffee in Berlin one Sunday morning in 2015, I instantly heard the howls of laughter back home at the impractical idealism of this thought, then realised no such laughter could break out because the piece simply would not appear. Impoverishment of intellectual environment, low expectations of public intelligence – another essay could be written on the role these might play in failures of innovation.

+

To climb back down from these heights to where I normally live: a simple tune that epitomises inherited tradition can be the most affecting of all. A voice that is not conventionally beautful can provoke the deepest response. A broken voice, a voice that is near dying, may have a bigger range than a voice fully fit and trained to scale mountains.

Sometimes it's good to just shut up and listen. This, by Scottish poet W N Herbert, explains to me why some of my favourite people are inveterate fans, and inveterately curious:

> . . . our society, no matter what the subject, is too keen to divide us into tourists and experts. Tourists are led through historical sites by a guide with an umbrella; experts peer out briefly from the museum windows. Tourists are intimidated by the mass of knowledge required to engage intellectually with any complex issue; experts wonder whether it's worth even starting to explain. Tourists' interests are temporary, and are therefore presumed not genuine; experts' are lifelong, and therefore must be convinced of their own authenticity. In this way every opening moment rapidly transmutes into another involuntary act of closure.
>
> Poets are neither tourists nor experts. Nor are they concerned overmuch with authenticity. They have engagement without especial expertise, and they are not intimidated by what they do not yet know. In other words they are perpetual amateurs. What fascinates them is the spark generated by language, any language, the life inherent in all codes of communication, and the various energies of linguistic

pattern. Whether you are a tourist or an expert, it can be good to encounter such an amateur. Certainly, it is hard to think of a field of intellectual endeavour which was not opened by the enthusiasm of amateurs.[12]

In my house, the best place to play music is the kitchen: by chance, the acoustics are conducive to hearing yourself and others clearly. In the kitchen, I have used jars of rice, the cardboard tubes at the centre of paper-towel rolls, empty wine bottles and glasses, matchboxes and knives as percussion implements. There is an Italian theatre company that has built an entire show around the sounds and processes of preparing food.

+

Your second string may not be musical. You might be a fruit picker or a software programmer, a gardener, flax weaver, kitchen-hand or geographer in your day job, and a ballroom dancer, a painter, a football player or classic car enthusiast in your other life. It doesn't really matter: any and every thing can be put to use in the experiment of making. But if everything is free now to the consumer of art, for the producer, nothing is. There are no shortcuts: whether you are trained or self-taught, only practising your instrument will enable you to join the conversation.

1   Robert Hass. (2012). 'Wallace Stevens in the World' in *What Light Can Do: Essays on Art, Imagination and the Natural World*. New York: Ecco Press.
2   In his book *Outliers*, *New Yorker* journalist Malcolm Gladwell argues that roughly ten thousand hours of practice are required in order to achieve high-level mastery of any given skill.
3   Natalya Anderson. (9 June 2016). 'The City Admits No Wrongdoing'. Interview with Harmony Holiday. *Prac Crit*. Web. Accessed 19 January 2017.
4   Stephen Brown. (28 May 2010). Review of *Jazz* (Gary Giddins and Scott DeVeaux [2009]. New York: Norton). *Times Literary Supplement*.
5   Jacques Derrida and Ornette Coleman, trans. Timothy S. Murphy. 'The other's language: Jacques Derrida interviews Ornette Coleman'. 23 June

1997. *Genre: Forms of Discourse and Culture* 37, no 2, Durham: Duke University Press. Accessed via *Jazz Studies Online*.

6   The 'Oblique Strategies' (1975) are a set of creative aphorisms devised by musician Brian Eno and artist Peter Schmidt to generate fresh approaches to a project. Although they worked in different artistic disciplines, Eno found that many of Schmidt's aphorisms were applicable to music, and vice versa. Originally produced as printed cards, they are now available online and in app form.

7   Alex Duebin. 'The Afterlife of the Voice: An Interview with Peter Gizzi'. *Paris Review*. March 2015.

8   Robert Hass. (1984). *Twentieth Century Pleasures: Prose on Poetry.* New York: Ecco Press.

9   John Gardner. (1984). *The Art of Fiction: Notes on Craft for Young Writers* (Reissue ed. 1991). New York: Vintage Books.

10 Thanks to Cherie Lacey for introducing me to anarchist writer and poet Hakim Bey's concept of the Temporary Autonomous Zone in relation to festivals.

11 'Europe must collaborate'. Conversation with Giorgio Agamben. (27 August 2015). *Die Zeit* 35. Translation author's own.

12 W N Herbert. (2006). 'Did Ernest Fenollosa and Ezra Pound Get It Wrong?' *Poetry London* 53, Spring.

Awkward and Golden

On silence in writing

Emily Perkins

Silence as we experience it might include human sounds – breathing, creaking, blood in the ears. It might be nothing more than a drop in the howling wind, the absence of talk or the end of a baby's cry. It could be silence through chatter, silence on a subject.

Silence exists in relief, in contrast, in flickering beats and aching stretches. Its qualities depend entirely on surrounding conditions. Silence is a frame around sound; sound is a frame around silence. Silence can't be touched but it can be felt.

Silence can be knowing, blank, charged, dull, friendly or hostile. Silence can be golden or awkward: masterful discretion, or the bliss when you've shut the door on overstaying visitors, or the excruciating ear-pulses after you've told a long joke that's fallen flat. How many writers does it take to have an awkward silence?

Silence is a precondition of emotional access. Emotions are soundless even when accompanied by laughter or a scream – that's part of their power. We use words to disperse pain or to share delight. Silence is an important site of uncontrol.

A writer wants to use silence in as many ways as she wants to use words. How can we use silence to grant readers access to thought and feeling, to have them 'thinking the thoughts of another', as Georges Poulet puts it[1] – these thoughts that are not even ours as written, because in the silent space of reading, writers cannot be dictators?

The Hayward Gallery's 2012 exhibition 'Invisible: Art About the Unseen 1957–2012' was an invitation to think about what participating in an invisible artwork means. The viewer is asked to provide meaning. Conventions of representation and even of abstraction are pulled away and we enter, sometimes to the point of becoming, the work.

Jeppe Hein's 2005 work *Invisible Labyrinth* is 'an imaginary labyrinth without physical walls directing the movement of the visitors'.[2] Gallery-goers traverse the empty space as though it were a maze, and infrared technology is used to 'buzz' each participant through a headset, to indicate they are walking into a non-existent 'wall'.[3] This is, of course, viewer-dependent. Experiencing this piece, I knew I could cross the invisible lines and walk like a ghost through the ghostlike walls, if I wanted to, but I obeyed the wordless instructions of the buzzing headset. It was a way of collaborating in the game, of choosing to make something rather than march through and make nothing.

When I was at drama school a lot of our training relied on seeing things that weren't there. In clown class, we often improvised around shark-infested waters or found ourselves on the moon. There we would be, nine clowns shivering on a cardboard raft, crocodiles waddling towards us over the cracking mud, and one clown – let's call him Bloop – would stomp across the linoleum floor shouting that we were stupid because 'There's nothing there!' Whether he was a spoilsport or an anarchist genius, I still don't know, but he's gone on to a successful international career: make of that what you will.

When we write, we know we're sending out something that will be more or less reader-dependent. There will always be at least one clown who doesn't want to play along. The more gaps and silences in our work, the more Bloops we risk in our readership. The *Invisible* exhibition leads me to connect invisibility, silence, and wordlessness, to draw on visual arts and other art forms to think about the powers of silence for good and ill, and how we can imaginatively harness, direct, suggest and evince different types of silence in writing and teaching to enhance the experience of those who play along.

In *A Book of Silence*, author Sara Maitland seeks silence in the desert, hills, forest and other places. For her, silence doesn't just mean quiet; it also means solitude, an absence of others. She is trying to resolve the question of whether writing is compatible with silence, and concludes that they don't really go together. I agree with her. The concept of writing as a solitary act is one I feel less and less connection with. As a teacher, I see how writing develops with the close engagement of other people. Even when writing alone, it's not just the characters – hazy as they may be – and the story-world that feel like active, audible company; it's the words themselves. Thought is silent and often wordless, in that we can arrive at awareness much more quickly than we could name it. But thought forming in your mind, unspooling from your fingers, and appearing before you on the page or screen – this is hearing as you think, with all the sound and rhythm reception of your inner ear. Writing is aural. It makes a silent noise.

+

Fine art representations of the invisible can be controversial, preying on anxieties about modern art and a fear of the emperor's new clothes. An art hoax, a photo of people actually looking at paintings that have been digitally removed, presented as a show of 'work' by an invented artist called Lana Newstrom, has fooled many in the art scene and confirmed the prejudices of those cynical about conceptual art. I sometimes wonder whether I'm being taken for a ride when I read experimental writing, until I remember that isn't important – the question is whether I'm prepared to go along, and what I might get out of it.

Modern art has tried to grapple with the unseen since at least 1915 and Malevich's painting *Black Square*. Robert

Rauschenberg followed in 1951 with his *White Paintings*. In the mid 1960s the influential artist Bruce Nauman famously cast the space beneath his chair. Sculptor Rachel Whiteread is known for her casts of architectural features, rooms and buildings, which fill in empty space and leave the viewer looking at its solid manifestation. One of the most affecting of these pieces is *Ghost* from 1993, which is the cast of an empty Victorian parlour. When exhibited in a small gallery, this cast room leaves the viewer little available space to walk around it, the nothingness now a something that pushes you to the edges. These are visual representations of negative space.

Negative *narrative* space can be identified by ellipses, jump cuts, elisions, lacunae and the missing links of contiguity, where connections are provided by the reader. I love this simple line from Paul Auster: 'there needs to be enough space in the text for the reader to inhabit'. This doesn't have to mean minimalism or leanness. I think it means having trust in the reader. Given the right kind of opening in the work, the reader's mind rushes in.

If negative narrative space can be identified and elaborated on, negative space can also be inserted *into* a narrative, in a sort of 'reversible jacket' move. Works that *remove* text, like erasure poetry, Tom Phillips's *A Humument*, or Mary Ruefle's whiteout books, use redaction and deletion to create something new.

Within the context of a fiction MA there can be pressure to produce volumes of words, and students can be reluctant to make cuts. It's often the case with new writers that the end of the work is where cuts are most needed, where they've lost their nerve and tried to make sure the reader 'gets it'. But when the writer stops trusting the reader, the reader usually responds in kind. Setting cut-up and erasure exercises for students is a useful way to get them over any feelings that a text is sacred and its meaning constant. And visualising negative space can be a way into thinking about what is not said, using silence as a presence rather than an absence.

+

Silence's power is particularly evident in performance. The breaking point between sound and silence can be a critical part of a work's impact. When the music stops and only non-speaking human noises are left, there's a powerful shift in mood and focus.

In Pina Bausch's seminal dance work *Café Müller*, the Henry Purcell score comes and goes throughout the piece, shifting the mood as the sounds of bodies are obscured or revealed. The effect is strange – the music stops and for a few seconds you are acutely aware of silence, then of breathing, scraping chairs, footsteps. A dropping sensation as the score falls away. A feeling almost like stroking of your inner ear when the music resumes. Your emotions are pushed and pulled by the music and silence as much as by the movements.

Performed silence is shared by everyone. Although here is art critic Jonathan Jones in the *Guardian*: 'This year, Marina Abramović caused a stir when she said her exhibition at London's Serpentine would be about "nothing". Yet the controversy was not about the potential invisibility of the idea – it was about plagiarism, for another artist claimed prior rights in nothing.'[4]

If embodied or performed silence is time-bound, could written silence then be space-bound? In the mid-eighteenth century, Lawrence Sterne's *Tristram Shandy* followed the death of Parson Yorick with a famous 'black page'. The minute's silence we observe to commemorate loss can be illustrated in text too. One Saturday in 2012 the back page of Australia's *Daily Telegraph* was blank, out of respect to the late cricketer Phillip Hughes.

White space on the page is traditionally a larger, more malleable ingredient of poetry than prose. As readers we've come to accept conventions of formatting, and rely on these to render the reading process invisible, one in which we can forget sight, forget even the marks on the page, and feel as though we are absorbing the work's content directly into our minds and bodies.

We must have white space for letters and words to exist and sense to be made. A crucial stage in early infant sight development is recognising the edges of things; that's why black and white mobiles are so fascinating. In learning a foreign language, we know we're getting somewhere when we can distinguish words from the babble-flow of conversational speech. Silence is crucial to distinction and separation.

A larger expanse of white space, or a break in the line, means something else. In prose, conventionally it means a shift in time, location or perspective, a move from summary to scene or equivalent change of mode. Why don't we use it more often within modes to achieve a different effect, to break with convention?

In his 'Lecture on Nothing', John Cage describes progressions known as 'deceptive cadences', and that they 'progress in such a way as to *imply the presence of a tone not actually present*, then fool everybody by not landing on it, but landing somewhere else. What is being fooled – not the ear, but the mind.'[5] He goes on to say, 'One had to avoid having progressions that would make one think of sounds that were not actually present to the ear.' But poet Andrew Johnston talks of being happily surprised when a 'third term', an unwritten word, hovers above a line of poetry – for instance in his poem 'Fool Heart'[6] the section titled 'Sensible Shoes' contains the following:

Here you are, and
here: note this footprint's
toehold on the real, the whole
an accurate absence: it's yours

It's sort of magic, the way the missing word 'heel' floats silently, textlessly, into the reader's ear.

Not going to the edge of the margin is thought of as poetry's territory, where it's the norm to promote the status of individual and clustered words, for their wordness to be considered of more value than that of those in prose. In prose we expect words to be corralled with one another, put to the work of significance by their relations, not their separateness. Is there any way to create a space-bound, wordless silence on the page? There must be new ways in which online formatting plays with and creates silence. What's it like to scroll through blank space on a screen, to go offline, to follow a hyperlink to a page not found? What both aural and textual blackouts rely on for significance is the usual stream of sound or visual information. There has to be something to interrupt.

Of course there's a distinction between literary representations of silence and concrete expressions of silence. We use interruptions, gaps, chasms, omissions, absences. We control tempo with ellipses, stretches and pauses. We switch tracks, open and close gaps within structures, use fragmentation, crumple sentences, make leaps. We play the writing as though it's music, even if we don't show a rest symbol or fermata. Most of us get worked up about when to choose a comma, a period, a semi-colon, a section break. Should the break be one line deep or three? Asterisk? What is the value, what is the weight, of the wordless textual gesture?

Cage's 'Lecture on Nothing' spaces the words on the page and suggests a reading rhythm: four measures per line and twelve lines per unit. This essay from the 1950s has been performed recently by both Robert Wilson and Kenneth Goldsmith; those are readings I would love to hear. But when I look at it on the page, left to my own devices, I become a disobedient reader, and revert to my conventions. I skip the breaks and read through for the sense. Does that make me a kind of Bloop-the-clown? Maybe concrete renditions of silence or gaps on the page, especially in prose, are underused because they're kind of . . . unappealing? But they're available, there for the taking. Someone could be having fun with them.

Maybe we are better off looking for less literal ways

to evoke silence or wordlessness. In figurative language, words describe the allegedly indescribable. From Barbara Ehrenreich's *Living with a Wild God*:

> And then it happened. Something peeled off the visible world, taking with it all meaning, inference, associations, labels, and words. I was looking at a tree, and if anyone had asked, that's what I would have said I was doing, but the word 'tree' was gone, along with all the notions of tree-ness that had accumulated in the last dozen or so years since I had acquired language. Was it a place that was suddenly revealed to me? or was it a substance – the indivisible, elemental material out of which the entire known and agreed-upon world arises as a fantastic elaboration?[7]

Those kinds of revelations, seeing-through-the-veil, slipping-from-meaning experiences are terrifying. They may or may not be a form of madness. They are certainly uncanny, and can give you vertigo or make you pass out. They might be connected with names that are too sacred to say, a step on the via negativa, the belief that the Divine cannot be of the named universe, that understanding must be surrendered. Such experiences as Ehrenreich's might involve a temporary shedding of the world. They are powerful and unforgettable, and intense emotion or concentration can set you on the path towards them. When it comes to triggering a similar wordlessness in a reader, a stunned or potent silence where words evaporate in the face of feeling, revelation or spiritual presence – it is the whole, not a part, of the text that works to achieve it. This is a writer's undertaking – to *suggest* enough through the work that the ideas and feelings bloom within the reader's mind and heart seemingly – and in large part truly – of their own volition.

+ .

Literary fiction is sometimes criticised for being about nothing, or worse, bringing about nothing. Its preoccupation with breaking form, and often using silence and gaps to achieve this, may give that illusion. So much of fiction's business is what's not said. Virginia Woolf wrote of 'Reality dwelling in what one saw and felt, but did not talk about'.[8]

Fiction is one of the crucial ways we learn about others' interiority, subtext and how to read it in life as well as books. What is not said is an essential engine of drama. One of the most devastating (and brutally funny) scenes in Chekhov's plays is a short non-exchange from *The Cherry Orchard*. In this encounter, near the play's end, Lopakhin the merchant has just bought the beloved cherry orchard and Ranevskaya's family estate, and Varya, whose home it was, is having to move to town and lose her role as mistress of the house. Her mother has just told Lopakhin that Varya is in love with him, and exhorts him to propose to her – in this way, Varya could remain in the family home. The audience knows Varya loves Lopakhin and we are prepared to believe he might love her too. And then he comes into the room and we wait for the proposal. And we wait, and we wait. And he talks about travel times, details of staffing, the weather . . . and then he leaves. In one minute, Varya's unrequited feelings, her dignity, and her home are all swept away in his silence.

Harold Pinter, in a speech at the National Student Drama Festival in 1962, said: 'There are two silences. One when no word is spoken. The other when perhaps a torrent of language is being employed. This speech is speaking of a language locked beneath it. That is its continual reference. The speech we hear is an indication of that which we don't hear.'[9]

It's common practice in workshop to set exercises designed to generate subtext within scenes. We are listening for the unsayable. Sometimes I wonder what would happen if the subtext were spoken, brought to the surface to become explicit – would another layer of subtext naturally be generated? Does meaning proliferate, or would the scene deflate? In *A Room of One's Own*, Woolf said of Galsworthy and Kipling: '. . . all their qualities seem to a woman, if one may generalize, crude and immature. They lack suggestive power. And when a book lacks suggestive power, however hard it hits the surface of the mind it cannot penetrate within.'

There's an exercise that Keith Johnstone writes about in his great book *Impro: Improvisation and the Theatre*, a word-at-a-time game where students tell a story or write a letter in a group, word by word. What often happens, he says, is that the first rounds quickly bring up social taboos: in his words, 'obscene and psychotic' storytelling.[10] (I've done this exercise as a drama student and, ahem, he's right.) From Johnstone I take that it's not until these taboos have been aired and dispersed that an interesting and new kind of storytelling, expressing an unexpected truth, can be created by the group.

There is a certain kind of freighted silence in a short story, commonly seen in workshop and elsewhere, where what was previously culturally suppressed, unacknowledged and unspoken – say, child abuse – is heavily implied. When cultural taboos are brought into the light and more openly acknowledged and discussed, does this literary silence lose its effect? Is this a kind of progress, and does it mean we have to be more interested in consequence than revelation? In redrafting it's often the case that the revelations of a narrative's second half, the little story-bombs, need to be dragged up to the beginning of a script or story, because the more fascinating thing is what happens *after* they've detonated.

Then there is the writing around a subject – to approach an atrocity obliquely, as, say, W G Sebald does with the Holocaust, because it cannot or should not be corralled or ordered by language. When does description become reduction rather than illumination? It seems obvious that certain storytelling tropes, the kind we see in Hollywood films, should have no role in discharging our feelings of

horror at human brutality. Silence can and should be used
differently in representing or alluding to these matters. The
silence relies on a set of indicators, however, and the shared
knowledge from the culture that readers can be relied upon
to bring. This is how we understand gestures, metaphors and
symbols, and feel the presence of the unspeakable through
gaps, allusions and silence.

In workshop, again, students may hear what's underneath
their writing for the first time – the cultural assumptions, the
literary influences, the moral implications, the attributes and
attitudes of the implied author. This can be one of the great
strengths of the workshop process – not to whip away a mask
and say, 'Aha, we see what you really think,' but to help us all
hear what the silences in our work are saying; the ones we
mean and the silences that are unintentional. Sometimes this
doesn't need to be explicitly stated. Silence in the workshop
is important, useful, as in all teaching. I'm in a constant
practice of trying to get better at allowing silence, to trust
the process, trust the students, trust the discoveries. It's
the same principle as trusting the reader, based in the belief
that knowledge that feels personally arrived at, rather than
imposed, is true learning.

+

A silence is like a hole, in that it only exists because of what
it is not. (Readers of Hone Tuwhare's poem 'Rain' will know
that 'small holes in the silence' are another thing.) Silence
wraps around sound, or sound wraps around silence. They
break and make each other. The way a story begins carries a
sense of the silence that it's breaking. Sometimes that silence
seems vast, cavernous, like a void. The blank page or screen is
alleged to carry a terrifying quality of silence, waiting for you
to fill it with your words. It is, for some writers, silencing. But
there is no nothing. We are in the constant torrent of life, the
immaterial as well as the observable. 'There's no such thing as
silence,' John Cage said, recalling the première of '4'33"', his

1952 composition that instructed the performers not to play anything. 'You could hear the wind stirring outside during the first movement. During the second, raindrops began pattering the roof, and during the third people themselves made all kinds of interesting sounds as they talked or walked out.'[10]

If you think about facing the page and listening, trying to catch the sounds that are there – all the noise of life and clamour of the day, the dreams, the imaginary worlds – the challenge becomes not to invent it but to get it down. Drawing a blank usually happens if you're being asked – or asking yourself – the wrong question. Once you're listening and hearing, silences, gaps, then become crucial – they are the selection process – as you draw your poem or story out of the ur-story that surrounds you, or wrestle the spirit that rises from the ground and through you.

There can be a funny readerly anxiety about endings. The end is approaching – I can feel it in the number of pages, or sense it in the poem's rhythm – but what comes over the page? If I'm reading a poem that might end at the bottom of the page, I want to ring that bell, feel that resonance, with the final words. But what if I do that and then turn the page and there are two more lines, or three more stanzas? Do I hold some of my feelings in abeyance just in case? With a novel or a story, if I can't see the end coming, it's the same – you're on the cusp of the ending, so you think, but not quite there – then there's that queer, impotent flatness when you turn the page and that's it, there's no more. Or the strange feeling of excess when you think the ending has arrived but over the page the story continues. It's the anticipation of silence, the desire for just the right kind of silence, which makes this fraught.

Sometimes I think of endings as awakenings – when the fictional dream is over – but another way to think of them is as the threshold to a particular kind of silence.

One of the richest silences is that between the end of a brilliant live performance – of a poem, or piece of music, or play – and the applause that follows to dispel the charge. I love being in the audience when this happens. It feels like a totally shared experience. There's also the cringey silence after a live performance that hasn't gone well. The unspoken 'What? Is that it?' followed by a smattering of applause. Nothing is discharged. Awkwardness reigns.

There is a silence, too, that's ever-present, carried within – the kind of intimate or communal silence that we tap into during meditation, a noticing, listening silence. The weird thing about this silence is that on it floats an inner voice – what we might call conscience, or perception. Denise Riley, in her essay 'A voice without a mouth: inner speech', asks, 'But is the inner voice merely a stifled form of outer speech; or is its true origin a meditative state, a mentalese preceding articulation and suggesting that there is thinking prior to words?'[11]

For writers, reaching the reader's inner voice is a matter of capture and release. This is where novels, short stories and poetry may have an advantage over other art forms – in the silence and free-time nature of their transmission, they get into the same territory as thought and create it so that it seems to germinate from within. Perhaps the great success of third person point of view and free indirect discourse in fiction has something to do with this too. The 'he' or 'she' we read is often so much more intimate, so much less performed, than any first person 'I' can be.

At the end of a meditation the silence (which might include the sounds of breath in unison, like wind in the trees) is often broken by the sound of a bell – a chime that resonates beyond the formalised part of the practice. This sound is intended as a focal point for stillness – a sound that emanates silence.

+

Another way of considering silence is as an opening in the cloth of culture, a space in the recorded arts for you to find your way towards and fill. Not the space that society has prepared for you, which is *already acceptable* and may not

challenge anything, but the gap – that silence – the shape and
size of you; not only your life, voice and experience, but your
curiosity. It is the dimensions of your imagination, the thing
you want to read. It is the stories and jokes and poems and
scripts and essays and words that speak to you and of you,
and which are not being made by anyone else. Sometimes,
to reach that silence and know its potential, you have to
make your way through a lot of white noise, inner and outer,
the static that tunes fitfully to a million frequencies – radio
stations like Who Asked You and You're Needed Elsewhere
and Thanks but We'll Decide the Classic Hits. Some of these
frequencies are more pervasive, damaging and insidious than
others. Some of them are only embarrassing. Not everything
can be dealt with by simply focusing on that eloquent silence
and tuning out as much other noise as you can. Maybe you
don't even need to reach the silence and fill it with your
writing; maybe you can't sense it, or you're satisfied by
everything else the culture provides, or you want to put your
energy into activities with more quantifiable results. Maybe
it's only when you step into the space of that silence that you
realise how much it can galvanise you.

Here's an exercise I've only ever imagined, that I would
like to assign students and myself: Write something that will
never be read: make a place on the page to write what you
wouldn't dare if you knew anyone was going to read it. What
will you write if you can say what can't be said?

1   Georges Poulet. (October 1969). 'Phenomenology of Reading'. *New
     Literary History* 1:1.
2   *Invisible Labyrinth*. Jeppe Hein. Accessed 10 May 2017. Web.
3   Ibid. 'The visitor thus combines the visual information with the
     technologically produced invisible leads, recreating the labyrinth in his
     imagination. The invisible labyrinth is a new form of architecture or
     sculpture, since it is no longer a visible or physical tangible object, but a
     work of the imagination and thus only becomes a sculpture through the
     interactivity and psychology of the viewer.' Accessed 10 May 2017.
4   Jonathan Jones. (September 2014). 'Invisible art: the gallery hoax that
     shows how much we hate the rich.' *The Guardian*.

5   John Cage. (August 1959). 'Lecture on Nothing'. *Incontri Musicali*.
6   Andrew Johnston. (1993). 'Fool Heart'. *How to Talk*. Wellington: Victoria
    University Press.
7   Barbara Ehrenreich. (2014). *Living with a Wild God: A Non-believer's
    Search for the Truth about Everything*. London: Granta Books.
8   Virginia Woolf. (1915). *The Voyage Out*. London: Penguin Books.
9   Leslie Kane. (1984). *The Language of Silence: On the Unspoken and
    the Unspeakable in Modern Drama*. Rutherford: Fairleigh Dickinson
    University Press; London: Associated University Press.
10 Keith Johnstone. (1979). *Impro: Improvisation and the Theatre*. London:
    Faber and Faber.
10 Alex Ross. 'Searching for Silence'. *The New Yorker*. 4 October 2010. Web.
11 Denise Riley. 'A voice without a mouth: inner speech'. *Qui Parle* 14:2,
    Spring/Summer 2004.

Controlled Experiments (in Poetry)

Stephen Burt

The majority of the following poems are to be considered as experiments. They were written chiefly with a view to ascertain how far the language of conversation in the middle and lower classes of society is adapted to the purposes of poetic pleasure. Readers accustomed to the gaudiness and inane phraseology of many modern writers, if they persist in reading this book to its conclusion, will perhaps frequently have to struggle with feelings of strangeness and awkwardness: they will look round for poetry, and will be induced to enquire by what species of courtesy these attempts can be permitted to assume that title. It is desirable that such readers, for their own sakes, should not suffer the solitary word Poetry, a word of very disputed meaning, to stand in the way of their gratification; but that, while they are perusing this book, they should ask themselves if it contains a natural delineation of human passions, human characters, and human incidents; and if the answer be favourable to the author's wishes, that they should consent to be pleased in spite of that most dreadful enemy to our pleasures, our own pre-established codes of decision.

—William Wordsworth, preface to *Lyrical Ballads* (1798)

> The real experiment is what you want to say. You can express a very freaky or experimental idea in a strict framework, or you can express a very trite, boring, oft-repeated idea within an experimental framework.
> —Mick Jagger (1972), quoted in Bill Janovitz, *Exile on Main Street*, 2005

'All poetry is experimental poetry,' Wallace Stevens quipped, and he was right, at least if 'experiment' means – as it seems to have meant for Wordsworth – 'trying something out' or 'trying to do something new'. Every time you try to write a poem you are at least trying to do something new, even if the results are in some sense a failure (negative results are still results), or if what you do comes far too close for comfort – or too close to hold your own interest – to what's been done before.

But 'experiment' has some clearer meanings, meanings closer to scientific practice as we learn about it in college, grade school or high school, and closer to (though – as science studies reminds us – not necessarily congruent with) what modern scientists often do: it seems to me that those meanings can tell us more about what we can do when we read poems. They might also work against some ways that present-day poets use the term.

In what we might call a classical paradigm of laboratory science (a paradigm that has of course been challenged and complicated by Bruno Latour, Paul Feyerabend and many later philosophers and sociologists) a scientist asks a question about a variable, attached to a falsifiable hypothesis. Does ultraviolet light make sprouts grow faster? Are red things more memorable than other things? Then the scientist conducts an experiment which isolates that variable: two sets of sprouts, one exposed to UV light; two sets of screens, with dozens of students in front of them, flashing with similar shapes, some red, some green or blue. (Some students may see no red shapes; some may see only red.)

The students who don't see red, and the shapes that aren't red, and the sprouts without the UV, are control groups: the same except for the absence of whatever the experiment pursues. The control group allows the classical scientist to test a hypothesis; without it, there would be no way to correlate the UV light with the difference in plant growth, no way to falsify the hypothesis that UV light could be the cause.

How, and when, are poems experimental, and what parts or aspects of poetry can poets test? A test, in this sense, requires a control: something that resembles the altered or new thing in all but one crucial respect. And that means that to have experimental poetry – to have poems that feel like experiments, that try out some sort of new thing to see how it will work – we have to be able to recognise a control group: poetry that feels like an experiment has to play off against poetry that resembles it in *most but not all* respects (it is tempting to say, though it would be too neat to say, in *all but one respect*) in order to do its experimental work.

That claim may seem abstract, or inconsequential, or too theoretical, or just wrong: can't we find poets who differed in many, many respects at once from what took place around them? Poets like Hopkins, for example? Or Stein? How does this sense of experiment compare with the current sense among poets, defined (to quote Canadian critic Dani Spinosa) by 'artifice, openness, chance' and left-wing politics, exemplified by Charles Bernstein or Jackson MacLow?

I'll get back to them in a minute, after some disclaimers. I do not mean to propose a general, monocausal explanation for literary history, for why (as Stein famously put it) some things are rejected and then suddenly accepted, much less for what Stein (or anyone else) called genius. I do want to propose a model for how we understand what counts as new in a poem. I do not want to propose that we should regard poets, or poetry critics, as perceptual psychologists, actually conducting valid and replicable laboratory experiments (though Randall Jarrell thought perceptual psychology like Wolfgang Köhler's could tell us a lot about how we read literature). I do mean that we should consider those experiments as an analogy, that the idea of experiments with control groups, testing one thing by holding other constant, and defining the thing by what we test it against, turns out to be a very useful analogy both for etic (from-the-outside) accounts of changes in how poems work, and for emic (from-the-inside) accounts of what we hear, and admire, in them.

To understand a poem as experimental – as a successful experiment – we need to recognise the ways in which it resembles whatever it seems to reject; what it has in common with the other poems of its lineage, and of its era; what its control group should be. If we can read poems that way, then the paradigm of experiments meant to test a specific hypothesis, with reference to a control group, can help us understand poetic invention, literary reception, and literary-historical change.

+

What sort of things can this paradigm help us understand? For one thing, it can help us see why some innovations get embraced right away, and others take a while to get widely noticed, or widely imitated, if they ever do.

Experiments in style, changes and innovations in how to write poetry, that have been recognised as such quite fast, that have been adopted and admired widely within a few years of their creation, have had control groups that their early readers could recognise: one thing changed radically, other things stayed the same. The early T S Eliot, for example, started from models recognisable to anyone who read French, or who had read Arthur Symons. Often it rhymed: 'In the room the women come and go / Talking of Michelangelo.' Most of the parts of *The Waste Land*, though their mode of assemblage was new, would have made sense as fragments of freestanding poems. When Eliot mused, in 1917, in 'Reflections on "Vers Libre"', 'that the division between Conservative Verse and *vers libre* does not exist', one of the reasons given was that all verse, good or bad, could be scanned, which is to say set beside, and examined as deviations from, regular norms. Eliot's own work, and the work he tended to quote (in that essay and elsewhere) as exemplary, usually made those comparisons clear.

Poems that we now regard as successful experiments, on the other hand, but that few people could appreciate on their own terms when they were created, have not had easily recognised control groups; it was hard for the first readers of these poems to understand what norm they were rejecting, what other norms they were (instead) accepting, what kind of thing they were to understand this new thing as a deviation *from*, or (harder still) as a new example *of*. Obvious examples are the book-length poems of William Blake and Gertrude Stein; other, less obvious examples still do not make sense to us now, and may never do.

Thinking about poetry as a series of experiments with a control group can also help us understand how style changes, how invention works, over more limited domains: for example, the domain of metre, and the shape of a poetic line. When you read late nineteenth- and early twentieth-century experiments in free verse, the control group is almost always in regular metre. The lines are end-stopped, and the iterative sense of how a line works has not changed much (it derives either from relatively closed, end-stopped metrical verse, or from the King James Bible). What has changed is the rhythmic pattern within the line.

Imagist poetry circa 1916 (to which the early Eliot reacted) did not change that pattern very much, though it took earlier free verse as its guide. Once the idea of the Imagist poem took hold, by the end of the 1910s, poets could take that idea as a given – the short, end-stopped, free verse poem organised around perception – and then vary other things in their poems (either about sound or about something else).

The innovative metrics of William Carlos Williams, which

he developed starting with *Sour Grapes* (1921) and kept on developing into the 1930s, take not the metred verse of the Georgians but the Imagist-era free verse, the New Poetry of the 1910s, as the starting point, or the control. Williams's free verse, in which most of the lines were enjambed, required – for him to invent them, and for us to hear them – the end-stopped free verse of the Imagists as *its* control.

I'll show you how this works with a few examples. First, some free verse from W E Henley's 'In Hospital' (1889):

> Now one can see.
> Case Number One
> Sits (rather pale) with his bedclothes
> Stripped up, and showing his foot
> (Alas for God's Image!)
> Swaddled in wet, white lint
> Brilliantly hideous with red.

Part of the point here, as Henley avoids standard metres, is that whatever seems conventionally beautiful will not fit this experience; it has to be disorganised, shocking and harsh. That is the kind of fallacy we get from undergraduates who think that free verse always implies disorganisation, but here it makes sense: free verse itself, in 1889, was novel enough, against the background of regular, recognisable metre, that it had to mean, if not disorganisation, then *something*. And because Henley's measures itself against metrical verse, it substitutes a syntactic principle for an aural one: each line ends at the end of a phrase. So does each line in H D's 'Sea Lily' (1916):

> Reed,
> slashed and torn,
> but doubly rich –
> such great heads as yours
> drift upon temple steps,
> but you are shattered
> in the wind.

The free verse still takes itself to be unusual but it no longer assumes itself ugly, and its imagined auditors are already familiar with free verse; you might say it uses enjambment (at 'yours'), but not much – the lines are stacks of phrases, and the phrases describe a kind of Romantic beauty. You could say the same about any number of Imagist poems – say Amy Lowell's 'Bright Sunlight' (1915):

> The wind has blown a corner of your shawl
> Into the fountain,
> Where it floats and drifts
> Among the lily-pads
> Like a tissue of sapphires.

Williams wrote this way too in 1915 and 1916. Here is an almost random example from a poem called 'A Love Song':

> I am alone.
> The weight of love
> Has buoyed me up
> Till my head
> Knocks against the sky.

It was only after this sort of free verse, these sort of Imagist stanzas, had become a recognisable norm that Williams and others could try to go beyond them, to write lines like these, from *Sour Grapes*:

> You know there is not much
> that I desire, a few chrysanthemums
> half lying on the grass, yellow
> and brown and white, the
> talk of a few people, the trees,
> an expanse of dried leaves perhaps
> with ditches among them.

It is because free verse that breaks on the phrase and highlights an image has become a new norm, a new control, that Williams can experiment by deviating from that norm, by breaking – for example – on 'the', on 'perhaps'. (For more

on Williams's metrical experiments – and on his ways of
making them into metaphors for other kinds of experiments
with point of view, with persona, with tone – see Stephen
Cushman's terrific monograph from the early 1980s, *Williams
Carlos Williams and the Meaning of Measure*.)

Other experiments – with sound, with rhythm, with scale
and subgenre and frame – become possible in the 1920s and
early 1930s once poets can take the free verse of the 1910s
(and also the free verse of Eliot, so immediately influential)
as control groups. First, Charles Reznikoff's celebrated
distich from *Jerusalem the Golden* (1934):

Among the heaps of brick and plaster lies
a girder, still itself among the rubbish.

These lines – so much admired by Zukofsky and others –
normally come up as part of the history of the Objectivists,
or of American modernist verse, but they are thoroughly
traditional: indeed they are both in iambic pentameter (with
an added unstressed syllable on 'rubbish'), and their control
groups – the things that they largely resemble – include
at the level of metre the entirety of the English blank verse
tradition, *as well as* the body of Imagist free verse.

But we do not normally encounter it as part of the history
of blank verse, alongside Tennyson and Frost; we encounter
it as a member of other classes of poetry, mostly the free
verse of the previous fifteen years. See it against one control
group and it is salient in one way; see it against another and
it is remarkable in another. Against Imagist and modernist
short-form free verse, the experiment has to do with its
rhythmic balance (which is actually a return to a metrical
norm) and with how very much has been left out. The poem
on its own makes the claim that it can be enough, that we
need no more than these two lines to admire the world as it
is. We do not even need the figurative language that earlier
very short modernist poems, such as Ezra Pound's, condition
us to require.

Then Williams's 'Between Walls' (also 1934): the title runs into the poem.

Between Walls

the back wings
of the

hospital where
nothing

will grow lie
cinders

in which shine
the broken

pieces of a green
bottle

The Imagist free verse poem of the 1910s is a negative here – it is what is discarded – at the level of line shape, or sound, even though that kind of poem is in other respects (focus on one image; beauty found in a discarded urban thing; analogies to photography) exactly the sort of poem that Imagists, and that Objectivists (who took Williams as a primary model) then wrote. Williams has held scene and genre constant in order to vary the shape of the phrase and the line.

You can, of course, come to this poem straight from reading Keats, or Langston Hughes, or Larkin, and get a lot out of it. But the poem sounds most interesting, and most inventing, if you are using the right control group, a group of poems *more like* this poem in respects other than line shape: that is, previous image-centred free verse.

+

The literary scholar Paul Stephens has traced the short history of 'experimentalism', the term, which he uses 'interchangeably with . . . "avant-gardism"'; he finds that the 'ism' noun emerges only after 1985. The word 'experiment', as you might expect, goes much further back: it becomes more prominent, and much more frequent, over the course of the eighteenth century, concurrent with the rise of laboratory practice and the first industrial revolution. Google Ngrams shows it very rare in 1700, rising to a peak in 1780, then rising again, more slowly, to an all-time high in 1965 (it has trended gently downward since). Now as in 1965 we can speak of experimental poetry, but also of experimental theatre or experimental film. We now associate the idea of experiment (impersonal? defamiliarising?) with modernism, or with an avant-garde, but we can find the word, and the idea (as in Wordsworth) among the Romantics, whose sometime romance with chemistry and the other natural sciences has been well documented (by Richard Holmes, among others): consider not only Wordsworth and Coleridge's experiments with the language of common farmers, but also Joseph Wright of Derby's 'An Experiment with an Air-Pump' (1768), or Coleridge's experiments with nitrous oxide.

There is nothing uniquely modernist about the notion of poetry as experiment. And it seems to me that the language of experiment, and of control groups and test cases, fits the practice of poetry in our time better than it fits some other art forms, because poetry – compared to theatre work, for example, or to film – seems to have fewer aspects, fewer dimensions, so that it is easier to isolate one and attempt to vary that one, as long as we are viewing poems primarily as verbal structures, 'a small (or large) machine made of words', in Williams's phrase. (We can also view them – sometimes we must also view them – as representations of unique personalities; I'll go back to that in a moment.)

And it seems to me especially useful to ask about control groups – to ask what the comparison group, what the background, for an innovation might be – when we are talking about the aspects of a poem that are relatively easy to isolate: particular images, or words, or sounds. (We can do the same thing with tone, for example, but it's harder.)

We can look for control groups in poetry too. Victorian poets and poetry critics conducted – as Dennis Taylor and others have shown – a complex debate about how to hear English metre, and what terms (classical, or if not classical, what?) could best describe it. We do not need to know the whole debate but we might remember that it exists in order to find the control group, the right comparisons, for a number of Victorians. It can be hard for us – and harder for our students – to hear what Swinburne is doing, because we can no longer bring to mind – we probably have not read lately – a control group of other poems that sound much like this:

> I have lived long enough, having seen one thing, that love
>   hath an end:
> Goddess and maiden and queen, be near me now and
>   befriend.
> Thou art more than the day or the morrow, the seasons
>   that laugh or that weep;
> For these give joy and sorrow; but thou, Proserpina,
>   sleep.

The experiment with metre here is literally the language in which it is written: Swinburne is adapting – nor is he the first to adapt – the single most recognisable among classical metres, the dactylic hexameter (with spondaic substitutions) of Homer. This metre – hard to recognise if you don't know Latin or Greek, not hard if you do – consists of spondees and dactyls and empty slots with additional rules about line-starts and line-ends: I HAVE LIVED-long-e NOUGH-having SEEN; GOD-dess-and MAID-en-and QUEEN [beat], BE-with-me NOW-and-be FRIEND . . .) Swinburne has asked us to figure out what changes when we hear the metre in English, rather than listening for it in Latin or Greek; and his persona, the last pagan emperor, Julian, has asked himself whether his way of life (analogous to his metre) can survive. (Julian's answer is 'no': that is why he loves death.)

We can think about experiments and about control groups with later poets as well. To find the right control group is to figure out what a particular poem, or a particular style, can do that its close relatives cannot do. James Wright's poetry looks more innovative the more we recognise, as its control group – the poetry that resembles it in all but one or two crucial respects – the poetry of the other 'Deep Image' writers, people like Robert Bly and Galway Kinnell; and Adrienne Rich, it may turn out, was running 'experiments' – taking some other poetry as her control group, and changing just one thing at a time – with all of the other poets on the political left, from Denise Levertov to Judy Grahn to her own earlier selves, as successive controls.

And if we return to the line of Williams, we can see (for example) Lorine Niedecker's work as a source of continuing interest, as a production of genius if you like, in part because it invites us to read it against so many control groups, makes sense in so many dimensions, resembles so many prior sorts of poems – Imagist lyric, post-Imagist Williams, folk ballad, Dickinsonian epigram, even pop song – in some, but not all, ways. Take this late love poem to Niedecker's husband:

> I knew a clean man
> but he was not for me
> Now I sew green aprons
> over covered seats. He
>
> wades the muddy water fishing,
> falls in, dries his last pay-check
> in the sun, smooths it out
> in *Leaves of Grass*. He's
> the one for me.

I could spend all day describing the various contexts that poem invokes, the various kinds of speech genres, popular texts and literary modernist poems against which we can view that poem as an experiment.

+

I'll sum up: to understand a poem as an experiment, we have
to be able to bring to mind a control group: we have to see
what kind of thing is here, to see its continuities with a class
of largely similar works, in order to understand what in it is
new. That claim applies to the individual aspects of poems
– to the shapes of their sentences, to the qualities of their
imagined speakers – as well as to poems as wholes: we ask
what kind of poem we have been reading almost as soon as
we can begin reading it, and if we do not know what kind of
poem we have, we may doubt whether we are reading a poem
at all.

Academics may recognise this claim – that to understand
a work as literary we must understand it as a particular kind,
and see where it *does not* deviate from others of its kind –
from the work of Alastair Fowler, who also claimed in 1982, in
Kinds of Literature, that we readers of contemporary poetry
have trained ourselves to recognise all sorts of subgenres to
which we have not given names. At this point we recognise
some of those subgenres not least by the names of their
publishers, or by the poets' locales: the US poets published
by Wave Books of Seattle, often post- or neo-Surrealist; the
Cambridge University School of rebarbative, semantically
tangled poetry led by J H Prynne. And this sense of poetic
kind, style and school is not a barrier to invention, but a
way to think about invention: against the background of a
particular kind, the extraordinary – or the just plain odd –
single poem can emerge.

Some experiments lead nowhere, or not right away: some
results are negative. But we have to be able to recognise them
as results in order to think about the possibilities for poetry
at a given time. We can experiment – and in this sense poets,
even medieval and Augustan poets for whom 'innovation'
was a negative word, have always experimented – with levels
of diction, with ways to arrange an image, with information
given or withheld. Each time a poet experiments with one
aspect, other (lines, images, sentences and so on) in other

poems, or in other parts of the same long poem, serve as control.

Only in certain periods, though, do we find experiments that take, as their control group, poetry in general, as the poet's contemporaries understood it: not experiments with how to break a line or how to insert a strange word or how to bring in extreme tones, but rather experiments with what a poem 'is'. Experiments at that higher level of generality are one way to think about revolutions in taste; about what we used to tell students to call 'Romanticism'; and about modernism as Pound and Williams – though not, for example, Wallace Stevens – understood it. These attempts or rehearsals for revolution – and not Wordsworth's, nor Swinburne's, nor Eliot's experiments – are what Stephens understands as 'experimentalism'; in them (as he writes) 'ultimately what is being experimented with are received notions of what constitutes literary value', of what we recognise as literature, or poetry, on the whole.

The way that we use the term 'experimental' when we talk about the arts, today, emerges from that modernist demand, the demand that we make 'it' new where 'it' refers not to one aspect of the work of art, but to our sense of the work of art as a whole, to our sense of what counts as a work of art, that we take as control group for this experiment, not some subgroup of similar works, some particular kind, but all of the examples of 'poetry' – or 'painting' or 'sculpture' or 'music' – before the present day.

Experimental poetry – or 'experimental' art of any sort – is in this sense poetry that might not count as poetry at all, poetry that sets itself apart from the entirety of whatever seemed like 'poetry' five or 25 years ago. Experimental music, in the same sense, is music that sounds like it might not be music, from Edgard Varèse's 'Ionisation' (1931) to the Dead C's atonal, low-fidelity, feedback-driven not-quite-rock.

When Wordsworth warned readers in 1798 that most of the poems in *Lyrical Ballads* were to be considered as experiments, he asked them to set the poems not only beside gaudier and (in his view) less natural poems by other late eighteenth-century poets, but beside the people, the human nature, that all these poems set out to depict; holding human nature constant, as it were, he changed the form of the poem to see what would happen. And – as you know if you have read much other poetry from Wordsworth's time – there were many aspects of late eighteenth-century poetry that Wordsworth did not change: the ballad stanza would have been familiar, and the succession of subgenres also familiar (poems on the naming of places; poems that retold local tales; short portraits of rural people), with precedents in Cowper, Smith, Gray, Burns.

In order to recognise Swinburne's experiments with English metre, you need to be able to recognise non-English metres, and to be able to scan English ones. In order to recognise Laura Kasischke's and Terrance Hayes's experiments with rhyme, you have to be used to hearing the less complicated rhyme in their control groups. But in order to recognise 'experiments' with the very idea of a poem, all you need is some sense of what other people have recently meant by 'poem'.

That is one reason (though only one reason) Conceptualism, in the early 2000s, especially in the United States, became such a big deal: it's easy to explain, and easy to render important, if you are talking to people who have not read the poetry that you have read. (It may be that the control group for conceptual poetry is not 'other poetry' but 'conceptual movements in other arts'.)

But we should be able to recognise other kinds of experiments within poetry, and not only at the category's edge.

There is something entirely wrong about this way of viewing poetry as an experiment, and I will tell you what it is: when we see poetry as technical experiment – the way that poets from Wordsworth to Pound to, say, Harryette Mullen sometimes expect us to see it – we are ignoring the part of poetry that seems to us, when the poetry seems worthwhile, inexplicable, irretrievable, irreducible to particular techniques: the part of poetry that Shelley intended when he compared the mind to a fading coal, the part of poetry travestied by TV and radio commentators who tell us that poetry is the essence of souls. Those commentators are embarrassing, but they are not entirely wrong: they echo – as Jarrell echoed – Goethe's quip, 'I deny that poetry is an art.' It is not only an art. But the language of experiment will help us see how it is an art; how the parts that can be described separately should be described separately, how they arise.

+

I'll end by suggesting that this way of thinking, not just about poetry, but about poetry and the idea of experiment, produces a counterintuitive result when we set it beside conventional accounts of schools, of lines of influence, within the Anglophone poetries of the last hundred years. A way of thinking about poetry as experiment (in which it needs a control group) takes as given what many of you probably question, what most of us – especially if we write poetry, or if we help other people write it – tacitly or explicitly reject: poetry as experiment (requiring control) is poetry as intellectual enterprise, and tends to make reading, evaluating and describing poetry uncommonly cerebral. Its emotional goal might be nothing more than what the critic Sianne Ngai, in her terrific study *Our Aesthetic Categories* (2012), names the 'merely interesting' as opposed to passionate transport or intimate revelation. A long line of poets and critics (Coleridge, for example) has treated poetry as something more ambitious: poetry for these critics must exalt the imagination, considered as Shelley's burning coal, or become (with Coleridge) esemplastic, representing the sacred creation of something new in the world, or incorporate a *cri de coeur*, making present some human feeling not quite articulated before. It seems to me that if we are reading poetry as poetry we have to keep both paradigms available: the paradigm of intellectual experiment and the paradigm of the potentially holy *cri de coeur*. It seems obvious that they conflict, and that the poems we keep talking about for a while have something to say to both.

But it also seems to me that once we recognise experiments need control groups, we find some unexpected misalignment between models *of* poetry (as intellectual experiment; as unique, unpredictable creation) on the one hand, and tastes *in* modern and contemporary poetry (avant-modernist versus Romantic-confessional). It turns out to be the Romantic confessional poetry readers who want clearly controlled experiments and the avant-modernists who want something truly ineffably indescribably new.

In fact, you can write – and the American-Canadian poet Adam Sol has recently written – a poem that lays bare the device, that makes clear the shared structure, of so many relatively conventional, post-Romantic poems and the aspects that these poems share with one another (so that you can alter one and keep the rest if you want them to serve as controls). Sol called his poem 'Template'. Here are the opening lines:

> Here I am at the specific location,
> with its world-infected familiarity,
> and its overlooked, unlikely beauty. It is here
> where, after a brief meditation on an esoteric topic,
> I will come to a realization at once profound
> and elementary, something we all know
> that had never before achieved itself in song.
> How exposed I am, here in these words,
> translating my insights into language both elaborate
> and brutal. And how hopeful of you
> to press on despite the odds,
> the paltry expense and frequent disappointments.
> But this isn't about you. You sit down.

I find these lines funny and thoughtful, and I do not find in them a plea that we write no more poems remotely like this one (though some critics – famously, Charles Altieri – have in fact entered such pleas). Rather, Sol's lines suggest a possibility for variation within them – as well as a frustration with their constraints. They show – again – that to use a template is not to merely copy it, and to use a convention in some ways is not to be 'conventional' in all ways. The existence of conventions – of potential small-scale control groups, of ways to keep many things constant while altering one thing, or a few – is *not a problem* if you want to read more of that sort of poem!

Indeed it is sometimes how that sort of poem gets made new – by Wordsworth, for example, when he learned from William Bowles and Charlotte Smith and William Cowper. It also suggests a way of thinking about artistic creativity identified not with any poetry critic but with the cognitive scientist and science writer Douglas Hofstatder, who compared works of art to mixing boards with faders or knobs for volume, brightness, attack, decay, reverb and so on; Hofstadter quipped that ordinary artists find new settings, or new combinations of settings, for knobs, but the trick of great art involves finding new knobs, figuring out how to vary some aspect of art that had seemed like a constant, or a requirement, or a given, until now.

That view of art is not a problem if you are trying to describe a relatively subtle change. It may be a problem if you are calling for poetry to advance, or to leave behind its predecessors, by doing something (even more) radically new. Yet as hundreds of years of literary theory, social theory and perceptual psychology (E H Gombrich's *Art and Illusion*, say) have shown, we can't make a wholly new template; what we can do is back up and take a larger control group, take greater distance from them, make it new *at a higher level of generality* than the Romantic-confessional or scenic poet can do.

And that is what partisans of the post-avant-garde or of

neo-modernism are asking poets to do: not 'to experiment' as opposed to not conducting an experiment, but to regard the experiment, and the control group, at a higher level of generality – altering not a location or a line shape or a relationship or a mode of address but the very definition of 'poem'.

That is one way to read what we now call 'modernism' in general, although when you look at it closely I think you can often see a series of shorter steps – as when Michele Leggott's line or Patience Agbabi's sestinas emerge within and against the horizon created by their peers and their own slightly earlier work. We can make an analogy here not only with laboratory science, but with Darwinian evolution, in which slight mutations that confer a reproductive advantage eventually add up, hive off and generate new species. Evolutionary biology, perhaps alas, by contrast with (say) inorganic chemistry, does not ordinarily lend itself to neatly controlled experiments: it accumulates evidence, its hypotheses admit disproofs, but it requires historical – and not, in the strictest sense, testable – explanations. And if the analogy with controlled laboratory experiments leads us to see new poetry against the horizon of the old, experiments against control, the analogy with Darwinian processes might remind us that poetry does not proceed linearly, or teleologically – there is no one 'front' for any avant-garde; rather, by finding new means of variation, new former constants now subject to change, poetry can proceed in all directions, like a cladogram or evolutionary tree, its segments and subgenres, its recognisable kinds, growing more and more numerous, and sometimes farther apart, until some other process brings some of the branches, some of the experiments, to an end.

Take Two

The psychology of the rewrite

Ken Duncum

Take Two is a simple game played with Scrabble tiles. Each player gets seven and tries to make their own word grid with them. As soon as someone has used their seven letters they say, 'Take two,' and everyone has to take another two tiles. Once there are no tiles left, the winner is the player who first succeeds in using all their letters. It's fast and it's easy – if this is the first you've heard of the game, try it sometime. One thing: if you play it and want to win, you will almost certainly have to adopt a particular strategy. That is, if you can't fit your new letters into your already-formed word grid, then you must break down what you've done and build anew. This feels like going backwards, can seem like wasting valuable time, and the temptation to stick with what you've got is strong. Who knows, if you wait – sit on your hands – the next couple of letters might make everything fit. And yes, that can happen. But generally, ordinarily, usually, only players who have the nerve and take the chance to break it down, reshape and rebuild, can and do win.

I can't speak for rewriting in other forms – prose, poetry, non-fiction – but in rewriting scripts that same open-minded, courageous willingness to pull what you've done apart and start again is the most fundamentally necessary attribute.

'I'm here for therapy,' says Sarah, collapsing into a chair

271

in my office. 'I can't do it, I don't know where to start. I can see it needs work – but I'm paralysed, terrified that if I pull a string the whole script will unravel and I'll have nothing.'

Writing is scary enough. For most scriptwriters you can double or triple that fear and anxiety when it comes to rewriting. Why? Probably because rewriting makes up at least ninety per cent of the overall process – films, plays and TV shows are rewritten far more than they're written – so writers approaching it (particularly for the first time) recognise rewriting as the most important phase, one requiring a completely new set of skills that they may or may not possess. Their twin nightmares each revolve around an inability to make the thing better: either that they will find themselves unable, unwilling, too self-satisfied to see what needs to be done, so will be reduced to doing a bit of editing, tidying up, making cosmetic changes – rearranging deck chairs on the *Titanic*; or that they will find themselves changing everything, rudderless in a storm of new and desperate inspiration, not rewriting but writing again, condemned to an eternal first-draft process, forever heaving the baby out the window because they're incapable of discerning the difference between it and the bathwater.

Fair enough. Those are real terrors, real monsters that cut a swathe through the ranks of would-be scriptwriters every day. While it's not true to say that anyone can write a first draft, anyone with the deep desire and stickability can. And they do. The real winnowing comes next, the real test of whether that writer is going to be able to 'succeed' in their chosen endeavour or not.

So what is it? When a scriptwriter is rewriting a script, what are they doing? And why is it so psychologically fearsome?

Maybe because when you look into the abyss, the abyss also looks into you. When you rewrite you must also rewrite yourself. And God knows no one likes doing that.

This all sounds very portentous. Let me explain what I've observed.

The first draft comes in a rush of invention and inspiration, it's a wild ride where you're hanging on by your fingertips, creating things out of the raw stuff of chaos. Indeed it's only six weeks since Sarah delivered her first draft, buzzing with excitement and adrenaline from the final forty-eight-hour dash. That's how it should be and needs to be; more than anything that first draft is a channelling of the writer's subconscious, a getting-out of what has been bubbling back there out of sight. One of the most important aspects in writing that first draft is to keep the channel open, to keep that download from the deeper recesses of the cave-where-story-dwells moving, without impeding it with analysis.

But once you've done that, once that first draft lies there covered in the blood of the newborn – and you've had a bit of a lie-down – then it is time for some analysis. It's time to fire up a different part of your brain in an attempt to objectively weigh up what you've written. In order to rewrite effectively, this more cold-blooded analytical aspect of your mind then needs to work together with the atavistic creative part that wrote the first draft. It may be that they can function together simultaneously (both light up on the brain scan at the same time), but more likely they will work together in phase, your consciousness flicking back and forth between them (sometimes at a leisurely pace, spending extended periods in each; at other times oscillating so quickly it becomes a white-hot blur). It's not easy, but neither is juggling, and practice will get you a long way at both skills.

Sarah and I have already talked about her first draft, done some structural analysis of the story and where it could go in the next stage, plus zeroed in on what she wants to achieve in this new draft (teasing out the potential for increased depth of character and relationship). My advice to her now, a week later, is all around making creative space for a fresh look at her story. I urge her to open a new file and write from scratch, only retrieving something from the first draft if she is absolutely sure she needs it – in other words to return as much as possible to the blank page rather than face a complete and completed script which gives her the sensation of shaping up to the carcass of a beached whale with a penknife. I tell her to keep in mind that her first draft is not being overwritten or erased – it will still exist, separate and inviolable. Whatever happens with the second draft, if she makes a complete and total mess of it, she can always go back to the first version. In other words, she has nothing to lose, only things to gain, if she wades back into the story in an experimental frame of mind and hopefully discovers the joy of re-creation.

Sarah looks at me somewhat sceptically, but goes back to her desk, takes a deep breath, and sets about demolition and rebuilding. The next time I see her she may look ecstatic – in love with the process – or she may have the fixed expression of someone plunging down a winding mountain road whose brakes have just failed. Either one is fine, as long as she's moving forward.

That, however, is the easy discussion about rewriting, operating on the 'morale' and 'giving yourself permission' level. The bigger challenge, in my opinion – and the psychological difficulty that many scriptwriters suffer – is to be able to see yourself in the story and take the appropriate action.

As Sarah departs, Ben is waiting to see me. In passing they give each other the sympathetic glance of soldiers in the trenches before Ben slides into the hot seat, dropping his bag and detaching his earbuds. His first draft is a wry and amusing tale of an adrift young man who observes a variety of different subcultures and beliefs without himself finding anything to believe in. Ben isn't happy with the end of the story, though. He feels something more significant or satisfying needs to happen, but he can't decide (or imagine) what. He's already aware his central character is based on himself – I don't have to persuade him of that – so we're able to save time and cut to the chase. But for any unbelievers out there . . .

The story is you. If you wrote it, your DNA is in it; your personality, your image of yourself. You can't dream without it being about you – it's the same when you write something. Knowingly or unknowingly, whether it's a zombie apocalypse movie, a TV series about the Romantic poets, or a stage farce full of hilarious bed-swapping shenanigans, your story is the mirror of you. And so it should be.

The challenge now is that in questioning your story, in seeking to analyse it and criticise it, you equally have to analyse and criticise your image of yourself. And this work begins in draft two.

Every draft should be written with a point of concentration, an awareness of what you're trying to achieve, but in the early stages of rewriting there are specific areas of focus. A solid second draft explores character and relationship. Necessary work is done to flesh out characters, make them more rounded, three-dimensional, authentic in their emotional states and choices rather than functioning as plot-puppets, active where they were passive, complex where they were simple, interesting where they were predictable. Relationships are overhauled to give them dramatic shape, light and shade, and (in the case of the most significant relationship) to embody the thematic meaning of the story (as best as that meaning is understood at this point in the process).

The fly in the ointment here is usually the protagonist. Often (perhaps always) more peripheral characters have jumped up fully formed, have come to life on the first-draft page, or will with comparative ease through this second-draft concentration on character. The protagonist, by contrast, often appears and remains a two-dimensional cypher – sketchy, unconvincing, sometimes infuriating in their seeming lack of self-awareness, their inability or unwillingness to really engage with anyone else. And – take it from me – this character-shaped vacuum at the centre of your script can stubbornly persist from the second through the twenty-second draft, the last bitter, lonely attempt to save this brilliant story and force the world to acknowledge your genius.

Why does that happen? Why do these scripts slowly and painfully sink in a welter of frustration and thwarted ambition? Because that protagonist is you. And if you can't learn the trick of seeing yourself, then you won't be able to see your character, and they won't be able to see themselves.

What I'm talking about here is the effort and insight required to move a story away from self-gratifying fantasy to complex and involving drama.

We all love to fantasise – and, if we're honest, the difference between doing that in the privacy of our own heads for our own enjoyment and writing a first draft of a story intended for the world is often negligible to non-existent. That's fine. But beyond that first draft stage, wish fulfilment is one of the greatest threats to any script or scriptwriter.

I've noticed that this pleasurable wish fulfilment comes in two forms: Superman and Cinderella. In the first, the protagonist is wildly admired and found attractive by virtually every other character. Romantic possibilities fall at his or her feet, peers are in awe of the protagonist's charisma and power (or in hysterics at their jokes). Of course there's some misguided antagonist who will learn the error of their ways, but otherwise the protagonist just has to show up to have others oohing and aahing at their impressive attributes. The problem is, besides that stupid, wrongheaded antagonist, there is one other dissenting party: the reader or audience member. They have a growing sense of annoyance and frustration with a protagonist who doesn't seem to have earned or be earning any of this approbation, who doesn't see any necessity to work to change themselves – accompanied by equal annoyance with the coterie of sycophantic surrounding characters feeding the protagonist's sense of smugness. This always reminds me of a Don McLean song entitled 'Everybody Loves Me, Baby (What's the Matter with You?)'. The matter with us – the audience – is that we can tell this is a fantasy; and it's not our fantasy, it's the writer's.

The Cinderella version of this is the opposite – virtually all the other characters are stupid and wrongheaded in not understanding and supporting the beautiful, tender-hearted, vulnerable (and right-thinking) lovely soul of the protagonist. This fantasy is a catalogue of neglect, cruelty, betrayal and dashed hopes heaped on the innocent protagonist – all of it completely undeserved. Ultimately, through a fluke or the intervention of the one character with their eyes open and their head screwed on, the qualities of the put-upon protagonist are recognised and he or she is raised to their proper position for all to see. Throughout, the audience – privy to all this injustice – is encouraged to feel great fountains of pity for the little-match-girl protagonist. And sometimes, they will – sometimes films like this get made. But it's just as likely the reader or audience will feel obscurely and progressively queasy about what's going on – that there's something bogus, even adolescent, about the 'poor me, nobody understands me' aura which seems to surround the protagonist (no matter how staunch and brave they're being). And once again that audience starts to trace back that sense of self-gratifying fantasy to its source, the self-gratifying author.

In both cases this represents a writer projecting themselves into a character who (they feel) doesn't need to change. And that's the hallmark of a fantasy. In a fantasy we stand in the middle and things happen to us – we win the Lotto or an Academy Award; really attractive people think we're amazing; really repellent people try to thwart us but don't succeed – but we remain the same. We don't have to do any work on ourselves, we're just there for others to respond to. The world changes to adapt to us, not the other way around. That's how fantasies function (that's why they're fun!) – but dramas are different.

Or are they? This 'change' thing all the script-whisperers

talk about – is it really that essential? In one word: yes. In a few sentences: okay, there are a thousand exceptions to this, often seen in comedy protagonists (where the joke is that the hilariously inappropriate central character carries on unashamedly being themselves, and what was funny about them at the beginning is still funny at the end) or the modern equivalent of tragedies, where the protagonist (possibly heroically) fails to change or changes too late to avoid their fate (Oedipus and Michael Corleone, I'm looking at you). For the most part though, stories are a means of conveying information about how we should live our lives. And that information is not about physical obstacles but moral and emotional ones. The most effective way of communicating this is by example, through an empathetic relationship we, as the audience, have with someone who is great in some ways but has one stunted, blocked, wrong-thinking, wrong-feeling part of themselves that they must confront and overcome in order to lead a full life. We are fascinated by other people's lives – but only because we hope to get a lead on our own lives. A failure to change or determination not to change can provide a negative lesson – don't be like this character – but positive change usually makes a more powerful and cathartic impression on the viewer. Which is what we want to do, right?

Back to the case in hand. Remember Ben, wondering what he can do about the somehow unsatisfying ending of his first draft? He knows something is missing as his slacker avatar drifts about, amused and bemused by others' desperation to find something to believe in, seduced by women and befriended by men who admire his natural poise and ability to be happy . . . right up to when the credits roll.

Usually with writers at this point I will start asking questions of and about their protagonists.

Questions for Superman: What's wrong with him, what are his flaws, weaknesses, deepest fear (kryptonite), internal conflict (shadow self)? How do you show those and play them out, how do you have other characters embody them, trigger them in the protagonist, externalise the protagonist's internal conflict so it is dramatised via conflict with other characters. What does this protagonist need to learn?

Questions for Cinderella: What's wrong with her? What makes people treat her this way? How does she bring this on herself? In what ways – actually – does she deserve this treatment, or in what ways are these perceived cruelties actually necessary challenges to her to change? What are her flaws, what about her is so irritating or alienating? In what ways (on closer examination) does she feel – and convey to others – that she is superior? What does she need to do to change, to actually join the rest of the human race? In what ways are her 'oppressors' in reality normal people who are trying to wake her up to herself?

That first question in both cases often knocks a writer sideways. They've never considered what might be wrong with their character – their protagonist is always in the right. I tend to take a devil's advocate position and side with the antagonists: this protagonist annoys me, makes me want to slap them; I don't blame Ming the Merciless for tormenting them (especially as Ming the Merciless seems more self-aware and fully rounded than your protagonist).

On further investigation into this question of what is wrong with the protagonist, usually we find that miraculously and unwittingly the writer (that's you) has left a trail of breadcrumbs through the first draft as clues for us. As it turns out, your subconscious has a fair idea of what is wrong with your protagonist (because guess what, it has a fair idea of what is wrong with you) and has cleverly woven that into the story.

So we begin unpicking, looking for the protagonist's shadow self (which is also your shadow self). Fault by fault, we chip away at the perfect Teflon hero who has no need to change, or interest in changing, in order to discover a more flawed and complex character who is constantly challenged to do exactly that; a 'hero' under pressure as much from their own fears as what the world throws at them. Clues towards understanding the character on a more complex level are often found in the form of contradictions in their behaviour – things that on the surface don't make sense. These are gold. Usually when they're pointed out, the writer sags in their chair like they've made a mistake; they promise they'll resolve the contradiction or take that bit out. No, I exclaim, that's the best bit – I love the fact that your character works at the SPCA but kicks her boyfriend's dog – don't remove it. Dig deeper into it, try to explore the contradiction as that will often be the key to the inner tension, the push and pull, the polarity that winds up the clock-spring inside your protagonist that then propels them forward.

Very rarely at this stage are my discussions with writers about changing what the character does. What we talk about is why the character does this and responds that way – what is going on inside them that gives rise to these actions. Don't change their (interesting, contradictory, infuriating or risky) actions; understand their motivations.

By drawing up a basic two-column positive–negative table, I will also encourage the writer to find the shadow self of their protagonist by a simple flipping of traits. List the attributes that make up your character's strengths and weaknesses. With luck, some will match. Stubbornness and determination are the same trait, just viewed positively or negatively. The same trait can be bad in one situation and useful in another. For the 'hanging' attributes that don't immediately come with a match, go looking for them. What's the negative 'shadow' of a positive attribute like 'self-belief' – it's arrogance, yes? What's the positive way of looking at 'suspicious' – it's alert or cautious, isn't it?

When Ben draws up this list he is interested to discover that his free-living, humorous, inquisitive, determined and forthright protagonist is also an aimless, lost, alienated eternal-observer who is stubbornly set in his ways, uses ironic detachment as a distancing defence mechanism, doesn't trust anyone, and refuses to hear the truth even though that is the very thing he is seeking. Suddenly the work that will define the second draft clicks into focus. Ben's protagonist will kick and scream to avoid looking at his own deficits, but look he must. And so must Ben.

The second question I will generally ask is, Where are you in this? How does this character, this story, relate to your life? Because it will, and now is the moment (definitely *not* in the first draft) to recognise that. I'm not advocating writing as therapy; it's just a fact that you will write about 'live questions' in your life. And exploring those questions in a drama where your protagonist must see themselves and grow also allows you to see yourself and grow. It's not (or shouldn't be) psychodrama – but it is an opportunity for you to get over yourself.

Ben looks sobered. He's starting to understand that writing this story may well involve working out what he personally believes in, nailing his colours to the mast not only in his script but in his life. In confronting his character with questions of 'Who are you?', 'What are you?', and 'What are you going to do about it?' he is also challenging himself to 'live out loud' (as Émile Zola describes the artist's purpose).

Stories are about the interface between the individual and the social world. They are about how we should act in regard to others, not the reverse. The world doesn't owe you or your protagonist a living. We are not baby birds waiting in the nest to be fed; we must fly and flock and in doing so face our own specific problems – which, all going well, will be not so unique after all. Through writing your own story – looking critically at your protagonist, identifying how they (and very possibly you) need to change, challenging them to step up to their responsibilities to themselves and others, and thereby arrive at that skin-splitting new stage of growth – you speak to an audience in the same position and give them a path they can also follow.

This is not easy. It may actually be the hardest thing of all in scriptwriting – it's certainly a contender for the most prevalent roadblock I see in the development of scripts and writing. And many are the scriptwriters who have stepped in my door looking for craft tips and instead found themselves fishing in dark, mysterious and much more personal wells than they anticipated. And (I have to say) things don't always end well – this symbiotic relationship between writer and central character can create tautological Gordian knots that strongly resist untangling.

One of the tightest knots I've seen was Andy's feature script – already years and many drafts in development before it passed across my desk – about a guy in his thirties making a last concerted effort to grasp his dream of being an Olympic ski-jumper. Haunted by this ambition, he has been unable to settle in a job, home or relationship, and shrugs off all these hindrances to attend a training camp high in the mountains, run by an intense guru who preaches a gospel of total mind and body devotion to your goal. After some obstacles, there's a breakthrough and the protagonist starts to soar, flying further and further with every jump. But he is also falling in love with the neglected daughter of his teacher, once groomed to be a champion by her father until a catastrophic injury sidelined her. With success looking like it's within reach for the protagonist, an awful dilemma rears its head: should he once again reject love, commitment and the possibility of a family in order to achieve that success, or risk losing it by embracing those things?

Andy couldn't decide what the ending should be – and that had bedevilled the project for years now. My conversation with him quickly revealed how stressed and worried he was. He was no longer a young man, and if this film could be a success it would convince him and others that he could make it as a scriptwriter. Everything was riding on it and he was giving it everything he had to the detriment of other things in his life, including his relationship – he wanted to marry his partner but had determined not to propose until he'd finished writing the script and the film was in production.

Does this sound familiar?

In his own life Andy didn't know whether self-actualisation should trump love, but he was resolute in maintaining his tunnel-vision focus on the film until it was finished. However he couldn't finish the film until he knew the answer about what was most important: personal ambition or love. And he couldn't know that without making a decision in his own life and living it out loud. But his life was on hold until the film was finished. He had created a closed circle, the snake eating its own tail.

One reason I mention this is as a cautionary tale. Don't do that. It doesn't have to be that hard. But also, Andy's dilemma serves to starkly exemplify the psychological dimensions of the rewrite, the added layer of complexity in what is already a tricky art. Writers who wish to turn a blind eye to this interconnectedness of the life they are living and the life they are writing do so at their own peril, and the peril of their script. The alternative is to embrace the opportunity to learn something about yourself, to resolve a nagging issue in your life. Whether you know it or not, that's why you had this idea, that's what this story is trying to blossom into – if only you'll let it, if you're able to give yourself up to the process of rewriting with an open mind and an open heart.

It'll Be Over Before
You Know It

Ashleigh Young

I work in a fake medieval turret on the roof of a campus building. When I come out and walk around, bumping into friends, they tend to ask me, 'What are you working on?' Which is one reason I don't often come out and walk around.
—John McPhee, 'Draft No. 4', *The New Yorker*, 29 April 2013

Before the poetry reading I put on a pair of tiny leather gloves. They had belonged to my grandmother and they were made for tiny 1930s hands. They were so small that my hands felt like mini Incredible Hulks about to burst out of their suits. But they were the only gloves I had at the time. They weren't some kind of lucky charm or ritual – it's just that I needed to cover my hands, because I'd broken out in wicked hives due to the stress of the impending poetry reading. I'd had 'nervous rashes' on my hands before – starting new jobs, first dates, an overseas trip – but nothing as bad as this. These were the kind of welts that are intriguing to touch: smooth and hot, like freshly hardened magma. It was like the hives knew I was about to enter the public writing life and had arranged a pyrotechnics display. They were Celebration Hives. And I doubted I would get any creative mileage out of them, like John Updike did when he published an essay about his psoriasis in *The New Yorker*.

There were about eight other poets at the reading that day

and we were gathered in the foyer of the National Library. I shook the poets' hands – no one mentioned my Hulk gloves; probably they'd seen it all before – and we chatted for a few minutes. I felt a bit like that guy who is mowing his lawn while a tornado goes back and forth on the plains nearby: let's just get on with things as planned. The poet Geoff Cochrane was there, and he must have seen that I was nervous because he leaned in and fixed me with a blue stare and said, 'It'll be over before you know it.' It was good to have that reminder. At the same time, I needed a way to deal with the present moment, in which there still existed the potential for me to mispronounce a word like 'leaves' or to start sobbing halfway through a stanza or to make an emphatic gesture and somehow accidentally punch myself in the neck.

I think now that there was something about that first poetry reading, the all-consuming dread of it, that mimicked the dread of writing a first draft. I mean a first draft of anything: a poem, a story, an essay, a song, maybe even a novel. Non-fiction writer John McPhee has called writing a first draft 'the phase of the pit and the pendulum' (referencing Edgar Allan Poe's short story in which an unnamed narrator vividly describes being tortured during the Spanish Inquisition), but he points out that the second, third and fourth drafts tend to be easier, almost as if some different person were taking over from you each time. As you progress, you start to think, 'Maybe I'll get out of this alive.' Sentences gain shape and intention. Panic breaks out less often. And, incredibly, at some point maybe you experience a tiny spark of eagerness: you begin to look forward to showing your work to someone. All this is by way of saying that somewhere along the line in the public writing life, maybe it would feel like someone else was taking charge. Maybe I would start to look forward to reading my work – some of it very personal, and written out of moments of deep confusion or loneliness or disconnection – in front of people. Maybe.

The other people at the reading were older and more

experienced writers than me. What most impressed me was their pre-poem banter – their ability to talk to the audience without seeming to weigh each word first. They'd say when they'd written the poem and why, who it was about, perhaps what other poem it was echoing. And the readings themselves were electric. These poems, these voices, were meant to be in the world. They were like simple technologies – the coat-hanger, the ironing board – that, as soon as they're in the world, you can't imagine them not being there. As James Brown began to read 'The Wicked', you could feel the audience's attention sharpen. 'It starts at the edge of your teeth / like a small stone caramelised within a black jellybean . . .' When Hinemoana Baker read 'A Walk with Your Father', it felt like we were all inside the person she was directing. 'Your feet, are they the right size? / If they're too large you will tire quickly, / too small and you'll be left behind.'

I read last of all. I gave no preamble, not because I had nothing to say but because I knew that if I stepped outside the poem itself – the safe house, as James calls it in his essay in this book – I would be lost. I held on tight to the lectern, my Hulk gloves providing extra purchase. My poem was called 'Visitations' and all of its flaws became apparent as it came into the room. It was just . . . *bad*. It went on too long, it was sentimental, it was trying too hard to be Carol Ann Duffy. I remember my voice as an eerie quivering sound, like a theremin solo. And then, as Geoff had predicted, the poem was finished. It really was over. There was a bit of dutiful clapping. Then the clapping was over too.

It's a rare privilege to get any attention in the first place, as a writer – to be invited to read, speak at an event, or say on the radio what you've done and why you've done it this way and not that other way and why it took so, so long to finish. Because of that privilege, it may seem disingenuous to fret that you're not doing it right. Maybe it seems silly or smug to talk about public attention, and how to regrow your skin afterwards and return to your writing. After all, you don't *have* to participate. You can be one of the elusive ones. And the world doesn't owe you anything. (There's beauty in that. It means that you're free.) But increasingly, writers *are* participating. And the attention doesn't have to be high-profile for it to change your sense of yourself and your work. Sharing your work with anyone, even a familiar writing group or an editor you trust, is bracing because of the way it can rearrange whatever you thought you'd got right. Silence can do this, too – the seeming lack of any response at all. It doesn't have to be momentous to shake you up; your world is the world.

There are some writers for whom it's easy. They share their work readily and they have interesting things to say about it; even their hesitations are eloquent. As grateful as I am for those writers, I'm here for the other ones. The mousy ones. The mumblers. The ones who trip up the steps or who notice halfway through speaking that they've got a hair stuck in their mouth. It's to them that I want to say that the self-doubt, the uncertainty, the celebration hives – these are all inescapable and necessary parts of the much bigger picture of having your writing in the world, and of being there alongside, owning up to it – and that this, in itself, is part of the even bigger picture of declaring without shame that writing is part of who you are. Let me be dramatic for a second: nothing can take that away from you. Not a bad review or a mean comment, not your deepest discomfort as your work is cross-examined or simply heard. And although I'm not sure whether any of this ever becomes entirely comfortable, it is possible to create small pockets of comfort and peace for yourself, even when you're onstage before a crowd. It's possible to let the rough moments roll past without being capsized by them, and afterwards put it all aside and go back into your writing.

I don't consider myself any kind of expert. I'm just an easily flustered person who has had to learn a few survival skills when venturing into public with my writing. Because, in terms of formal advice from the people who organise public events, probably the best you can hope for is a brief pep talk, delivered conspiratorially, from someone more jaded. *It'll be over before you know it*. If the event is well organised, you will receive an email saying the same thing. So the first thing to know, if you are to take part in a public event, is that you need to look after yourself. Here are a few basic things to keep in mind.

- If we extend James Brown's metaphor of the 'safe house' – as in, the poem that a poet will read at a reading – there are other safe houses you can build in preparation. What other safe houses – let's call these ones cabins – can you set up for yourself? What ideas, observations or stories do you feel comfortable expressing, in terms of your own work? Have two or three. Before your event, take some time to wander through each cabin. Rummage gently; don't ransack the place. And during the event, don't be in a big rush to go outside. It's okay to enjoy your cabin.

- Think how frustrating it is when politicians don't answer the question they've been asked in an interview, and instead repeat inanities because they are basically forbidden to say 'I don't know'. For writers, the rules are reversed. If you've been asked a question about your writing, and after some searching you honestly don't have an answer, it's more interesting to say that you don't know than to do forward rolls and roly-polies around the words. I don't know why that is. It just is. Perhaps it's just refreshing to hear a person say that they don't know, especially a person who's in the business of words. By the same token, don't be afraid to pause if you need a moment to formulate a sentence. Luxuriate in your pause, if you want. Some of the most compelling speakers also do the best pauses, because they permit themselves to collect their thoughts.

- Your voice may sound strange in the room. It may even sound monstrous. But, consider this: people are here for it. They want to hear that voice. Consider how, in art and comics, work that is less technically 'good' can be memorable. Think of Shrigley's wonky cows, or Allie Brosh's lopsided dogs drawn in PaintBrush. Artists don't have to be 'good at drawing' to make good work. If there's an interesting idea or feeling underneath, it actually doesn't matter that the body is too big for the legs.

- Make sure you feel as physically comfortable as possible – within reason; under no circumstances wear thick socks with sandals. My Hulk gloves were uncomfortable, but it would've been more uncomfortable for me to have my celebration hives on display.

- Do not let anyone tell you to 'Just relax'. The words 'Just relax and enjoy it' are guaranteed to make most writers' eyeballs bulge out like Ren's and Stimpy's. If you're nervous, you cannot afford to wait until you're relaxed before you participate. In this world far too much emphasis is placed on how to be 'relaxed and confident' when we enter nerve-wracking situations. As the incredibly prolific and productive author Roxane Gay has said: 'If I were to wait to be confident, I would never get anything done.' So a part of you will need to actively hijack the feeling of never *quite* being ready. (This goes for starting your next first draft, too.) Maybe all I'm talking about is gumption. 'Gumption,' said philosopher Robert Pirsig, 'is the psychic gasoline that keeps the whole thing going.'

After my first poetry reading, everything suddenly felt overwhelmingly ordinary. I just felt a bit . . . lame. That poem that I had worked so hard on, and that secretly I was proud of, was unremarkable out there. Not a disaster, not a triumph. I felt like the tide had come in and blithely swallowed a sandcastle I'd worked on all day. My poem had been eaten by the world. And this is a feeling I've had many times since, after events, and after showing someone my work – a feeling of flatness, of being unremarkable.

If only someone had reminded me that *your whole worth*

as a writer is not bound up with a single response. That this one response is not the final response! That in fact a final response does not exist, because your work may be found over and over again by different people, many of whom won't express their feelings about it. You cannot afford to wait for praise or condemnation to know whether or not you should continue. And survival, simple survival, is to be celebrated. As Paul Ewen, author of *Francis Plug: How to Be a Public Author* has said, 'We're expected to hit the ground running, confident and ready, loaded with banter, quips and answers. It's a disaster waiting to happen.' And yes, it can feel like jumping into a supermarket trolley and careening down a hill in Dunedin. So if you have avoided grievous injury, celebrate.

Perhaps more importantly, after any kind of exposure, you eventually need to come back to your writing. After that poetry reading, whenever I tried to go back into my usual writing routine, which at that time meant wrapping myself in a duvet and hunching over my computer like a big larva, my mind kept drifting back to the stage. Back to being seen and heard. I thought about how my voice had sounded, and I never wanted to hear that sound again. By extension, I didn't want to see my voice on a page.

In terms of getting over this, there are two approaches that have worked for me. The first is an aggressive approach, and it is my favourite. Write as if you were doing a frantic last-minute tidy-up before a flat inspection: fast and forcefully. Don't try to ignore any discomfort. Instead, write directly at it, the same way you should directly confront a manspreader on the bus. You're going to have to face your inner critic at some point – there are only so many days you can get up at 5am in order to 'catch it out', a routine some writers swear by – so shoot words at it as if you were in a game of paintball. 'Sometimes in a nervous frenzy I just fling words as if I were flinging mud at a wall,' John McPhee says. This is not a delicate process. We are talking about one of the most powerful forces within ourselves – self-doubt, and let's be honest, probably some self-loathing in there as well – and to face it as an equal, you must use force. You won't overwhelm it for good, but you will put up a good fight, and you can subdue it.

The second way is to write as if you were fidgeting. As if you were building something out of pipe-cleaners or doodling while on hold: just follow the line, and keep adding detail that pleases you. The detail *must please you on some level.* It is not for anyone else, it is just for you. Don't take your eye off the line. And do not insist that it reaches a destination. Insist only that it delights you. I once had a student in a creative writing class who had written a first-person piece about first-year student drunkenness (ostensibly it was a piece of science writing about what alcohol does to the brain). It was a lengthy piece and he wasn't sure how to end it. Ultimately he came up with the narrator at work in the morning, facing a long day ahead. Out of nowhere, the narrator looks at a piece of bad art on a wall: 'It was of an old man motorcycling through hell.' When I came to it, I laughed out loud. Sometimes, when I'm trying to think of what to write next, I think of that old man motorcycling through hell. What's *your* old man motorcycling through hell?

Above all, know that you're safe inside your writing. Nobody can touch you there. Continuing to write even as your own uncertainties yammer away, and even as you know that not everyone likes what you're doing, can be a glorious act of subversion. Fiction writer Pip Adam has talked about this, in the light of receiving a harsh review:

There was this really odd moment when I suddenly realised I was by myself, in my house in front of my computer and no matter how loud they shouted they couldn't stop me from writing. Maybe they could stop me from being read, but they couldn't stop me from writing and suddenly the writing felt a bit like a subversive act, like it always does really, like everyone is saying, 'BE QUIET!' 'WE DON'T WANT TO LOOK

AT THAT!' and I'm like, 'Um. No.' And I think that is
how I 'shrug it off', by remembering . . . all that other
shit, that takes place in another room. I get to write
in this room and what happens in that other room
I don't even have to go into. I can invite the people I
want into this room, and I have so many people who I
trust and who are supportive and often when I invite
them into this room they bring some of their work and
we celebrate and get excited about the work, and it's
great. I can shut the door and just get that weird kind
of fulfilment that I get out of writing.

In McPhee's 'Draft No. 4' he describes a feeling that comes
over him sometime into the writing. He's crossed the electric
fence from the actual world into the writing world – a fence
that writers have to cross when they go the other way, too –
and is at work. And then there's this feeling that something
'seems to be working and is not going to go away. The feeling
is more than welcome, yes, but it is hardly euphoria. It's just
a new lease on life, a sense that I'm going to survive until the
middle of next month.' And sometimes when you're out in the
world with your writing, that feeling will come over you too
– maybe very faint, but nonetheless there – that you're going
to survive, and that you're not going to go away.

Untitled 404

Hera Lindsay Bird

I have called this poem Untitled 404, because that is the
    name of the photo I have chosen to talk about
But I have less to say about this photo than this photo has to
    say about itself
To describe art in public is a great personal dumbassery
The best response to this poem would be to pick up a bottle
    of gin on the way home

I like this picture because it reminds me of loneliness
And the great, unspecific boredom of life
It's the expression I get every time someone tries to hold me
    accountable for my artistic wrongdoings
The critical theorists advancing, with black leather
    pompoms

Recently someone scolded me for speaking about Cindy
    Sherman because Cindy Sherman was an instrument of
    the patriarchy
Like an evil saxophone that only plays hold music for a bank
Bad financial jazz pouring out of the telephone
Oh sometimes I get so tired I want to blow the stars out, one
    by one

Every year people demand to know what art is feminist and
    what art is unfeminist

Sometimes I wonder if it's ethical to be a woman at all
It's a great aesthetic stupidity to waste your life on right-
    seeming behaviour
Like putting a coin in a jukebox that only plays whale song
Once there was a time in which I too had many ideologies
Many self-pleasing ideologies, with which to chastise others
The theme of these ideologies was: however wrong you are,
    that is the exact amount I am right by
I felt them in my blood like too much money

Once upon a time, I had many ideologies
Many superior ideologies with which to cheerfully educate
    my family and friends
Forget crying myself to sleep, I wanted to cry everyone else
    there
Then drive off in my Cadillac, my blond wig blowing

Once upon a time I had many ideologies
And by ideologies I mean specific ideas about things that
    other people should and shouldn't do
But proving yourself right is a bad career
Then you have to prove yourself even righter, in a blue satin
    pantsuit

Sometimes the world is so backwards all you can do is stare
Stare and stare, from out behind your waterproof mascara
Oh it's a great responsibility to be your own misogynist
There are so many beaded handbags with which to oppress
    yourself

I do not think the great project of art is ideological
    messaging time
Like Monet, spelling 'Fuck you' in waterlilies
The great project of art is to pour your eyes into the world
The sunset blazing overhead like too much eyeshadow

Untitled 404 is like a stock photo for loneliness
Or a pin-up girl for Great Forgotten Blouses of the Midwest
You stare out past the camera, into the great abyss of
    Western democracy
And the great abyss of Western democracy stares back

There are a lot of punishments in this world
And some of these punishments look a lot like day to day life
Some things cannot be transformed, only endured
You unbutton your blouse, like a Ukrainian tap-dance
    instructor in exile

People are always on the lookout for new ideologies with
    which to punish themselves
Contemporary ideologies, studded with hashtags
It's like not being able to wear a sexy nurse outfit unless you
    apply for a sexy medical licence
You have to take someone's blood pressure with your skirt
    hiked up

Untitled 404 is the moment between weeping and
    preweeping
Your eyes get hotter and hotter, like a faulty laptop charger
It's a mundane aesthetic, like changing the font on your
    family newsletter
Tossing up between Times New Roman, and Times Even
    Newer Roman

I will never be a good critic because I love too much what is
    ugly with the world
The moon shining over all of us, with its soft white handrail
It's like hanging a mirror on the side of your death to make
    your life look bigger
Or the wet, black cellulite of the ocean

Untitled 404 is a secondhand nostalgia
You think back to your childhood, but the past has been
    cordoned off
You start to wonder about the future and the great untitled
    project of your life
It keeps you up at night, like a big fluorescent sadness

The imperative to be correct is the great failure of the Left
Sometimes you just want to wash iceberg lettuce in quiet
    despair
It's like buying a second wig, and putting it on over the wig
    you're already wearing
You cry and cry, impressing no one